DIGITAL LEARNING AND COLLABORATIVE PRACTICES

T0373550

Digital Learning and Collaborative Practices offers a comprehensive overview of design-based, technology-enhanced approaches to teaching and learning in virtual settings. Today's digital communications foster new opportunities for sharing culture and knowledge while also prompting concerns over division, disinformation and surveillance. This book uniquely emphasises playful, collaborative experiences and democratic values in a variety of environments—adaptive, augmented, dialogic, game-based and beyond. Graduate students and researchers of educational technology, the learning sciences and interaction design will discover rich theories, interventions, models and approaches for concretising emerging practices and competencies in digital learning spaces.

Eva Brooks is Professor with Special Responsibilities towards IT-Based Design, Learning and Innovation and Director of Xlab in the Department of Culture and Learning at Aalborg University, Denmark.

Susanne Dau is Docent (Associate Professor) and research manager at the Professional Development and Educational Research Programme in the Department of Research & Development at the University College of Northern Denmark, Denmark.

Staffan Selander is Senior Professor in Education and Didactic Science in the Department of Computer and Systems Sciences at Stockholm University, Sweden.

DIGITAL LEARNING AND COLLABORATIVE PRACTICES

Lessons from Inclusive and Empowering Participation with Emerging Technologies

*Edited by Eva Brooks, Susanne Dau
and Staffan Selander*

Routledge
Taylor & Francis Group

NEW YORK AND LONDON

First published 2022
by Routledge
52 Vanderbilt Avenue, New York, NY 10017

and by Routledge
2 Park Square, Milton Park, Abingdon, Oxon, OX14 4RN

Routledge is an imprint of the Taylor & Francis Group, an informa business

British Library Cataloguing-in-Publication Data
A catalogue record for this book is available from the British Library

Library of Congress Cataloging-in-Publication Data
A catalog record for this title has been requested

ISBN: 978-0-367-62255-8 (hbk)
ISBN: 978-0-367-61775-2 (pbk)
ISBN: 978-1-003-10857-3 (ebk)

Typeset in Bembo
by SPi Global, India

CONTENTS

FOREWORD

Eva Brooks, Susanne Dau and Staffan Selander

A space can only be made into a place by its occupants. The best that the designer can do is put the tools into their hands.

Steve Harrison and Paul Dourish (1996)

A main aim of this book lies in the vital role that collaborative practices play as drivers for inclusive and participative digital learning as well as for new innovations in emergent technologies. Technology has changed the society we live in at an accelerating pace, which has created challenges for implementing them not only efficiently but also in meaningful ways. We can see an increased societal interest in collaboration, e.g. through the current widely spread application of co-creation in different contexts and organisational practices, in particular in the Nordic countries where it is used as guidelines for, among others, development of educational and welfare solutions.

This book has been in the writing for a few years and we hope that it has been for the better. Aligned with societal and technological developments, themes, content, nuances and orchestrations have matured and given way to a more stringent and accessible edition. The book discusses, and demonstrates, new challenges and possibilities in relation to learning, both in terms of participation and in terms of establishing inclusive design approaches. This is done from diverse and multidisciplinary perspectives, which we mean carry great potential for developing new knowledge, as well as new forms of practice together with new ways of learning.

We would like to acknowledge all researchers that in different ways have helped in shaping this book, both in discussions and informal conversations. We would also like to direct our sincere thanks to all authors that have contributed to this book. You are all in one way or another colleagues, research partners and/or like-minded friends – we are grateful for your knowledge, insights and trust. The book as such emerged from discussions in the *Xlab – Design, Learning Innovation* at the department of Culture and Learning, Aalborg University. Hence, we have been lucky to have had the Xlab teams' support, in particular when it comes to acknowledging playful explorations as essential parts of academic work. We also like to express our thanks to Stockholm University and University College North for their support. Last but not the least remains to thank the supportive and patient editor Daniel Schwarz. His supportive pushing has meant a lot for the finalisation of this book.

Aalborg and Stockholm in December 2020

PREFACE

Digital Learning and Collaborative Practices

Eva Brooks, Susanne Dau and Staffan Selander

We live in an era that can be characterised by its strongly expanding digital presence, which encompasses more or less everything that matters in our lives: may it be play and learning, work and production, economy and consumption, leisure time and hobbies, healthcare and medicine, information storage or guiding apps or even love. The ubiquity of digital programs and devices are nowadays so integrated and intertwined with the physical world that it seems relevant to talk about our society in terms of a hybrid society. This development supports new solutions for social communication and institutional practices. The use of adaptive, augmented, dialogic and game-based environments, as well as multimodal and multimedia communication tools, are examples of this in different learning contexts.

The emerging and expanding digital technologies are even accelerating at such a pace that current technological hypes (e.g. Internet of Things and Virtual Reality) soon may become obsolete. Therefore, we see it as a challenge to explore potentials in new enabling technologies, which require involvement of various disciplines as well as stakeholders across existing disciplines and practices. Not the least Europe faces a considerable challenge in fostering new ecosystems of innovation to harness holistic learning processes and a development of more inclusive societies.

It seems obvious that the digital systems now are so smart and so integrated, and to an ever-increasing scale so dependent on mass data, that they not only can "co-operate" with each other but also serve as a tool to map out individual patterns and preferences (of learning, consumption… etc.). Thus, digital tools and programs are not only serving our individual interests and preferences, but can also to some extent steer them. And this is a democratic challenge for an open society.

The digital revolution can also, in some aspects, draw the society apart, where small groups can preserve their (sometimes violent) political ideas behind a shield of "fake news" and conspiracies. Therefore, current changes of our societies open up for massive critique and dystopic discussions, as well as for technical optimism and naive visons of a bright, technological future. In this book, we are doing neither of these things. What we want to do is to show and discuss new, emerging practices that entail democratic and collaborative work and values, and to underline the importance of an ongoing dialogue about the digital technology, its ethics and social consequences.

This book is first and foremost an introduction to a broader, social understanding of emerging practices in an era of digitisation. We present some interrelated theoretical frameworks that especially focus on technology in use and on emerging practices in different social fields. Hopefully, we can learn from these examples and get inspired to take even newer steps towards future, democratic and inclusive digital solutions of learning environments.

In Part 1 we introduce some different, but interrelated, *theoretical approaches* on collaborative designs with a broader focus on: play and learning, learning ecologies, the importance of a dialogue-oriented digital environment and participatory designs in and for learning. In Part 2, we focus on some empirical examples of *inclusive practices* through digital technologies, like adaptive games, how you can learn music by way of composing and also a model for in-action interventions. Part 3 offers examples from different *empowering practices* with a focus on reflective learning based on gaming principles, VR, robots and programming and the role of virtual cases for learning and assessment. And finally, in the epilogue, we will discuss what there is to learn from these examples and perspectives – for a future development of digital tools and solutions.

CONTRIBUTORS

Hanne Voldborg Andersen holds a PhD in the field of innovative designs including technology-based interventions for learners with developmental and attention difficulties in K1–10 practices. As an expert in ICT, learning and inclusion, she currently works as a national coordinator for FabLab@SCHOOL network in Denmark. FabLab@SCHOOLdk is an initiative for development of 21st-century skills in a context of emerging digital technologies and design thinking for teachers and learners in Danish primary and secondary schools. FabLab@SCHOOLdk collaborates internationally with the FabLearn network at Stanford University.

Bjørn-Terje Bandlien, PhD, holds a position as an associate professor in music at Norwegian University of Technology and Science NTNU, Department of Teacher Education. He has many years of experience as a music teacher in secondary school, primary school and Nordic folk high school, where creative activities such as concert and performance production, composing and studio work have been frequent and important forms of work. As a teacher educator, Bandlien teaches music didactics, composition and music theory. Bandlien's doctoral research which was finished in 2019 was about secondary school students' composition on the iPad informed by a design theoretical perspective. The purpose of the project was to contribute to increased knowledge and critical awareness about the school's digital composition teaching.

Lykke Brogaard Bertel received her PhD in Human-Computer Communication & Interaction in 2016, specialising in Persuasive Educational and Entertainment Robotics (PEERs). She has a background in digital technologies and persuasive design and has worked as a specialist in robot-mediated motivation and learning since 2011. She holds a position as an associate professor at the Department of Planning, Aalborg University and is affiliated with the UNESCO Centre for Problem-Based Learning as well as the Aalborg University Robotics research group. Her research interests are in the fields of human–robot relationships, motivational psychology and participatory design. In her PhD thesis, she studied design aspects of robot-supported learning in primary and special education.

Anthony Lewis Brooks holds a PhD and is an associate professor at Aalborg University, Denmark where he is director/founder of the "SensoramaLab" (Virtual Reality, HCI and Playful Learning Complex) and a founding team member of the Medialogy education. In the 1980s he created bespoke instruments and volumetric invisible sensing systems for unencumbered gesture-control of digital media to stimulate meaningful causal interactions that could be tailored to individuals, their needs, preferences and desires alongside the outcome goals of facilitators, therapists and educators. He is an active keynote speaker at international events and has presented globally. He is an ambassador for accessibility and is a Danish representative for UNESCO's International Federation for Information Processing (IFIP) Technical committee (WG14).

Eva Brooks, PhD and professor with special responsibilities towards IT-based Design, Learning and Innovation and Director of Xlab in the Department of Culture and Learning at Aalborg University, Denmark. Her research has a design focus on participation, social interaction and the use of digital technologies including their implications for play and learning in formal and informal learning practices. Her research includes an innovation dimension, where she applies a co-creation approach to children's participation in developing state of the art technologies. She has been leading several research projects and is steering co-chair of the EAI International Conference on Design, Learning & Innovation (DLI).

Susanne Dau is an associate professor and research manager at the Research Program Professional Development and Educational research at the University College of Northern Denmark, Department of Research and Development. She holds a PhD in Blended Learning. Her research interest includes: Professional Development & Judgement, Educational Research, Blended Learning and ICT for Learning & Inclusion.

Uno Fors, PhD, head of department, and professor in computer science with a focus on IT and learning at the Department of Computer- and Systems Sciences, Stockholm University, Sweden, with more than 35 years of experience in developing and studying VCs in many different domains. His research interest concerns IT-based visualisations related to virtual patients and simulated meeting with patients. Simulations offer opportunities to train and solve medical and related problem, i.e. problem-based learning. Here, his focus is on the pedagogical factors – to create user motivation and engagement.

Pauline Fredskilde is educated as a teacher and holds a MSc in Product Design with an honorary degree in entrepreneurship. She has worked as a learning consultant at the Department of Design and Communication, Southern Denmark University, Denmark where she designed courses for teachers in technology literacy and computational thinking and researched the same topics as a research assistant. Currently, she runs the company Guldastronaut, which specialises in designing toys, activities and skill development courses for children and their educational staff. She is a team leader and member of the board of the NGO DigiPippi, which works to bridge the gender gap in IT and technology. She is also a co-founder of the online digital platform, Pixelplaneten, which is a portal and platform for educators who want to work more with technology, design and invention. She is active in the debate within women in technology, children's creativity and ingenuity.

Thorkild Hanghøj has a PhD from the University of Southern Denmark (*Playful Knowledge – An Explorative Study of Educational Gaming*) and is an associate professor at the Department of Communication and Psychology, Aalborg University, Denmark. His research focuses on the educational use of games, which both include digital games (e.g. *Minecraft*, *LIMBO* or *Torchlight II*) and analogue games such as debate games or board games. Research areas include: the design of educational games and game-related learning materials, the crucial role of teachers in adapting games to pedagogical approaches and curricular aims, students' development of game-related literacies through game journalism and the use of co-operative games for supporting inclusion through increased motivation for at-risk students. His current work explores the educational impact of games through a mixed methods approach.

Camilla Gyldendahl Jensen, holds a PhD from Aalborg University and is an associate professor at the Department of Architectural Technology and Construction Management, University College North (UCN). Her research focuses on topics such as integrated building design, sustainability, concept development and problem analysis. In addition, she is an internal innovation coordinator and thus responsible for the development and execution of innovation courses in the education at UCN.

Rune Hagel Skaarup Jensen, Digital learning consultant at Centre for Digitally Supported Learning at Aalborg University and Master of Science in Techno-Anthropology from Aalborg University. He has participated in research and projects within the fields of learning, technology, inclusion, digital didactic and problem-based learning from primary school till higher education in Denmark. Jensen is currently a digital learning consultant where he supports teachers in developing digital supported learning activities at Aalborg University. For further information: https://vbn.aau.dk/da/persons/119078

Anu Kajamaa, PhD, is an associate professor and a research group leader at the Faculty of Educational Sciences, University of Helsinki. She received her PhD in 2012. Her award-winning doctoral dissertation is a study of change management and long-term evaluation of organisational change efforts within formative interventions. She has conducted extensive collaborative research and intervention projects in schools, teacher education, healthcare and social care and entrepreneurship contexts. Kajamaa has produced 40 refereed publications in national and international journals. Her current research focuses on children's learning, development and creativity in school-based makerspaces. For more information: https://tuhat.helsinki.fi/portal/en/persons/anu-kajamaa(1a0b7f2e-4201-44e3-9cc4-96dab1d6993d).html

Susanne Kjällander, PhD in Didactic Science at Department of Child- and Youth Studies at Stockholm University. Kjällander has a background as a primary teacher but now works as a senior lecturer within teacher education. She has been doing research on digital learning environments for almost 15 years. Her expertise is digital competence, digital literacy, programming and adaptive games along with children's creative, explorative and sustainable learning with digital resources. She has led several research projects in both school and preschool and just recently had a postdoc position at Stanford University, California. She is the founder of a new national research network about digitisation in preschool in Sweden and editor of the *International Journal of Designs for Learning*. She often lectures about her research, has written several books and articles and took part in writing the national curriculum in Sweden.

Ola Knutsson has a PhD in Human-Computer Interaction and is an associate professor at Stockholm University. His research focuses on participatory design of learning and work environments, the use of design patterns and research on digital literacy.

Kristiina Kumpulainen, PhD, is Professor of Education at the Faculty of Educational Sciences, University of Helsinki. Recognized internationally for her scholarship Kumpulainen is the author of over 100 articles and ten books. Her research interests focus on children's learning, development and well-being in their communities, formal and informal education, dialogic learning, agency and identity, multiliteracies and professional development of teachers. She is the recipient of numerous research and development grants. Her current research projects include the Joy of learning multiliteracies (funded by the Finnish Ministry of Education and Culture) and school-based makerspaces for promoting young learners' digital literacies and creativity (funded by the Academy of Finland). She is a regular keynote speaker in national and international conferences and venues. For more information: https://tuhat.helsinki.fi/portal/en/person/krkumpul

Markus Löchtefeld is an associate professor at Aalborg University at the Technical Faculty of IT and Design, Department of Architecture, Design and Media Technology. He received his PhD degree from Saarland University in Saarbrücken, Germany with the title: Spatial Interaction with Mobile Projected Displays Within the fields of Computer Science and Human Computer Interaction. He has previously been affiliated with Lancaster University, United Kingdom and University of Saarbrücken, Germany. He is currently Principal Investigator for the H2020 DecoChrom project, investigating personal fabrication of printed electrochromic displays and printed electronics. He teaches at the Medialogy education in Interaction Design, and Prototyping and Fabrication Techniques as well as in Art and Technology.

Anders Kalsgaard Møller is an assistant professor at Aalborg University, Faculty of Humanities, Department of Culture and Learning. He is part of the research group IT Learning and Design (ILD). He obtained his PhD degree with the title "Evaluating 3D Positioned Sound in Multimodal Scenarios" at Aalborg University, Department of Electronic Systems. He is associated with the laboratory Xlab. His research focus is on user research methods, interaction design and evaluation. He has been working with the development of health technology, Virtual Reality applications, assistive technology for people with dementia, 3D binaural sound evaluation in multimodal environments, learning and vocational training and computational thinking. He teaches as the master of IT, Learning and Organizational Change.

Kristen Pilner Blair, PhD, is a senior research scholar at Stanford University's Graduate School of Education and is the Director of Research for Stanford's Digital Learning Initiative. Her research focuses on improving STEM instruction and assessment in both formal educational settings like classrooms and informal settings, like camps and museums. Dr. Blair has collaborated with cross-institutional partners to develop new learning technologies and instructional materials for helping to teach math and science. She also examines fundamental learning questions, such as how students learn from both positive and negative feedback. Dr. Blair holds a PhD in Learning Sciences and Technology Design and an undergraduate degree in Mathematical and Computational Science, both from Stanford University. She is co-author of the book, *the ABCs of How We Learn: 26 Scientifically Proven Approaches, How They Work, and When to Use Them.*

Robert Ramberg earned his PhD in cognitive psychology at the Department of Psychology, Stockholm University and holds a position as professor at the Department of Computer- and Systems Sciences, Stockholm University (Technology enhanced learning and collaboration). Ramberg also holds a position as a research director at the Swedish air force simulation center (FLSC), Swedish Defense Research Agency. His research focuses on the design and evaluation of representations and representational artefacts to support learning, training and collaboration. Of particular interest to his research are socio-cultural perspectives on learning and cognition and how theories must be adapted when designing and evaluating technology enhanced learning and training environments. And more specifically how artefacts of various kinds (information technology and other tools) mediate human action, collaboration and learning. His research has been published in international journals.

Staffan Selander, PhD and professor emeritus in Education at the Department of Computer- and Systems Sciences at Stockholm University. His research has focused on designs for learning, multimodal knowledge representations and digital learning environments. He has been leading several external, international research projects and has tutored 45 doctoral students. In 2008, he initiated the open access journal *Designs for Learning* (www.designsforlearning.nu). He has been a visiting professor in Australia, Brazil, Chile, Denmark, Finland and Norway. Latest books: *Games and Education: Designs in and for learning* (Arnseth et al., Ed. 2019, Brill/Sense), *Multimodal texts in education, A comprehensive framework* (Danielsson & Selander, 2021, Springer) and *Learning as Social Practice: Beyond Education as an Individual Enterprise* (with Kress, Säljö & Wulf, Eds., 2021, Routledge).

Jeanette Sjöberg is a senior lecturer in pedagogy at the School of Learning, Humanities and Social Sciences, and a pedagogical developer, at Halmstad University, Sweden. Her research focuses on children and young people's learning in relation to digital technology, and on students and teachers in higher education in relation to digital technology, and it includes areas such as digital game-based learning (DGBL), collaborative learning, teaching design and practical research. In summary, her research revolves around contemporary challenges for children, young people and adults' learning in relation to digital technology.

Elsebeth Korsgaard Sorensen is professor emerita in Digital Communication & Learning and head of the former research unit, D4Learning (http://d4learning.aau.dk) at the Dept. of Culture and Learning, Aalborg University. Currently, her research is focusing intensively on the challenge of inclusion in schools. As head of the project, iDIDAKT, funded by the Danish Ministry of Education, she investigates the potential and use of digital technology for enhancing the process of inclusion in schools of children with difficulties in focusing attention. Her research topic includes a strong focus on promoting dialogue and reflection in creative learning designs that utilise the power of digital and mobile technologies to address and advance learner empowerment and digital democratic citizenship. She has been involved in a long list of research projects. She presents her research at international conferences, frequently as a keynote speaker, and she has published extensively in international journals and books within the field.

Tobias Alexander Bang Tretow-Fish, is a PhD student at the Technical University of Denmark (DTU). Tretow-Fish has written about games in atypical environments and has been connected to an extensive research project on Problem Based Learning (PBL) Digital before beginning as a PhD. In his PhD, Tretow-Fish's research tries to examine the Rhapsode TM adaptive learning system-mediated quality improvement of nursing education.

PART 1

Designing for Collaboration

Frameworks of Learning

Eva Brooks and Staffan Selander

Introduction: Designing for Collaboration: Frameworks of Learning

This first part of the book provides frameworks and theories that can guide those interested in designing for particular collaborative experiences. It also provides operational frameworks on how to involve participants in processes of social activity. When aligned with participation, communication can be considered as an essential feature of collaboration as well as an interpersonal capacity that comes into play when individuals are provided with opportunities for social interaction. It is also argued that to empower interdependence, collaboration should be encouraged rather than enforced. Hence, designing for collaboration involves considering participants' mutual engagement, in particular related to joint problem solving. To foster collaboration, problem solving tasks are suggested to be ambiguous and playful to instigate dialogue rather than obvious and straightforward accomplishments.

Relative to digital learning, the aspect of collaboration is often associated with a social nature of interactions evolving from social demands of collaborative activities. This kind of processes can be associated with a foundational participatory character, where participants become increasingly involved in collaborative undertakings. Expressed differently, we acknowledge that evolving collaborative processes among participants could be considered as a democratic and empowering involvement. This participatory character of collaboration is a well-established aspect within the field of participatory design and other design-oriented approaches, in particular within the Nordic countries. Currently, the term co-creation is often used interchangeably with participatory design. Other crucial elements to consider when designing for collaboration are boundaries and situational constraints that can hinder eco-social trajectories towards meaningful participation in collaborative settings. Here, playfulness is explicated as generating a mindset that can cross-cut different experienced constraints as well as opportunities.

The forthcoming chapters present mainly Scandinavian, design-oriented approaches in research, built on social and democratic perspectives focusing on theoretical frameworks and tools for research, reflection and deeper understanding of emergent practices. Through the various contributions, we aim to add to the understanding of what is unique about these theoretical perspectives, and what emerge as more generic dimensions across different design and research practices.

The first chapter *Designing as play* by Eva Brooks, illustrates how designing can be described as a play activity and as such contribute to the shaping of interactions and environments of creative collaborations among children. She uncovers characteristics of design and play, respectively, in terms of their material and immaterial resources and discusses in which ways they are linked to participants' interests to foster participation and social dimensions of learning. Theoretically, Brooks leans on the conceptual ideas of co-creative exploration and participation, which entails aspects of play, dialogue and interaction, which are put forward as material and immaterial processes contributing to change and diversity.

Central to the chapter is an attempt to, in a concrete form, outline how designing as play can be practiced and theorised underlining the ethos of participants' voices to be heard and considered. This is done through empirical examples carried out in digital as well as non-digital play and learning practices. Here, the author emphasises the material manifestation of children's interaction, which moves beyond representation as a way of understanding designing as play.

The second chapter, *Designs for learning and knowledge representations in collaborative settings* by Ola Knutsson, Robert Ramberg and Staffan Selander, outlines a perspective on participatory designs for learning as a social activity that can be used not only to analyse and understand new learning sites and practices, but also to organise new collaborative learning environments. In doing so, they elaborate on the concepts of designs *in* and *for* learning including a focus on material and semiotic resources and how these can be applied during different learning sequences. Throughout the chapter, the authors argue for an understanding of learning as a dialogical process, where representations and representational artefacts can be used to relieve or reinforce cognitive processes. This is exemplified through a case study inspired by participatory design methodology where sketches, design patterns and design workshops are used as representational formats. The authors conclude by emphasising the importance of including communicative aspects when designing for learning and knowledge representation.

Chapter three, *A learning ecology design* by Susanne Dau, addresses current complex learning situations, which span across different physical and digital domains and which involve an increased personalised use of digital technologies. She does so by applying a learning ecology perspective on orientation and wayfinding in physical and digital environments. In her description of a learning ecology, she draws on the concepts of spaces, places, tools, techniques, technology, affordances and narratives and points to the interrelatedness of these different features and how they influence peoples' orientation in different learning environments.

Furthermore, the chapter reveals how people orient themselves from a learning ecology perspective, which the author describes by means of the concept of way-finding as a process of mapping the physical, mental and social environment. In this way, wayfinding as a concept emphasises emotional, physical, social, cognitive and psychological orientations of people moving, acting and interacting in and across different environments and structures. Dau argues that this ecology offers an understanding of identity formation and of the sociality of learning.

The fourth and last chapter in this part of the book, *Designing for digital col-laboration and knowledge building through meta-learning, dialogue and collaboration* by Elsebeth Korsgaard Sorensen, presents a theoretical framework based on a peda-gogical design perspective, namely the dialogic knowledge building interaction model (D-CKB). The perspective implies a view on learning as mediated by democratic interaction between learners in digital environments, in particular in the form of student-centred collaborative processes of negotiation. The chapter illustrates the conceptual idea behind the D-CKB learning design approach and discusses how it fosters participation and engagement. The author describes how the model has been implemented in an online course, where she details a set of assessment criteria including quantitative as well as qualitative requirements targeting both scaffolding and assessing of dialogic processes. Sorensen concludes her chapter by promoting the model's generic opportunities to promote meta-learning and learning-to-learn as a consequence of the democratically oriented student engagement in D-CKB.

To sum up, the four chapters theoretically emphasise different lenses to exam-ine and propose frameworks for learning. Nevertheless, the chapters are unified by shedding light on learning as a social activity, where participation creates inclusive and empowering qualities when designing for collaboration in play and learning activities targeting different stakeholder groups.

1

DESIGNING AS PLAY

Eva Brooks

Introduction

Design and play share similarities, yet are at odds with each other. On the one hand, both promote curiosity and exploration, which supports motivation and the acquisition of knowledge. On the other hand, design typically leads to concrete solutions for specific situations, whereas play is seen as an open-ended natural asset where people imaginatively interact with the world. Similarly, designers are curious to ask the question "how" in order to get to the intended solution, whereas playing humans imaginarily ask the question "what if". Yet, both questions reflect a wonder about the creation of a possible future. In this regard, Stappers (2007) refers to the act of designing as the locus where new ideas get created by confronting them with the world. These confrontations lead to the instantiation of a designed idea in the form of a prototype. Zimmerman et al. (2007, p. 493) state that designers in this way have skills to create "a product that transforms the world from its current state to a preferred state". While the term "design" has a built-in ambiguous character and often treated as either a noun or a verb, this chapter is concerned with the acting of design rather that the outcome of this acting. Hereby, I refer to the etymological source of *disignare* and *designare* (Côrte-Real, 2010), which I interpret as "giving form" to something while being occupied in an activity of *designing*. Within this interpretation lies an understanding of designing as a matter of exploring a material as well as immaterial world.

In his groundbreaking book *The Ambiguity of Play*, Brian Sutton-Smith acknowledged the variability of play and stated that play is characterised by its quirkiness, redundancy and flexibility (1997). He continues by stating that play is not any frivolous act, but rather a powerful human asset for explorative and creative interactions between people and the surrounding environment. Hence, the concept of play can be considered as a somewhat disruptive activity that fosters novel idea generation by *making and breaking* down traditional ways of approaching the world. This chapter promotes such making and breaking processes as pivotal to play processes by reinforcing that they enable us to ask questions of *what if* to support actions of connecting and reconnecting ideas and hypotheses. In play, thus, people are able to explore and sustain creative actions of making and breaking, stimulating opportunities for self-expression, problem solving and building social relationships. This also offers meaningful ways of using ideas and other resources in new ways, which widens people's sense of participation (Rogers, 2000). This puts forward play and imagination as material as well immaterial processes.

Based on the author's empirical studies over a range of years, the goal of this chapter is to argue for, discuss and outline conditions for how designing and play can achieve a unity through aspects of *exploration* and *material interaction*. *Designing as play*, I believe, forms a fruitful way forward generating new insights into the theoretical and practical fields of design and play. This set of binary pairs of concepts is presented to shed light on a curiosity about what the characteristics of designing as play will be. As such, the importance of material interaction is highlighted. Next section will describe the empirical field included in this chapter. This is followed by unfolding designing as play in terms of exploration and through a material lens. Each of these are revealed theoretically and followed by an empirical exemplification. Finally, the chapter concludes by putting forward designing as play as a *melded phenomenon* framed by *making and breaking processes*.

Empirical Field

The empirical field included in this chapter is based on the author's several years of research within the field of child–computer interaction. The empirical examples however are based on a case study including four design workshops with a total of 120 children between 6 and 9 years of age. It was part of a project, *Architecture is Play*, where children's interaction with technologies and creative material targeting architectural learning in terms of math, science and design skills were investigated. Data was collected from observations, interviews and informal conversations with the participating children and their educators. The workshop was led by two facilitators from the design centre and to some extent supported by the participating educators.

When the children entered the design workshops, their task was to become architects and design a house for a fantasy animal. The children worked in groups and each group should design a specific room of the house, which together should form a house where it was possible to move around and seamlessly walk between the different rooms. With introductory knowledge about additive systems and scales, the groups built a room for a fantasy animal (a "crocoraff", a "eledile", or a different third animal). Hence, the children built the room to a specific animal with a specific size and with specific needs. The first step was to build the room out of foam-brick modules (size 1:10 and conceptualised as "centicube-model") and the next step was to build together these different rooms to a house for the animal. The house was built with cardboard boxes in natural size (1:1). Herein was the challenge for the children, i.e. to convert the foam-brick model to a room suitable for a "crocoraff". How could the children measure the size of the room – by means of, e.g. their own bodies or transfer the centicube-model to a scale (1:100)? The session was structured according to a simple cycle of scientific reasoning, where the children could reflect and ask, plan and predict, act and observe and report and reflect.

Exploration: Acts of Making and Breaking

Exploratory practices can be driven by imagination and doings. Linnell (2009) describes how people in explorative activities orient themselves in a material, sensational and symbolic world. In this way, the matter of exploration can be expressed and understood as a complex and often unexpected chain of expressions. In the field of design, such events might be described as emergent, while in a play context they could be described as social forms of imagination. Either way, these can be considered as dynamic procedures representing processes of making and breaking.

The context of exploration, i.e. how people can make sense of what they are doing and engage with, is a contributing factor in how designing as play develops and is sustained (Brooks & Sjöberg, 2019; Pramling Samuelsson & Carlsson, 2008). Vygotsky (1978, p. 11) stated that "A child's play is not simply a reproduction of what he has experienced, but a creative reworking of the impressions he has acquired". Understanding exploration in this way means that what a child does is combining prior experiences to create a new concrete situation, which is the essence of imagination. Thus, the significance of exploration has to do with being motivated to follow one's interest and imaginary experimentation with ideas. In giving space for designing as play processes, designers and educators have to constantly explore the interests, ideas and motives of children.

Design has for several years taken the form of participatory design or co-creation (Sanders & Stappers, 2008), and in Scandinavia, there is a strong tradition of working with design in close collaboration with stakeholders (cf. Ehn, 1993). Co-creation and participatory design processes constitute fruitful ways to foster exploration. Such processes are mediated by different tools, e.g. toys, technology or construction material, which connect exploration closely to acts of making and breaking. Such acts are characterised by being open to existing ideas and a willingness to imagine ways in which things could be done differently (i.e. considering *what if*). In this way, a "making and breaking" approach corresponds to a design process by offering participants to proceed through iterative cycles of designing and implementing ideas, where each implementation becomes an opportunity to promote explorative, critical and playful actions. Expressed differently, through acts of making and breaking, children can make their own choices and decisions and, thereby, find their ways of dealing with what they already know and their creative imagination of *what could be*. Eisner (1990) states that tensions between a desire to invent and explore and a need to share with others is a way for individuals to become social requiring learning of social conventions and working within their limits. Coping with tensions like this include what Zimmerman et al. (2007) have termed as a perceived fuzziness of design work. This is how I consider exploration as corresponding to designing through its uncertainty and to play through its open-ended character. Either way, having opportunities for exploration that stimulate imagination and encourage co-creation opens up for contextualising learning and using innovative approaches of expression.

Empirical Example

A group of two girls and two boys were building a bedroom for a bear named Berry using the cardboard boxes and were partially finished with their construction when the following discussions between the girls (Lisa and Annie) evolved:

LISA: We have no roof. If it rains Berry will be wet.
ANNIE: Yeah, if it starts raining and Berry wants to go inside, it doesn't help, he will still be wet. It should be dry in here, no matter what weather.
LISA: Ok then, let's build a roof.
ANNIE: We cannot use the cardboard boxes for it though.

The girls grabbed one of the facilitators and asked for a large piece of textile. When they got it, they found out that it was not big enough to cover the whole bedroom, but big enough to cover the area where they have placed Berry's bed. The girls then crouched down, side by side on the floor next to the cardboard bed.

ANNIE: It's dry in here.
LISA: Is here room enough for Berry to keep dry? He doesn't like rain.
ANNIE: I think so. I have a blanket here too.

At this moment, the boys (David and Ben) enter the room.

DAVID: Come on, I think this room is too small.
ANNIE: Why? All that is needed for the bedroom is here.
BEN: Yes, but it would be nice for the bear to also be able to easily get out. There is space on the other side of this wall [pointing]. Let's make another door and create an outdoor space.
ANNIE: But we are not supposed to build there.

DAVID: But there is space, so why can't we do it?

BEN: Let's do it and we put a nice carpet and chairs too.

An overriding factor in this example was that the children found ways to use the workshop environment to imagine future situations such as *what if* it rains and there is no roof on top of the bedroom? The support from the facilitator was crucial as this determined the way in which children could secure the situation. The boys' idea of breaking the rules of the building area that was designated for the bedroom and create an outdoor space gave an insight into how the children negotiated and used strategies to sustain their imaginative exploration. While children's exploration was influenced by the immediate space where they could build and decorate the bedroom, they also explored the boundaries of it by being creative to make a world that of make-believe. They became increasingly inspired through making and breaking these boundaries as it gave them opportunity to try new things. The children pushed their creation beyond simply constructing a bedroom for Berry, developing ideas and sustaining their own imaginative exploration. Therefore, it is pivotal to foster different types of *what if* spaces for children to explore and not just the content of resources in the space.

Material Interaction: Acts of Prototyping

Considering designing as a play through a lens of material interaction opens up for considering the crafting of ideas as a process of working back and forth between materialising ideas and the manifestations of ideas through an act of design (Brooks & Sjöberg, 2020; Wiberg, 2014). That is, to consider both details and wholeness and materials and textures. Wiberg (2014) unfolds this by describing *details* as aesthetic qualities, *wholeness* and compositional meanings, *materials* as giving character to properties and *texture* as appearance authenticity. This way of considering materiality not only makes it a practical lens, but also an analytical one enabling researchers and practitioners to grasp a material-centred interaction design. This extends Schön's (1983) statement that materials talk back to designers.

Material properties demonstrate how an understanding of the material can help in envisioning new design and how this helps in reimagining the material itself. *Texture* communicates material properties through its material appearance and becomes an issue of authenticity when this appearance is true given what it is made of. Attention to *details* can be regarded in terms of their aesthetic quality and has a focus on implementation, i.e. how materials have been selected and used in giving form to a design. A focus on *wholeness* has to do with the overall composition (Wiberg, 2014). Wiberg (2014) stresses that this conceptual framing goes beyond representation to also account for how it is experienced.

Considering Wiberg's approach, this chapter puts forward prototyping as a central anchor to bring material interaction to life as well as framing the ideas and imagination which are in play. Prototypes force people to evoke discussion and reflection. The role of prototyping, such as being unfinished and open for experimentation, opens up a way to experience future situation, to connect abstract theories to experience and a prop to imagination and telling stories (Stappers, 2013). Hence, material interaction becomes more than a reasoning with material and more than a representation of concepts or ideas.

Empirical Example

All groups started to design their specific room by means of foam-brick modules (centicube-model) and, then, using cardboard boxes to transform the centicube-model to natural size. In this process, the foam-bricks and cardboard boxes provided a greater in-depth understanding about concepts and materials. The children went back and forth between the two kinds of resources to experiment with different ways of manifesting their centicube-model into a full-size cardboard model. In this way, this prototyping activity of going back and forth, as well as dealing with materials that included different experiential properties, facilitated the children's material interactions, for example regarding limits, possibilities and properties of the different materials as well as compositional resources in terms of making specific qualities of the designs. The children were concerned about how they could communicate the full-size room through the material properties so that it could be understood properly by the other children, facilitators and educators. It was visible how this spurred, directed and inspired their prototyping activity.

Conclusive Remarks

Overall, the empirical examples have shed light on how the activity of *designing as play* can be understood as melded interactions, where *what if explorations* and *prototyping* by means of different kinds of material came together in experiential *making and breaking* endeavours. The way in which the children initiated and sustained imaginative designs and creative doings were visible within all groups. What I have termed as *melded interaction* stimulated their reflection and recursive actions with regard to how designing as play supported imaginative and material experiences and manifestations. In this regard, it was not only the environment and material resources that offered these experiences, but also the way in which the facilitators stood back and enabled sufficient space for the children to explore and to break boundaries. Following the children's ideas and interests meant that the facilitators were not only flexible in their support of the children's designing as play activities, but also that they themselves explored possibilities to support the children's experiences in the pursuit of continuous learning and participation.

Exploration and participation entail aspects of play and participation, where material (prototyping) and immaterial (imagination) interactions meld together and contribute to change and diversity. Keeping to this conceptualisation of designing as play, I emphasise the ethos of participants' voices to be heard and considered through material manifestation of their interactions with each other and with the recourses at hand. By applying the theoretical tools of explorative and material interactions, it is possible to study processes of designing as plays in which participants are able to experiment and experience different aspects of learning.

Acknowledgements

I thank all the children, teachers, and workshop facilitators. I gratefully acknowledge the grant from Nordea Foundation. I acknowledge Utzon Center for, in collaboration with DR School and pedagogical consultants from Aalborg Municipality, designing the workshop material as part of the project Architecture is play.

References

Brooks, E., & Sjöberg, J. (2019). Evolving playful and creative activities when school children develop game-based designs. In: A. Brooks, E. Brooks, & C. Sylla (Eds.), *Interactivity, game creation, design, learning, and innovation*. ArtsIT 2018, DLI 2018. Lecture notes of the institute for computer sciences, social informatics and telecommunications engineering, vol. 265, 485–495. Springer, Cham. https://doi.org/10.1007/978-3-030-06134-0_51

Brooks, E., & Sjöberg, J. (2020). *A designerly approach as a foundation for school children's computational thinking skills while developing digital games*. IDC '20: Proceedings of the Interaction Design and Children Conference, ACM, 87–95. https://doi.org/10.1145/3392063.3394402

Côrte-Real, E. (2010). The word "design": Early modern English dictionaries and literature on design, 1604–1837. Working Papers on Design Working Papers on Design, 4, ed. Grace Lees-Maffei, Retrieved 10.12.2020 from http://sitem.herts.ac.uk/artdes_research/papers/wpdesign/index.html

Ehn, P. (1993). Scandinavian design: On participation and Skill. In D. Schuler & A. Namioka (Eds.), *Participatory design. Principles and practices*. Boca Raton: CRC Press/Taylor & Francis Group. https://doi.org/10.1201/9780203744338

Eisner, W. E. (1990). Discipline-based art education: Conceptions and misconceptions. *Educational Theory, 40*(4), 423–440. https://doi.org/10.1111/j.1741-5446.1990.00423.x

Linnell, P. (2009). *Rethinking language, mind and world, dialogically: Interactional and contextual of theories of human sense-making*. North Carolina: Information Age Publishing.

Pramling Samuelsson, I. & Carlsson, M. (2008). The playing learning child: Towards a pedagogy of early childhood. *Scandinavian Journal of Educational Research, 52*(6), 623–641. https://doi.org/10.1080/00313830802497265

Rogers, N. (2000). *The creative connection: Expressive arts as healing*. Palo Alto: PCCS Books.

Sanders, E. B. N., & Stappers, P. J. (2008). Co-creation and the new landscapes of design. *Co-design, 4*(1), 5–18.

Schön, D. (1983). *The reflective practitioner: How professionals think in action*. New York: Basic Books.

Stappers, P. J. (2007). Doing design as a part of doing research. In R. Michel (Ed.), *Design research now. Board of International Research in Design*, 81–91. Basel: Birkhäuser. https://doi.org/10.1007/978-3-7643-8472-2_6

Stappers, P. J. (2013). Prototypes as central vein for knowledge development. In L. Valentine (Ed.), *Prototyping: Design and craft in the 21st century*, 85–97. Bloomsbury.

Sutton-Smith, B. (1997). *The ambiguity of play*. Cambridge, MA: Harvard University Press.

Vygotsky, L. S. (1978). *Mind and society*. Cambridge, MA: Harvard University Press.

Wiberg, M. (2014). Methodology for materiality: Interaction design research through a material lens. *Personal and Ubiquitous Computing*, 18, 625–636. https://doi.org/10.1007/s00779-013-0686-7

Zimmerman, J., Forlizzi, J., & Evenson, S. (2007). *Research through design as a method for interaction design research in HCI*. In *Proceeding of the SIGCHI conferences on Human factors in computing systems*, San Jose, CA, 493–501. ACM. https://doi.org/10.1145/1240624.1240704

2

DESIGNS FOR LEARNING AND KNOWLEDGE REPRESENTATIONS IN COLLABORATIVE SETTINGS

Ola Knutsson, Robert Ramberg and Staffan Selander

Introduction

In this chapter, we will outline a perspective on designs for learning as a social activity, beyond an understanding of learning as (only) an individual endeavour. Since some decades we can notice both globally and digitally distributed multimodal resources for communication and information storing, as well as new patterns for collaborative work to solve different kinds of problems (like crowdsourcing). This chapter gives a theoretical overview of a design-theoretic approach to learning that can be used not only to analyse and understand new learning sites and practices, but also to organise new collaborative learning environments. We will give one example of how this could be done: design patterns for sustainable change of technologies for learning in a professional group of teachers.

Designs for Learning and Knowledge

The concept of design can be given many different meanings. It is both a verb and a noun, and it can denote a process as well as a product, and a profession. It could further denote a field of research as well as a theoretic approach or a method that is used for doing research (Bannon & Ehn, 2013). Design could be understood as a way to construct a prototype for mass production of a specific artefact, but it could also be the very process of investigating a phenomenon anew, and to build up a new theoretic understanding – design (practice) as the prerequisite for theory-building (Redström, 2017).

   The traditional idea of design as "giving the thought a form" focused on form and function, and on the aesthetics and usability of a product. Contemporary, collaborative and process-oriented perspectives challenge this view, with a focus on function and meaning. This means an interest in how design can be a means to reframe a problem and construct new, shared meanings and practices (c.f. Dorst, 2015).

Designs for Learning – Designs of Knowledge Representations

Designs for learning, likewise, could mean script for acting in a given learning environment (Gagnon & Collay, 2001). As an alternative, we would like to put a more theoretically grounded perspective at the fore: designs *for learning* in terms of buildings, learning resources, allocation of time and money, curricula, the organisation of the learning space and the teaching, etc. and designs *in learning* with a focus on the individual- and group-oriented learning paths (Kress, Selander, Säljö, & Wulf, n.d.). The focus is both on *material and semiotic resources* and how these are *used during different learning sequences.*[1]

We cannot "see" learning as such, only the traces of learning and new knowledge in terms of new representation – how the learners are be able to show what they have learnt and how they have understood a phenomenon or a field of knowledge (Laurillard, 2012; Selander, 2008, 2015). This is also a question of understanding how knowledge can be represented multimodally in different ways (Bessemer & Kress, 2016), and an understanding of learning as a fundamentally dialogical process (epistemologically as well as ontologically; Selander, 2018).

To study learning from this point of view is to focus on context and sequences, framing and fixing points, and on the choice of material and semiotic resources to express/represent knowledge. Designs for learning thus also highlight existing "cultures of recognition": i.e. what is "seen as", and "recognised as", learning and knowledge (Kress & Selander, 2012).

Representations and representational artefacts can be used to relieve or reinforce cognitive processes, and also to coordinate different information units. In the research field of computer supported collaborative learning (CSCL), special attention has been focused on how representations are not only used naturally in human action, but how representations can be designed to support different types of learning. This leads us further to the idea of *sketching* and the construction of new *design patterns*.

Sketching

From a design-oriented perspective on learning, as shortly outlined above, learning can only be studied in terms of sign-making and how knowledge has been transformed (or re-designed) into a new representation. Thus, learning can be conceptualised in terms of the (time-based) difference between someone's capability to express things anew, to do new kinds of analysis, to use new techniques or to use established techniques in a new way. A way to study how someone conceptualises, shows and finalises something learnt (or a new idea) is by collecting information from the very process itself, highlighting which elements that have been of most importance, which decisions that have been made, as well as which expressions that are most sufficient for (relevant) others to understand the new idea (or what was learnt; Selander, 2013).

Representations, in the format of design sketches, have within the fields of HCI and interaction design (IxD) proven to support both individual design work and collaborative design work, as well as communication with stakeholders. In shared and collaborative design work, design representations aid to express thoughts and ideas, and there is something shared and inspectable to critique and collaboratively develop further (Ramberg, Artman, & Karlgren, 2013). And in communication with stakeholders, to communicate and present ideas of future systems and artefacts, their functionality and future use (Tholander, Karlgren, Ramberg, & Sökjer, 2008). Hence, the process of creating design representations as well as the results from it serves many complementary purposes.

Design Patterns

The concept of design pattern as originally introduced by architect Christopher Alexander, consists of a three-part rule, which expresses a relation between a *context*, a *problem* and a *solution* (Alexander, Ishikawa, & Silverstein, 1977). In his work on design patterns, Alexander attempted to document collective knowledge about urban design at different scales ranging from regions and cities, to buildings, rooms and even to the detailed level of doorknobs. The idea of using design patterns to share good examples of solutions to recurring problems has been picked up in several and different fields of research and practice, e.g. within the fields of interaction design (I×D), technology enhanced learning (TEL) and education.

When design patterns have been used within the field of interaction design, design patterns as a resource in the design work have proven to work both as a starting point for design by providing with examples, as well as an inspiration for the design of certain products or processes. In a study on student's collaborative interaction design, design patterns not only functioned as examples and inspiration for reuse of design ideas, but also aided the students to observe and articulate differences in opinions and difficulties the students had in understanding the design problem, each other's ideas and proposed solutions (Karlgren & Ramberg, 2012). This could also be expressed in terms of going "beyond the individual to integrate social networks and digital tools in a networked society" (Kafai, 2016) which redirects attention from tools to communities.

The Representational Format of Design Patterns

Much research within the fields of TEL (see for example Goodyear & Retalis, 2010), interaction design (e.g. Mor & Winters, 2008) and education (e.g. Kress

& Selander, 2012; Laurillard, 2012; Selander, 2015) has focused on design as a dialogic, participatory process. Here, we have added the use of design patterns to capture and document good examples of how to use technology in education. The approaches used vary and design methodologies and tools that are used often have their origin within the fields of HCI and IxD (e.g. participatory design and future workshops). Problems and difficulties have been observed both in the writing of design patterns, as well as in putting them into use. What concerns the writing of design patterns, based on experiences from writing design patterns together with teachers, an adapted participatory design methodology has been suggested (Mor & Winters, 2008).

When design patterns are written and elaborated by researchers, it is reported that these often become too extensive and abstracted from practice and as a result become difficult for teachers to use and put into practice. When design patterns on the other hand are written by teachers, research report that design patterns that are written can spark new ideas of not only how to use technology in education (Knutsson & Ramberg, 2018), but also that the design patterns risk becoming incomplete and fragmented, which in its turn present new challenges for other teachers to put them into use (Rolf, Knutsson, & Ramberg, 2019). Incomplete and fragmented patterns and the need to fill in missing gaps, may however not be an entirely bad thing. This could be described as a process of re-design in which the teacher can adjust the design pattern according to specific goals and regulations. This also points to a design practice that grows in collaboration with the partakers. It is not a script to follow, rather a pattern for thinking and acting in relation to specific circumstances, possible to change during the process.

Participatory Pattern Design

Participatory pattern design, as rooted in the Scandinavian school of participatory design, views (in this case) teachers as domain experts on teaching, who are invited into a design process of developing a common resource of solutions to teaching problems. Into this process, teachers bring their design problems or solutions having their origin in their own teaching practice. Work and research within participatory design use a range of techniques, methods and practices including different types of workshops, design games, multimodal narratives and constructions. By interacting and learning in each other's contexts, a mutual understanding between designers and participants is developed (Muller, 2007) involving people in design of processes and artefacts central to participatory design.

Goodyear and Retalis (2010) point out that a pattern-based approach to technology used in teaching and learning could capture teachers' design experiences by providing a way to connect recognisable problems with tested solutions, and the patterns could relate to design problems on any level (cf. larger and smaller patterns). In addition to this, the patterns could improve design performance as well as educate the designer/teacher. They also argue that there are not only practical gains of capturing teaching experience in the format of design patterns, but also of the designing of "learning places" (i.e. learning environments that are wanted by teachers and students and constitute a coherent whole) for both teachers and learners.

Participatory Pattern Design – A Case Study

In writing of design patterns of technology used in teaching and learning, the teachers are in command, developing their future "learn-places and -spaces", by way of documenting solutions they have already designed as well sketching on new ones. As researchers, we are facilitating a process of documentation of already existing pedagogical designs, as well as a creative process of developing new pedagogical designs.

It can be assumed that teachers and pupils in schools already equipped with laptops and tablets, are not in immediate need of new and contemporary applications, or presumably not even the best possible application. The sheer number of applications possible to use in the context of teaching and learning are to say the least, numerous. However, *how to use* available technology and how to put it into good use in contexts of teaching and learning is a different and more complex question. The approach taken was to identify tools and techniques that support the process of digitalisation of education. Based on pedagogical and didactical motives a guiding question was, what activities are to be supported with technology and why, and which are not? An intention was to develop a sharing culture between teachers (similar to e.g. the work by Laurillard, 2012), inspired by cultures of open source, and to connect this with the democratic movement of participatory design. This includes providing means to access, maintain and (preferably) further develop knowledge on how to use technology in teaching crucial aspects that need to be supported within an organisation such as the school.

In this case, design workshops were used. A group of teachers were involved in the digitalisation of the school. The researchers' idea was to get closer to practice on a long-term basis in comparison to intervention studies. In addition, the idea of "design patterns" was introduced as a tool to document and communicate solutions of recurrent problems. In this case, five workshops were designed, each with its own specific purpose. A sixth workshop was later developed by the participating teachers, in order to invite other teachers at the school and show the design patterns that they had documented, as well as a pattern language illustrating how to traverse and navigate among the collection of different design patterns. The first workshop focused on more formal aspects of what a design pattern could be, and look like (for a more detailed presentation, see Knutsson & Ramberg, 2018):

Title: pattern name.

Problem: a description of the problem that the pattern is meant to solve.

Context: a description of the context in which the problem occurs.

Solution: a suggested solution to the problem.

Maturity: the level to which the suggested solution has been tried out.

Other info: other information relevant to understanding of the pattern.

The second workshop focused on documenting new patterns, and collected patterns from the previous workshop was presented. A slightly different pattern template was introduced including "achieve goals" and "pedagogical possibilities" to the category "problem". In addition, "proposed solution" was now used instead of "solution". The reason for this development of the pattern template was that we perceived the teachers to be too problem oriented, i.e. they documented problems they were experiencing but put less emphasis on proposing and detailing solutions to these. Also, the strong focus on problems seemed to get in the way of thinking of possibilities.

Workshop 3 started with a presentation on what a pattern language could look like, and how the teachers' patterns could fit into the structure of a pattern language. The teachers were presented with printed copies of all patterns they had written, and started to work on how the patterns were connected.

At the fourth workshop, Schuler's method for pattern language development was presented, in order to show the teachers that a method for the development of design patterns and pattern languages (Schuler, 2002) was followed. The presentation gave an overview of the whole process, our current position in it, and the long-term goals with the process. In our case these consisted both in collecting and writing design patterns and languages based on experienced problems and suggested solutions, as well as to collaboratively adapt design methods and techniques to fit within the context of the school.

The purpose of the fifth pattern workshop was to familiarise the teachers to work with the design patterns and the pattern language in a wiki tool, to facilitate continued and collaborative work with the patterns outside of the workshop context. Another purpose was to facilitate and enable a presentation of the results of the workshop series to a larger group of teachers at the school.

For the last workshop it was decided that three teachers should be responsible and run it. The purpose with this workshop was to show the results of the process of creating the pattern language, to introduce the concept of design patterns to other teachers, as well as to present different ways to work with design patterns.

The teachers were also invited to write new or to do complementary design patterns, using an adapted design pattern template. Different design techniques were also tested during these workshops, as well as the collaborative documentation of design patterns using a wiki tool. The newly introduced digital learning platform at the school was also a key player for pedagogical development supported by different cloud services of educational technology.

After the Design Process: Infra-structuring and Design Patterns

The concept of infra-structuring was introduced into participatory design to mitigate problems of what happens after a design project is ended. What is strived for is to put things in place for long-term commitment from stakeholders and to work with an open-ended design structure (Hillgren, Seravalli, & Emilson, 2011). In the school context, we could discuss, metaphorically, a pattern language in terms of a railroad, and the design patterns as the stations – constituting the infrastructure. Trains travelling on the railroad, on the other hand, are metaphors for such design processes that seemed necessary to initiate based on what has been found on the earlier stations (patterns). If such infrastructure could be set up in schools, teachers could deal with the introduction of new technology and policies. In putting design patterns into use, the design patterns via a process of re-design connect the existing design to future designs by its potential of identifying problems. A challenge is to make it become an "eternal" design process where the pattern language becomes as alive as a real language is.

Who is the Designer? Reflections on Participatory Design and Knowledge Representations

In the academic discourse within TEL, interaction design and designs for learning, teachers are often portrayed as designers. However, what does that entail and what does it mean to be a designer? Is it a matter of trait, competence, or perspective? Is e.g. the core competence of a designer to master design methods and tools that originate in "traditional fields of design" such as industrial design, architecture, human–computer interaction and interaction design? Is it the mastering of the methodologies and tools that define and make up the designer, or is it something else or something more? Is it the ability to create/build/prepare something in a chosen material with the support of methods and tools available in the domain in question, e.g. education?

To design something (partially) unknown (an artefact, a lesson, a learning activity), is a process supported by domain-specific methods and tools. An endeavour has long been to train and support teachers to do their designs (and become designers in the sense of using methods and tools having their origin in "traditional fields of design") by providing with design methodology and different types of design tools (e.g. TPAC), including design patterns. If the starting point is not to "train teachers to become designers", but rather to see them as designers and experts in their field – with their own tools and processes – a central question would be how we could use this perspective for systematic and collaborative development in educational settings?

To develop existing pedagogical practices, it seems necessary to existing problem-solving practices and routines, and to encourage the development of new, documented and shared practices. A question is also if design patterns should deliberately be kept incomplete, so that there is a clear space for teachers to "fill in gaps" based on their own experience, creativity and ideas? The rational being that it is not possible to copy already existing solutions – only to reframe and re-design them.

A Dialogic Approach

Learning is a living process, not a machine process. When we design for learning and knowledge representation, the communicative aspect cannot be left aside. This is both a theoretic approach and a way to organise developmental work, to take part in a developmental process – in other words: to design *for* such a process *with* the interested parties.

Note

1 For more information of the model Learning Design Sequences, see for example Selander (2008, 2015).

References

Alexander, C., Ishikawa, S., & Silverstein, M. (1977). *A pattern language: Towns, buildings, construction*. New York: Oxford University Press.

Bannon, L. J., & Ehn, P. (2013). Design matters in participatory design. In: J. Simonsen, & T. Robertson (Eds.), *Routledge international handbook of participatory design* (pp. 37–63). New York: Routledge.

Bessemer, J., & Kress, G. (2016). *Multimodality, learning and communication. A social semiotic frame*. London/New York: Routledge.

Dorst, K. (2015). *Frame innovation. Create new thinking by design*. Cambridge, MA: The MIT Press.

Gagnon, G. W., & Collay, M. (2001). *Design for learning. Six elements in constructivist classrooms*. Thousands Oaks, CA; Corwin Press Inc.

Goodyear, P., & Retalis, S. (2010). Learning, technology and design. In: Goodyear, P. & Retalis, S. (Eds.) *Technology-enhanced learning: Design patterns and pattern languages*. Rotterdam: Sense, 1–28.

Hillgren, P. A., Seravalli, A., & Emilson, A. (2011) Prototyping and infrastructuring in design for social innovation, *CoDesign, 7*(3–4), 169–183. doi:10.1080/15710882.2011.630474

Kafai, Y. (2016). Seeking to reframe computational thinking as computational participation. *Communications of the ACM, 59*(8), 26–27. doi:10.1145/2955114

Karlgren, K., & Ramberg, R., (2012). The use of design patterns in overcoming misunderstandings in collaborative interaction design. *CoDesign, 8*(4), 231–246, doi:10.1080/15710882.2012.734829

Knutsson, O., & Ramberg, R., (2018). Teachers' collaborative pattern language design. *Designs for Learning, 10*(1), 1–17. doi:http://doi.org/10.16993/dfl.76

Kress, G., & Selander, S. (2012). Multimodal design, learning and cultures of recognition. *The Internet and Higher Education*. doi:10.1016/j.iheduc.2011.12.003

Kress, G., Selander, S., Säljö, R., & Wulf, C. (Eds.) (n.d.). *Learning as social practice. Beyond education as an individual enterprise.* London: Routledge.

Laurillard, D. (2012). *Teaching as a design science: Building pedagogical patterns for learning and technology.* New York and London: Routledge.

Mor, Y., & Winters, N. (2008). Participatory design in open education: a workshop model for developing a pattern language. *Journal of Interactive Media in Education, 2008*(1), 1–16.

Muller, M. J. (2007) Participatory design: The third space in HCI (revised). In J. Jacko and A. Sears (eds.), *Handbook of human-computer interaction*, 2nd Edition. Mahway NJ USA: Erlbaum.

Ramberg, R., Artman, H., & Karlgren, K. (2013). Designing learning opportunities in interaction design: Interactionaries as a means to study and teach student design processes. *Designs for Learning, 6*(1–2), 30–57.

Redström, J. (2017). *Making design theory.* Cambridge Mass.: The MIT Press.

Rolf, E., Knutsson, O., & Ramberg, R. (2019). An analysis of digital competence as expressed in design patterns for technology use in teaching. *British Journal of Educational Technology, 50*(6), 3361–3375.

Schuler, D. (2002). *A pattern language for living communication. Proceedings of Participatory Design Conference (PDC 2002)*, 23–25 June, Malmö, Sweden, 51–61.

Selander, S. (2008). Designs for learning and ludic engagement. *Digital Creativity, 19*(3), 199–208.

Selander, S. (2013). Transformation and sign-making. The principles of sketching in designs for learning. In M. Böck & N. Pachler (Eds.) *Multimodality and social semiotics.* New York & London: Routledge 121–130.

Selander, S. (2015). Conceptualization of multimodal and distributed designs for learning. In: G. B. Kinshuk & M. Maina (Eds.) *The futures of ubiquitous learning: Learning designs for emerging pedagogies*, Heidelberg, New York, Dordrecht & London: Springer, 97–113.

Selander, S. (2018). Can a sign reveal its meaning? On the question of interpretation and epistemic contexts. In: S. Zhao, E. Djonov, A. Björkvall, & M. Boeriis, (Eds.) *Advancing multimodal and critical discourse studies* (pp. 67–79). New York & London: Routledge.

Tholander, J., Karlgren, K., & Ramberg, R., Sökjer, P. (2008). Where all the interaction is: sketching in interaction design as an embodied practice. *In Proceedings of the 7th ACM conference on Designing interactive systems*, pp. 445–454.

3

A LEARNING ECOLOGY DESIGN

Susanne Dau

Learning Ecology

Learning ecology is a compound and complex term, and in this chapter, the understanding draws on the epistemology and ontology of orientation, and hence, how people orient themselves. The orientation ontology is the philosophical foundation for the epistemological descriptions and concerns of being with references to primarily Heidegger (1973), Ricoeur's (1981) and Ahmed (2006) and it includes questions of "what" and "how". Thus, orientation is the umbrella that frames the fundamental epistemological basis of the learning ecology and the theoretical underpinning of wayfinding later in this chapter.

The concept of learning ecology is two-parted and complex. It contains two different concepts respectively learning and ecology. Learning can be understood from different epistemological directions and perspectives and ecology stems from a biological understanding of the relations and interactions between organisms and their surroundings, including other organisms. Thus, the ecological perspective includes the practical world, the environment and living and working with others (O'Sullivan & Taylor, 2004).

The learning ecology approach has been suggested as an answer to today's learning as it offers a way of understanding the complexity of knowledge creation in a complex, dynamic, chaotic and interconnected world where emerging technologies, network and new knowledge modes are continually evolving and where digital literacy, creativity, connectivity and other lifelong learning skills have become more essential than ever. Therefore, a learning ecology and networks become a foundation for continuous growth in educations (Siemens, 2007).

An ecological approach to learning and teaching is not a new phenomenon. Already in the seventies, Doyle (1977) conceptualised an ecological approach to teaching. Doyle's (1977) ecological model described the classroom as an ecological system where relationships and environment interacts.

Later, Siemens (2007) described learning ecology as the space in which learning occurs. However, he unpacks the ideal learning ecology as a space where:"… –learner's access to information is not hampered… – experiment and failures are tolerated… – knowledge is shared and transparent, allowing for co-creation and recreation by others" (Siemens, 2007, p. 54).

Moreover, Siemens (2007) elaborated on the conceptualisation of learning ecologies with the reference to Brown (1999) and Solomon (2000) finding several aspects of learning ecology, e.g., that learning ecologies are dynamic, living, adaptive, self-organising, informal, loosely structured, changeable and evolving. Siemens (2007) stressed that there is a need to look at learning from an ecological point of view where learning becomes a process of exploration and a dialogue scaffolding flexibility and adaptability. Where Siemens (2007) explicitly conceptualises a learning ecology as a process with a fluid structure and several possibilities, Barron (2004) has a more precise framing of the concept of learning related to ecology in the original understanding. She stresses that a learning ecology is closely associated with the environment's opportunities for learning. She defines a learning ecology as "the accessed set of contexts, comprised of configurations of activities, material resources and relationships, found in collocated physical or virtual spaces that provide opportunities for learning" (Barron, 2004, p. 6). Hence, Barron's descriptions seem to include both the flexible environment, sociality, tools and thus materiality and the configured activities. According to configured activities, the acknowledgement of configuration opens up for an understanding related to a narrative approach and a reflective understanding as suggested by Ricoeur (1984).

The learning ecology perspectives add a conceptual frame to the existing challenges of navigating in a technologically rich and a continuously developing society, as it offers a language for peoples' interactions and activities across the different environments. A learning ecology perspective acknowledges that boundaries are blurred, multiple and permeable and that the environment affects people and their identities and development (Barron, 2006). Thus, a learning ecology perspective is a relevant approach that can support a society of continual change where technology and digital competencies must be continually developed and changed, accordingly. A learning ecology offers an adaptive and dynamic perspective on learning where learning is regarded to be ubiquitous, flexible and contextualised. Moreover, a learning ecology perspective provides access to knowledge dimensions of habits, identity, behaviour and narratives as relevant conditions. Accordingly, it raises possibilities to research the complexity of peoples' interactions with emergent technologies across different settings, spaces and places.

Space and Place

Space and place are conditional for understanding the learning ecology and peoples' orientation. However, the concepts "of spaces and places" overlap and are difficult to separate: the fact that they are intertwined is also a prominent understanding among the theoretical descriptions of space and place referred to below. In this paragraph, a geographical, a cognitive, an ethnographic and social constructivist and a narrative phenomenological perspective are included to address the various approaches framing the ecological understanding.

From a geographical perspective spaces concern the following:

- The actual location represented by the position and the terrestrial coordinates
- The perceived lived and represented space of the individual
- The heterogeneous property of being directionally dependent in space and the aggregate of individuals' compositions of their interactions in space

(Pumain, 2004, p. 2)

Pumain's (2004) geographical descriptions of space are, despite acknowledgement of the perceived, lived and represented space of individuals and their interactions, limited to geography.

Ingold underlines that places have centres or are centres, as stressing that places have no borders (Ingold, 2011). However, when it comes to borders and places, I suggest that the understanding of expanding and blurred borders is more appropriate to capture the continual expanding, development and changes of places (Dau & Ryberg, 2014). For instance, spaces and places are blurred when people navigate in the physical and digital environment and when the physical environment influences the online navigation and visa verse, or, e.g. when students' study work is messed with daily living activities or online leisure activities, e.g. when notification from social media affect or influence the process of studying.

Places can be physical and virtual, but they can also be represented mentally and by mapping. However, the map and the representation are not the world, but constructed images that help people recognise, navigate, recall and find places. Hence, places can be real or imagined and they might have a spatial component – a locus. Moreover, some places can be difficult to locate (Golledge, 1999), such as the beaches of Denmark even with the use of global positioning system (GPS). Peoples' knowledge of places is cognitively mapped through experiences of the place, the read of the place, peoples' movement in the place, the objects and the subjects and spatial formations. For example, when people come to the place of an airport for the first time, they are oriented by the signs available, the flight information, the paths of the arrival and departure gates, the shops and restaurants, the movements and actions of other people in relation to security and their knowledge from prior experiences with airports.

There are no places without paths (Ingold, 2011). People move from place to place following the paths and marks of the landscape. For instance, when hiking in the Norwegian mountains following the paths of others, the cairns and the trails mark routes for the pathfinder. Hence, the landscape, marked by the people, is part of the historical traces to follow, following the ancestors' movements and traces and at the same time adding mental and embodied knowledge of the landscape and how to navigate it. Thus, peoples' traces are deposited in nature and affect the landscape. Similarly, virtual online spaces are marked by people's navigation online and vice versa. Movements, pictures, comments and more are in most cases stored or tracked by others. An example is Facebook's tracking of people's online footprint, deposited not in nature but in databases, which is something that Mark Zuckerberg was accused of in 2018. Zuckerberg consequently promised to act to protect of people's personal information acknowledging that security had been handled badly (Zuckerberg, 2018). Places and spaces accordingly have meanings at different levels (Ingold, 2011), but has also different representations and related actions.

Spaces are nevertheless more than physical or virtual settings. Spaces are according to Massey (2005) poststructuralist contours of space:

- A product of interrelations constituted by interactions
- A sphere of possibilities of the existence of multiplicity and thus contemporaneous plurality
- A sphere under continuous construction

Space is thus: "the dimension of multiple trajectories, a simultaneity of stories-so-far. Space as the dimension of the multiplicity of durations" (Massey, 2005, p. 24).

Spaces thus include spatiality. Spaces can accordingly be mental, social, acoustic, visual and spiritual. Spaces relate to time, but not in a graspable time and clock-sense, rather it is a continuously developing present of the past, pointing towards the future, as Ricoeur (1984) has suggested. This understanding of space is consistent with the Japanese notion of Ba (Basho) as a shared mental, physical and virtual space (Von Krogh, Ichijo, & Nonaka, 2000) characterised by the dynamic and relationality and based on human actions and sociality. Ba can exist in any kind of spaces afforded by humans' orientation and activities such as mental representation stored in cognitive schemes shared by narratives from generation to generation; physical places connecting people's knowledge, like schools, football fields, courts and more; and virtual spaces such as ResearchGate or LinkedIn where the people share their knowledge and experiences. Knowledge is therefore stressed to be embedded in Ba (Von Krogh et al., 2000). Thus, spaces constitute and are constituted by humans. Thrift (1996) agree on the social dimension of space: "Space and time is always and everywhere social". He describes the interrelatedness between time and space, and emphasises how spaces are socially constructed and how human, things and spaces are interconnected. However, Ba seems to include a broader perspective as it also acknowledges the mental space and the cyberspace.

Ahmed (2006) approaches the issue of space from a phenomenological understanding. She focuses on orientation in her description of spaces, stressing that spaces acquire direction and accordingly orientation towards something (Ahmed, 2006). The process of inhabiting space is "a dynamic interaction between what is familiar and unfamiliar" (Ahmed, 2006) similarly to the cases of navigating the airport and following trails for the first time. The sociality of space, therefore, depends on people's agreement on how to measure the world and thus time and space (Ahmed, 2006). The directional entity of space thus includes something new and something old, something known and something unknown and something in the past and for the future. Spatiality creates a frame for the directional actions carried out. Hence, Ahmed (2006) seems to follow the ideas of time presented by Thrift (1996) and Ricoeur (1984) where time and space are intertwined as space represent both the past, the present and the future. However, Ahmed seems to put more effort on the human's perspectives as she connects the time-space navigation and spatial movements to the people's agreement and familiarity.

Spatiality

Spatiality comes from the Latin "spati(um)" meaning space. Spatiality is defined on Dictionary.Com (n.d.) as "relating to space and existing or occurring in space; having extension in space". Spatiality includes humans' and animals' orientation in spaces both vertical and horizontal. However, as described above this chapter's descriptions of movements in space are grounded in a more thorough understanding. Pumain's (2004) geographical description of spatiality reflects the author's explanation of space:

> Spatiality is one of the two main explanatory paradigms constructed by geography in order to contribute to explaining differentiation of use of the globe surface by human societies, it forms an interpretation by means of 'horizontal' relations, which complements explanations based on 'vertical' relations of societies with the diverse conditions and resources offered by natural environments.
>
> (Pumain, 2004)

Spatiality is a foundation for orientation in emerging practices. Without spatiality, there is no possibility for movement and orientation in space. Spatiality becomes a matter of the movements made by people and afforded by the space, the setting and the artefact. According to Simonsen's (2007) geography of practice, human practice and spatiality are based on a social ontology, where moving bodies are measuring space in an active construction of a meaningful world affected by the where of that. However, turning to biology, Jander's (1975) definition of spatial orientation as a self-controlled maintenance of change in the body position relative to the environmental space gives a more concrete description of spatiality. Jander (1975) outlines different types of orientation among animals and humans where the most important in humans' development seems to be the topographical orientation where the movements are extended by learning (Dau & Ryberg, 2014). These movements, coupled with the learning processes and the cognitive spatial orientation, are both bodily scaffolded and mentally represented in the cognitive schemes, forming a foundation for the orientation and thus the knowledge development.

In cultural studies and literacy, spatiality has become a central concept focusing on the metaphor of "the spatial turn" and thus adding a new approach to the prior literary analyses of time and history. The spatial turn describes an intellectual movement that emphasis place and space in social sciences and the humanities (Guldi, 2011). The terms of mapping, mapmaking, space and place are only conceptual in the spatial turn which is more complex involving space and time in humans' activities and social engagement. The way people approach, understand and traverse space are depending on how people conceptualise, frame and communicate. For instance, can a zoo for some people represent a park of entertainment, for another a place for animal conservation or a workplace and for another again a prison for animals, and accordingly different mindset affect different behaviour among people in the park. However, when something happens it can change the same peoples' understanding and navigation in the zoo, for instance, when visitors experience the killing of some of the animals as a part of preservation of others.

The spatial turn offers a way of analysing emerging practices in spaces under continual construction and reconstruction by adding geographical and ecological perspectives to the understanding of ongoing production and processes going on. Hence, space is always under construction (Massey, 2005). Therefore, the spatial turn implies a transformation where space and places matter to identity, adding further knowledge to peoples' practices across disciplines. Arias (2010) stresses that:

> Globalization, spaces of flows, actor-networks, poststructuralist encounters, identity theories, gender relations, queer theories, postcolonialism, cyberspace, hybridity, these—to one extent or another, in varying ways – incorporate some variant of geography as humanly created, as filled with uneven relations of power, as implicated in the constitution of self and other....
>
> (Arias, 2010)

Arias (2010) agree with Massey's (2005) notion of spaces as unfinished and under construction and reflection, in the social relations and processes, where humans influence space and vice versa. Therefore, Arias (2010) is underpinning the dynamic between human and space. Arias' description is justified in a post-structuralist understanding of space as situated and negotiable and accordingly, it is framed by the ideas suggested in the spatial turn. Nevertheless, the reader will notice some similarities to other authors' notion on space in the above section.

The Spatial Turn and the Ecological Thinking

The spatial turn represents a movement from a simple and uniformed understanding of knowledge development approaching the research from one perspective to a more multidimensional understanding acknowledging that spaces and places matter for the full understanding of knowledge development. Hence, the geography adds an understanding of the where to the understanding of the how and why question raised within different research fields, e.g. cultural studies, sociology, pedagogy, literacy, history and more (Arias & Warf, 2009). Thereby, the spatial turn adds a more complete understanding of the research area addressed in contemporary studies based on an ecological thinking.

The spatial turn relates to ecological thinking and biological environmental study of the relationship between humans and animal's relationship and with the environment. Ecological thinking has been deemed useful in studies of human resource development in spaces that combine people and technologies (Bennett & Bierema, 2010). Similarly, design studies have adopted the thinking to specific research areas such as blended learning (Dau & Konnerup, 2017), serious games (Deterding, Dixon, Khaled, & Nacke, 2011), assistive robotics (Forlizzi, DiSalvo, & Gemperle, 2004) and human-centred informatics (HCI) (Culén & van der Velden, 2015). The ecological understanding offers a holistic perspective on understanding humans' spatial orientation in spaces of emerging technologies. Accordingly, ecological learning is described by Barron (2006, p. 195) as a "set of contexts found in physical or virtual spaces that provide opportunities for learning". The ecological approach thus offers a frame to understand the interrelatedness, and interactions of humans entwined with the environment whether it is online or offline acknowledging the importance of humans' activities, spatial behaviour and sociality in the mapping of life. Nevertheless, the humans' mind and the representation of the environments narratives also plays a crucial role in mapping humans' orientation. De Certeau (1991), for instance, has suggested that spatial narratives are essential for the construction of practices. The role of narratives and representations will be revealed in the next section.

Representation and Narratives

The understanding of representation as a mirror of nature underlined by Rorty (2009) and others has been questioned. Hence, the understanding of representation in a mimetic sense can also be understood as un-representable, e.g. when the space of the world is not similar to representation, but dislocated (e.g. Bergson,

1991). Representation is the mental pictures made by stories gained from prior experiences of traversing space. However, these representations are often influenced or limited by the human's feelings, other representations, the visual angle range and the cognitive capacity. Representation is stressed being contrary to fixation, instead it is regarded as a continuous process of becoming and creating.

Narratives represent a representation of an event or sequence either fictitiously or autobiographically, mostly, either on text or in image form. Adding a dynamic dimension to the mimetic narratives' connecting text and world is suggested by Ingold (1993), Ricoeur (1989) and Thrift (1996). The mimetic narratives in the text therefore point to the future in a fictive manner and are part of the identity formation in space and time (Ricoeur, 1989). Massey (2005) gives an example of understanding narratives from a European historical point of view:

> Recognising spatiality involves… recognising coevalness, the existence of trajectories… the spatial, crucially, is the realm of the configuration of potentially dissonant (or concordant) narratives. The spatial in its role of bringing distinct temporalities into new configurations set off new social processes. And in turn, this emphasises the nature of narratives, of time itself, as being not about the unfolding of some internalised story (some already-established identities) – the self-producing story… but about interaction and the process of the constitution of identities….
>
> (Massey, 2005, p. 71)

The quotation illustrates how narratives play a role in peoples' understanding of time and space and simultaneously raises new understanding, productions, interactions and identity comprehension. This is aligned with the spatial turn and Ricoeur's descriptions of narratives as a reflective activity and his descriptions of oneself as another where he outlines the narrative activity as mimesis understood as prefiguration, configuration and refiguration pointing both forwards and backwards in a fictive and historical manner. Moreover, the narrative aims at a deeper reflective basis for understanding and judgements, adding new dimensions to the self through the reading and interpretation of the narrative. Narratives, therefore, offer a basis for understanding spaces, orientation and spatiality both in a historical sense and in a fictive and futures sense without an aim of direct transfer into practice. Therefore, the narratives are not a map to follow but a reflective foundation for future orientation in the landscape of emerging practices just as stories have survived from generation to generation helping to prevent diseases and offering new generation skills without committing the mistakes of their ancestors.

The cognitive representations of stories lived, reflected and read are partly consolidated in mind and/or body. Other parts of the stories are not cognitively consolidated but are discarded or found irrelevant in the processing of information, however, the written narratives have its own permanent life offering a distanced description of life lived and lives to live, adding possibilities to adapt usable and meaningful knowledge for the reader of the text, however, not necessary to follow the "map" made by others but to give information for use in humans' own mapmaking. Accordingly, Ingold (2000) stresses that: "knowing is like mapping, not because knowledge is a map, but because the product of mapping (geographic inscription), as those of knowing (stories) are fundamentally un-maplike". Thus, the map (or the narrative) is not the landscape, but a simplified constructed image offering guidance for the map-reader's orientation. However, tools, technique and technology also play a role in the guidance and actions.

Tools, Technique, Technology and Affordance

Tools, technique and technology are passive entities until they activate a perceived, an unconscious or a real affordance. Gibson (1979) is the originator of the concept affordance: "The affordances of the environment are what it offers the animal. What it provides or furnishes for good or ill" (Gibson, 1979, p. 129). However, in this chapter I follow a more holistic understanding and thus Dohn's (2009) argument that affordance is embodied and Ingold's (2000) addition of enmindment; thereby affordance seems to concern a mix of the physical, the mental and the conceptual relations that the environment offers the human or not. However, affordance is also determined by humans' preconditions, prior experiences and capacity. Tools, techniques and technology are therefore elements in the process of affordance and the background affordance. Dohn (2009) describe background affordance as a form of environmental entity which plays a role perhaps in the bodily position and behaviour in an unconscious way, such as when the laptop camera affords a concrete behaviour or limits the behaviour of the laptop user (Dau & Rask, 2017), e.g. when the eyes are fixed to the camera's picture of oneself rather than the picture of the other person participating in the virtual communication, or when the camera becomes the focus and locus rather than the virtual communication. Hence, an awareness of affordance becomes essential in the use of tools, techniques and technology. However, a definition of those concepts is needed.

Technology represents objects and according to Mumford (1946) include tools, artefacts, machines, utensils and utilities. Mitcham (1978) and others include a process perspective to technology. Ingold (2000) more precisely distinguishes between techniques and technology. Technique according to Ingold, is a matter of subjectivity, as he places the subject at the centre of the activity rather than the technology, which is regarded as independent of humans' subjectivity. Hence, technique includes the use of skills dependent on the humans' competences and capacity from which technology is detached. Accordingly, Ingold (2000) distinguishes between tools and techniques. He stresses that a tool is an object used by an animal or human in the realisation of a project, e.g. in training a swimming technique; "A tool… is an object that extends the capacity of an agent to operate within a given environment in the understanding of tools. But you do not necessarily have to use a tool to implement a technique" (Ingold, 2000, p. 315). Craftsmanship is, therefore, a central aspect of proper tool use, for instance, in the use of a hammer, a bicycle, a fishing rod and more.

Technique is embedded in the experiences of humans – just like the process of separating the yolk from the albumen when baking. However, today it is possible to buy a tool to overcome the process of separating an egg. In contrast to technique, technology is not dependent on subjectivity but exist independent of the subjectivity and specific skills of the human. Ingold (2000) stresses, accordingly, that technology is a product of a modern machine-theoretical cosmology placing a critique of the risk of determination of practice . Techniques differ from technology as it represents a process involving the skills of the acting subject, with or without a tool – for instance, using the body in performance, in dance or swimming. Technology thus represents an activity that can be independent of techniques, for instance, in the general systems of guidelines and manuals or in entering the world of algorithms without any specific knowledge of the system behind. Technology then becomes a matter of production independent of human subjectivity, skills and craftsmanship.

Turning back to the perspective of affordance, technology might thus play a role, especially in background affordance, as technology sometimes creates room for certain behaviour mentally, socially and physically, such as in the case of augmented reality and the Pokémon release where people of all ages suddenly turned to behave spatially differently from prior behaviour in the physical environment. When walking along the street, people were less attentive to other people's movement as they followed their paths of the augmented roadmap offered by the smartphones and the application. Their visual orientation afforded by the physical environment and other people's movement was replaced by the technological features. Similarly, when they reached the attractions they were guided to, most of them did not even look at it: instead, they were concerned with situated lures and their possibility of achieving a rare Pokémon. Also, for some people, social affordance became displaced by matters of competitions, acknowledgement and reaching new levels being part of a certain community of practice in the augmented reality. For some people, the game is still a part of their daily routines and is becoming a part of their biography – for instance, when young people routinely have their mobile phone attuned to the application whenever they are on the move or when they automatically turn to a daily update from the most popular i-tuners talking about news from the game. Pokémon-seekers' orientation thus becomes directed towards certain predetermined practices limiting humans' ordinary map using. There have been examples of how Pokémon users have disrupted the current traffic rules and agreements in their efforts to gain new Pokémon. Awareness of the technologies' influence on people's spatial navigation, therefore, becomes very important.

Wayfinding

In contrast to the example of orientation behaviour among Pokémon followers, Ingold (2000, p. 55) underlines that "in wayfinding, people do not traverse the surface of the world whose layout is fixed in advance – as represented on the cartographic map. Rather, they 'feel their way' through a world that is itself in motion, continually coming into being through the combined action of human and non-human agencies". Wayfinding is a movement in time like music playing and storytelling (Ingold). Ingold differentiates between wayfinding, mapmaking and navigation (Ingold, 2000). He juxtaposes wayfinding and mapping as an ongoing cartography process which can also involve mental representations. However, navigation is compared to map using, and thus following paths already made or represented. Mapmaking is about the inscription practice afforded by prior mapping and mapmaking. Mapmaking is related to humans' capacity to make a map. Nevertheless, it is not about drawing a cartographic map on a paper, but about processes of remembering, sensing, structuring, consolidating and comparing. Questions of, where am I? and which way should I go? are found in narratives of prior movements (Ingold, 2000). How people find their way is thus characterised as complex structures holding complex processes (Ingold, 2011). For example, research of campus student's orientation (Dau, 2015) reveals that it is formed by the students' prior study trails, practice, habits and movements. The students seem to find their academic and professional way on the basis of instructions, the peers' movements and approaches, artefacts and the teachers acting and guiding. Social connections and co-constructed knowledge are parts of a common mapmaking process affording student's wayfinding and professional identity development (Dau, 2015).

Turning from Ingold's anthropological ecological understanding of wayfinding to a more geographical and psychological perspective, wayfinding means an oriented search, following marked trails, piloting between landmarks, paths integration, habitual locomotion and integrated internal representations referred to as cognitive maps (Allen, 1999). Despite these meanings of wayfinding emphasising different types of wayfinding according to different tasks such as travel to a familiar destination, exploratory travel and travel to new destinations, there seems to be a shortcoming when it comes to addressing the individual aspects that Ingold (2000) highlights. Allen (1999) suggests that the individual perspective concerns spatial ability, visual and mental capacity, the ability to interpret maps, the ability to store appropriate information and other orientation skills. Thus, wayfinding is suggested to be conditioned by knowledge, information processing capabilities, spatial perception and motor capabilities (Allen, 1999). In this chapter, a more complex understanding of wayfinding is emphasised, drawing on the perspective of mapping revealed by Ingold (2000). It includes the behavioural, ecological and narrative perspectives represented in the above sections and is based on the empirical research confirming the idea (Dau, 2015). Before turning to the empirical research supporting the conceptualisation of wayfinding as a central element in the knowledge creation process, the next paragraph describes contemporary research within the field of orientation and thus wayfinding.

Contemporary Studies on Wayfinding

Much research seems to ignore the difference between wayfinding, navigation and mapmaking, and often suggests that wayfinding is a matter of movement of users in physical spaces between certain points. Also, much research seems to ignore the embodied, social and emotional aspects of wayfinding. Nevertheless, the many attempts to address different perspectives on wayfinding, tools, techniques and navigation add pieces to a broad "research patchwork" of multidimensional wayfinding matters. A small selection of contemporary research is presented here to give a picture of wayfinding in use from different perspectives and related to various issues at different levels, starting with concrete empirical research, moving to a learning perspective and an example related to embodied social lifeline knots and ending with a study on students' wayfinding in blended learning environments.

Wayfinding and Research in Writing

Contemporary research (Strantz, 2015) on empirical methods suggests, for instance, the inclusion of mapped navigational data using local knowledge and mobile technology, thereby mapping students' mobility and working context to understand the context of writing and the complexity of technologies and networks. Access to students heuristic memory and visual representation offers opportunities to externalise stories and thus the knowledge of the researchers and the participants. Moreover, the author Strantz (2015) reveals that the mapped wayfinding of students studying abroad might provide a framework for understanding the use of tools and practices framing writing in situated and navigated spaces. Strantz (2015) provides a framework for understanding movements and actions and thus gives a perspective of students´ needs when they struggle to collect data and conduct research in non-classroom settings. However, the description of wayfinding is more related to the notion of navigation from a geographical perspective than the complex understanding of wayfinding suggested above.

Wayfinding and Adaptive Learning

Dziuban, Moskal, Cassisi, and Fawcett (2016) connect wayfinding in the digital age to the concept of adaptive learning. Referring to, e.g. Morville's (2005) description of wayfinding and Turchi's (2011) metaphorical framing of adaptiveness as a process of mapmaking, the authors establish a foundation for their conceptualisation of adaptive learning. Drawing on Hall's (2004) writing on an adaptive learning geography as a reorienting process improving students' learning processes and Carpman and Grant's (2012) functional hierarchy for personal geographies, they describe their understanding of adaptive learning as a wayfinding process, divided into the following recommendations:

- Know where you are (baseline measures)
- Know your destination (desired outcomes)
- Follow the best route (learning path)
- Recognise your destination (knowledge state)
- Find your way back (repeat, revise and reassess)

(Dziuban et al., 2016)

The recommendations are clearly grounded in a learning geography drawing on concepts therefrom and reflecting some of the essential movement and steps in the learning process by the conceptualisation of destinations, paths and routes addressing the questions of why, how and what, which are elementary in any learning process.

Wayfinding and the Embodied and Socio-cultural Lifeline knots

A more nuanced view on wayfinding has been presented by some authors.

For instance, Symonds, Brown, and Lo Iacono (2017) recently emphasised how wayfinding must be understood as an embodied and socio-culturally directed process, referring to Ingold (2011) in the revelation of wayfinding as an entwined knot of routes made by oneself and others' lifelines. Moreover, Symonds et al. (2017) draw on Bourdieu's (1990, p. 56) notion of habitus to explain how wayfinding behaviour is part of an embodied historical behaviour. The authors underline that embodied movements and the embodied socio-cultural approach are beneficial for understanding the wayfinding experience. Hence, Symonds et al. (2017) suggest an understanding of wayfinding that includes the embodied individual, experience and sociocultural elements. They thereby extend the narrated cognitive and geographical understanding of wayfinding, arguing that wayfinding is socially and habitually interdependent: "In a wayfinding context, our own routes thus impact other people's routes. We do not, in other words, find our way in social vacuums, but in a socially dynamic environment" (Symonds et al., 2017, p. 1). Thus, they stress that wayfinding includes groups of individuals entwined in lifeline knots created by the socially dynamic environment of people's wayfinding.

Students' Wayfinding in the Blended Learning Environment

The conceptualisation of wayfinding, according to Dau (2015, 2016), is based on a phenomenological ecological approach and draws on behaviourism, humanism and sociality. Wayfinding is in this study described as an ongoing learning process of mapping the physical, the psychological and the conceptual terrain in the learning landscape. The learning process involves psychological, embodied, emotional, spiritual, social and virtual spaces where narratives affect how people orient themselves and creates knowledge. Learning as wayfinding is underlined to address how people find their way by continuous cognitive development, and the development of attitudes and skills through embodied and cognitive movements in physical, mental or virtual spaces that are in motion. Learning as wayfinding can according to Dau (2015) result in the restructuring or development of prior knowledge (tacit or explicit). Moreover, learning as wayfinding can be described as knowledge development through qualifying and clarifying prior mapping of knowledge paths (e.g. cognitive and physical patterns) and as adding new knowledge and competencies (e.g. skills attitudes, values and information) or as an accommodative reconstruction of prior knowledge and competencies, for instance, by gaining new or better ways of handling, thinking, assessing, feeling and being. It is suggested that wayfinding accommodates a learning perspective that involves mental and embodied orientation processes in interaction with spaces, subjects and objects and their affordance, where architecture, stimuli, interruptions, habits, culture and behaviour, as well as indistinct borders, are affecting peoples' orientation or disorientation and thus learning (Dau, 2015).

A Reflective Basis for Design for Learning

According to the Larnaca Declaration on Learning Design (Dalziel et al., 2016), learning design originates from a desire to contribute to the emerging field of full or partly technology-mediated instruction and learning. The reflective basis described below is primarily related to educational philosophy, theories and methodologies in the Learning Design Conceptual Map suggested in the article (Dalziel et al., 2016). However, it is relevant to the reflective basis considered in every element of the learning design process.

The reflective basis is retrieved from the longitudinal case study on blended learning among undergraduate students at University College of Northern Denmark (Dau, 2015). The reflective basis is adding perspectives to consider in any learning design process.

The reflective frame generated from the study (Dau, 2015) is presented in Figure 3.1.

The different dimensions revealed in Figure 3.1 are related to the students' understanding of their orientation in blended learning environments. The presented dimension of wayfinding is validated by the informants, confirmed in the empirical data and tested in practice and theory (Dau, 2015). The figure illustrates the wayfinding entities to consider in any contemporary design for learning.

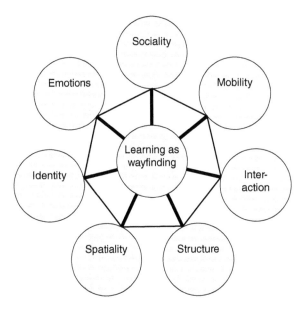

FIGURE 3.1   A reflective basis for learning design where learning is understood as a process of wayfinding. Retrieved and translated from Dau (2015).

The seven wayfinding entities illustrated in Figure 3.1 are all interrelated; together, they offer a reflective basis for the design for learning or considerations to include.

- Sociality is a relational process of collaboration. It involves sharing of tacit knowledge and experiences. Sociality appears in shared reflections, dialogues and discussions. Sociality is based on the communities such as communities of practice. Sociality act as a driver for the commitment between people.
- Mobility is physical, embodied, mental or virtual movements' patterns, geographical and spatial orientations and spatial positions, including a mapmaking process. Mobility is situated and coupled with habits, experiences, identity, sociality, interactions and preferences. Mobility appears as movements or lack of movements. Mobility occurs in physical and virtual settings and includes physical, mental and emotional movements and search behaviour.
- Spatiality refers to the spatial orientation, in which objects and subjects do different types of activity depending on the situation and context. Spatiality is spatial and topo-geographical behaviour in spaces. It is dependent on the virtual or physical architecture and artefacts and their affordances. Spatiality frames the contextualised embodied, cognitive, social and emotional behaviour. It concerns the possibilities of mapmaking and navigation in spaces

including their borders and limits. Spatiality is the possible movements in settings and can be both directional and misleading.

- Interaction is interactive relationships, e.g. interactions with spaces, media, objects and subjects such as peers. Interactions are, e.g. dialogical, communicative and narrative-facilitated. They are, e.g. influenced by access, role models, practices, crafts, reflections, exercises, opportunities for interaction, resources, hierarchies, action rooms, mental performances, habits, cultures and structures. Interactions can be directional but also misleading depending on the form, function and correctness of the interaction.
- Structure is about mental, physical and virtual maps and navigation tools which support the orientation and experience of coherence. Structure acts as a guiding principle as well as a management tool. It involves goals, incentives and frameworks for the orientation. These may be externally or internally based and concern self-management or external management. Structures can be directional, but also restrictive.
- Identity is about the self and its interactions with the surroundings. It concerns elements of identity seeking, creation and stabilisation. Identity stabilisation deals, e.g. with valuation, preferences and habits. Identity can be a guiding principle and a prerequisite for knowledge formation, but also the opposite. Identity may appear in different forms in different spaces. These partial identities provide direction for the different space-related orientation processes.
- Emotionality relates to the experience of positions in professional communities and in relationships, and to the significance of the mental, virtual and physical orientation. Emotionality is important in relation to the spatial emotions associated with the spatial orientation in the approximation of objects and subjects. It is a mobility either towards emotional pleasure or in relation to the management of discomfort. Emotionality can facilitate activities in terms of motivation, commitment and emotions.

The seven entities described above and illustrated in Figure 3.1 reveals the complexity to consider in any design for learning based on an ecological understanding (Dau, 2015). The model extends the complexity suggested by other researchers such as Wozniak, Mahony, Lever, and Pizzica's (2009) dimensions of reflectivity, interpersonally and technology. The seven wayfinding entities supplement and expand the existing understanding of learning ecology as they include specific entities that encompass anthropological, psychological, sociological, phenomenological and narrative understandings of the overall learning ecological landscape. The perspectives of wayfinding acknowledge the emotional, physical, social, cognitive and psychological orientation of people moving, acting and interacting in and across different environments and structures. It offers an understanding of the importance of identity and sociality for learning.

Mapping the Chapter and Concluding Remarks

This chapter has addressed a learning ecology perspective on orientation and wayfinding in digital and analogue environments and emerging practices. Firstly, it has described the learning ecology as a complex concept that draws on research conducted in biology, geography, anthropology and narrativity. In the descriptions of a learning ecology, related concepts such as spaces, places, tools, techniques, technology, affordance and narratives have been included to give the reader an understanding of the complexity and interrelatedness of the different entities influencing peoples' orientation in emerging practices and learning environments. Secondly, the question of how people orient themselves from a learning ecology perspective has been revealed and described by the concept of wayfinding as a process of mapping the physical, mental and social environment. The concept of wayfinding has further been mapped by the findings from a Danish research study (Dau, 2015) followed by a reflective frame for design for learning (Figure 3.1). The "landscape" mapped in the chapter is illustrated in Figure 3.2.

Figure 3.2 is an attempt, to sum up, and map the conceptualised landscape of a learning ecology, orientation and wayfinding in digital and analogue environments and emerging practices as presented in the chapter.

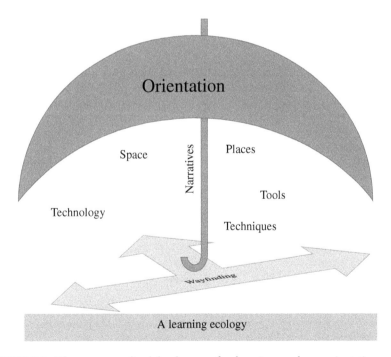

FIGURE 3.2 The conceptualised landscape of a learning ecology, orientation and wayfinding in digital and analogue environments and emerging practices.

The bottom of the figure is marked with a green colour, representing the basis for the understanding presented. People's orientation is the philosophical umbrella that "shadows" and frames people's wayfinding: it is constituted by the narratives and the biographies of themselves and others, with the environment and thus places, spaces, tools and techniques (concepts under the umbrella). Hence, Figure 3.2 pictures the structure of the chapter, the conceptual context revealed and the landscape of a learning ecology, orientation and wayfinding in digital and analogue environments and emerging practices as stated in the chapter.

The chapter has offered a frame to understand how people are interdependent with the environment and other people and their orientation and wayfinding. The chapter derives a conceptual and reflective basis of design for learning based on a theoretical conceptualisation and a research study. The overall theoretical mapping and the empirical examples of the learning ecology presented is thus a contribution to the theme of the book and it might act as a reflective basis reading the following chapters.

References

Ahmed, S. (2006). *Queer phenomenology, orientation, object, others*. Durham & London: Dale University Press.

Allen, G. L. (1999). Spatial abilities, cognitive maps, and wayfinding. *Wayfinding Behavior: Cognitive Mapping and Other Spatial Processes, 1*, 46–80.

Arias, S. (2010). Rethinking space: An outsider's view of the spatial turn. *GeoJournal, 75*(1), 29–41.

Arias, S., & Warf, B. (2009). Introduction: The reinsertion of space into the social sciences and humanities. In *The spatial turn: Interdisciplinary perspectives*. Routledge, London.

Barron, B. (2004). Learning ecologies for technological fluency: Gender and experience differences. *Journal of Educational Computing Research, 31*(1), 1–36.

Barron, B. (2006). Interest and self-sustained learning as catalysts of development: A learning ecology perspective. *Human Development, 49*(4), 193–224.

Bennett, E. E., & Bierema, L. L. (2010). The ecology of virtual human resource development. *Advances in Developing Human Resources, 12*(6), 632–647.

Bergson, H. (1991). *Matter and memory*, trans. N. M. Paul and W. S. Palmer New York: Zone, 21.

Bourdieu, P. (1990). *The logic of practice*. Trans. R. Nice Cambridge: Polity Press.

Brown, J. S. (1999, March). *Learning, working & playing in the digital age*. In *American Association for Higher Education Conference on Higher Education*, Washington, DC. Retrieved April (Vol. 24, p. 2007).

Carpman, J. R., & Grant, M. A. (2012). *Directional Sense: How to find your way around*. Boston, MA: Institute for Human Centered Design.

Culén, A. L., & van der Velden, M. (2015). Making context specific card sets-a visual methodology approach: Capturing user experiences with urban public transportation. *International Journal on Advances in Intelligent Systems, 8*(1&2), 17–26.

Dalziel, J., Conole, G., Wills, S., Walker, S., Bennett, S., Dobozy, E., … Bower, M. (2016). The larnaca declaration on learning design. *Journal of Interactive Media in Education, 1*, 1–24. doi:10.5334/jime.407

Dau, S. (2015). Studerendes orientering i fleksible professionsuddannelsers læringsrum: Et narrativt casestudie af vidensudviklingens veje og afveje. Ph.d.-afhandling. Aalborg Universitetsforlag.

Dau, S. (2016). Blended learning: An epistemic conceptualization of "learning as wayfinding" in blended environments. In EDUlearn16. IATED.

Dau, S., & Konnerup, U. (2017). Engagerende didaktiske design i blendede læringsrum–et grundlag for facilitering af læreprocesser. *Tidsskriftet Læring Og Medier (lom), 9*(16).

Dau, S., & Rask, A. B. (2017, October). *Connecting eye to eye: The challenge of computer supported contact*. In *European Conference on e-Learning* (pp. 124–131). Academic Conferences International Limited.

Dau, S., & Ryberg, T. (2014, October). *Disruptions and disturbance as challenges in a blended learning (BL) environment and the role of embodied habit orientation*. In *European Conference on E-Learning* (pp. 156). Academic Conferences International Limited.

De Certeau, M. (1991). Travel narratives of the French to Brazil: Sixteenth to eighteenth centuries. *Representations, 33*, 221–226.

Deterding, S., Dixon, D., Khaled, R., & Nacke, L. (2011, September). *From game design elements to gamefulness: Defining "gamification"*. In *Proceedings of the 15th International Academic MindTrek Conference: Envisioning Future Media Environments* (pp. 9–15).

Dohn, N. B. (2009). Affordances revisited: Articulating a Merleau-Pontian view. *International Journal of Computer-Supported Collaborative Learning, 4*(2), 151–170.

Doyle, W. (1977). 4: Paradigms for research on teacher effectiveness. *Review of research in education, 5*(1), 163–198.

Dziuban, C. D., Moskal, P. D., Cassisi, J., & Fawcett, A. (2016). Adaptive learning in psychology: Wayfinding in the digital age. *Online Learning, 20*(3), 74–96.

Forlizzi, J., DiSalvo, C., & Gemperle, F. (2004). Assistive robotics and an ecology of elders living independently in their homes. *Human–Computer Interaction, 19*(1–2), 25–59.

Gibson, J. J. (1979). *The theory of affordances. The ecological approach to visual perception*. Boston: Houghton-Mifflin.

Golledge, R. G. (1999). Human wayfinding and cognitive maps. *Wayfinding Behavior: Cognitive mapping and other spatial processes, 1*, 5–45.

Guldi, J. (2011). *The spatial turn in history. Spatial Humanities: A Project of the Institute for EnablingGeospatial Scholarship at the Scholars' Lab at the University of Virginia Library, Charlottesville, VA*. Retrieved the July 13, 2019 from http://spatial.scholarslab.org/spatial-turn/disciplinary-perspectives/the-spatialturn-in-history/.

Hall, S. S. (2004). I Mercator. In K. Harmon & K. A. Harman (Eds.), *You are here: Personal geographies and other maps of the imagination* (pp. 15–19). New York, NY: Princeton Architectural Press.

Heidegger, M. (1973). *Being and time, translated by John Macquarrie and Edward Robinson*. Oxford: Basil Blackwell.

Ingold, T. (1993). The temporality of the landscape. *World Archaeology, 25*(2), 152–174.

Ingold, T. (2000). *The perception of the environment: essays on livelihood, dwelling and skill*. London & New York: Psychology Press.

Ingold, T. (2011). *Being alive: Essays on movement, knowledge and description*. London & New York: Taylor & Francis Group.

Jander, R. (1975). Ecological aspects of spatial orientation. *Annual Review of Ecology and Systematics, 6*(1), 171–188.

Massey, D. (2005). *For space*. Los Angeles, London, New Delhi, Singapore & Washington DC: Sage Publications Ltd.

Mitcham, C. (1978). Types of technology. *Research in Philosophy and Technology*, *1*(1), 229–294.

Morville, P. (2005). A brief history of wayfinding. In *Ambient findability: What we find changes who we become*. California: O'Reilly Media. Safari Books.

Mumford, L. (1946). *Technics and civilization*. London: Routledge.

O'Sullivan, E., & Taylor, M. M. (Eds.). (2004). *Learning toward an ecological consciousness: Selected transformative practices*. New York: Palgrave Macmillan.

Pumain, D. (2004). *Hypergéo* – Spatial Analysis – Epistemological Foundations. Retrieved July 14, 2017 from http://www.hypergeo.eu/spip.php?article181#.

Ricoeur, P. (1981). *Hermeneutics and the human sciences: Essays on language, action and interpretation*. Cambridge: Cambridge University Press.

Ricoeur, P. (1984). *Time and narrative* (Vol. 1), (Trans. K. McLaughlin and David Pellaur). Chicago: University of Chicago Press.

Ricoeur, P. (1989). *The conflict of interpretation*. Great Britain: Abalone Press.

Rorty, R. (2009). *Philosophy and the mirror of nature* (Vol. 81). New Jersey: Princeton University Press.

Siemens, G. (2007). Connectivism: Creating a learning ecology in distributed environments. In *Didactics of microlearning: Concepts, discourses and examples* (pp. 53–68). Germany: Waxman Verlag.

Simonsen, K. (2007). Practice, spatiality and embodied emotions: An outline of a geography of practice. *Human Affairs*, *17*(2), 168–181.

Solomon, D. L. (2000). *Philosophy and the learning ecology. Presidential Session on in Search of the Meaning of Learning*, Denver, October 25–28. Retrieved February 1, 2007, from http://www.learndev.org

Spatiality. (n.d.). The american heritage® science dictionary. Retrieved July 27, 2017, from Dictionary.com website http://www.dictionary.com/browse/spatiality

Strantz, A. (2015). Wayfinding in global contexts–mapping localized research practices with mobile devices. *Computers and Composition*, *38*, 164–176.

Symonds, P., Brown, D. H., & Lo Iacono, V. (2017). Exploring an absent presence: Wayfinding as an embodied sociocultural experience. *Sociological Research Online*, *22*(1), 48–67. Retrieved July 21, 2017 from http://www.socresonline.org.uk/22/1/5.html

Thrift, N. (1996). *Spatial formations* (Vol. 42). London, Thousand Oak, New Delhi: Sage.

Turchi, P. (2011). *Maps of the imagination: The writer as cartographer*. Trinity University Press.

Von Krogh, G., Ichijo, K., & Nonaka, I. (2000). *Enabling knowledge creation: How to unlock the mystery of tacit knowledge and release the power of innovation*. New York: Oxford University Press on Demand.

Wozniak, H., Mahony, M. J., Lever, T., & Pizzica, J. (2009). Stepping through the orientation looking glass: A staged approach for postgraduate students. *Australasian Journal of Educational Technology*, *25*(2), 221–234.

Zuckerberg, M. (2018). Hearing before the United States House of representatives committee on energy and commerce. Testimony of Mark Zuckerberg Chairman and Chief Executive Officer, Facebook. Retrieved July 11, 2018 from https://docs.house.gov/meetings/IF/IF00/20180411/108090/HHRG-115-IF00-Wstate-ZuckerbergM-20180411.pdf

4

COLLABORATIVE LEARNING IN DIALOGIC DIGITAL ENVIRONMENTS

Elsebeth Korsgaard Sorensen

Introduction

The focused contribution of this chapter is to describe, discuss, elucidate and demonstrate – theoretically and through its implementation in practice – the concepts of collaboration, dialogue and meta-learning in a digital collaborative knowledge building (D-CKB) learning context of higher education in the field of user-driven innovation. Moreover, the chapter tries to capture the characteristics and values from learning through digital negotiation and collaborative construction of – in particular, NEW knowledge as it unfolds in a process, which denote the involvement of all stakeholders of a learning context in higher education (employees, partners, customers, learners, citizens, etc.). As opposed to traditional learning designs, learners in this understanding are not being exposed to an already designed curriculum. They are actually creatively involved in the actual design and creation of their own learning process.

The author argues that the D-CKB perspective presented and discussed in this chapter is essential in order to produce a kind of learning that generates ownership – simply a must for a society to grow and prosper. She presents a generic theoretical framework with features and theoretical assumptions, which – when employed in teaching and learning – are likely to possess a potential for furthering such prospering learning society.

Implied in D-CKB is a view on learning as mediated by democratic interaction and dialogue between learners. The author is using the term "democratic" to denote a collaborative process of negotiation, and when used in this context, the term is concerned with learning as a negotiation process and points to flat principles of communication and interaction between learners – a challenge for instructional designers to pursue.

D-CKB as a pedagogic design approach is interesting. Not only because it carries along a fresh view on the field of user-driven innovation it also adds another element to the trajectory and tradition started decades ago of involving the end users (the learners) themselves in the process of innovative creations. It implies the inclusion of learners as "responsible agents" for the quality of the collaborative learning process in terms of both ethical attitudes and democratic engagement. This approach is correlated with a set of underlying values. These, in turn, give birth to novel creative models and methods for employing digital technologies and architectures in learning processes in teaching and learning practices of higher education.

Digital Collaborative Knowledge Building (D-CKB)

Approaching the challenge of designing online learning from a perspective of democratic collaborative knowledge building (D-CKB) inspires our pedagogic design thinking to follow a set of alternative qualities and aspirations (including creative thinking), when envisioning alternative frameworks for the translation into practice of these pedagogic visions for the use of technology enhanced educational practices in digital environments.

Wegerif (2006b) underlines that understanding is an event within a dialogue between perspectives and states that is not reducible to a constructed representation, and that to teach the learning challenge of thinking is much easier to understand through a dialogic perspective, which focuses on the opening, deepening and broadening of reflective spaces (Wegerif, 2006b).

The notion of dialogic collaborative knowledge building (D-CKB) with its emphasis on meta-learning and learning-to-learn (L2L) (Bateson, 1976) represents one choice of pedagogical direction. Following this train of thoughts Wegerif (2006b) captures the qualities in the following wording:

> This dialogic interpretative framework implies the need for a pedagogy of teaching dialogic, that is the ability to sustain more than one perspective simultaneously, as an end in itself and as the primary thinking skill upon which all other thinking skills are derivative. This pedagogy can be described in terms of moving learners into the space of dialogue.
>
> (Wegerif, 2006b, np)

Reminding ourselves that we *cannot* design learning (Wenger, 1998) –but only *for* learning – leaves us as educational designers with the option of taking qualitative meta-pedagogical initiatives, which cultivate growth through a quality of L2L, and for practicing learning methods which prepare for learning to take place in "flat" ways in order to support the development of learner agency.

The Notion of Dialogic

In a dialogic perspective, "dialogue" is understood as *a way of knowing*; in other words, as a kind of epistemology (Wegerif, 2016). The view is put forward that there are no fixed meanings that can be obtained or learned. Rather, meaning is situated in a dialogic context. And a dialogic context always appears open to potentially new comments and reassessing views. There is neither a first nor a last word. There is no limit at all to the dialogic context, as it extends retrospectively into infinity.

A "dialogue" is understood as being any kind of social interaction. It may also in a linguistic context be perceived as a piece of sequence (utterance) in the context of other utterances. "Dialogic" may also be an adjective, describing anything relating to or in the form of dialogue – as opposed to "monologic – denoting that everything has one correct meaning in one true perspective on the world. The dialogue is never closed, and the questions we ask will change, and so, what counts as knowledge is never final. The dialogue is never closed, because any succeeding reflection will become a new element in the dialogue". "Dialogic knowledge" is never direct knowledge of an external world, but always emerges only within dialogue as an aspect of dialogue (Bakhtin, 1981; Wegerif, 2016).

Dialogic teaching draws students into the process of co-creative construction of knowledge (epistemological focus), whereas engagement in dialogue is a way to change ourselves and to change our reality (ontological focus). Consequently, moving learners away from a monologic notion in learning into the "space of dialogue", i.e. learners' *engagement in dialogue* and their interaction in the space of dialogue, should be considered a medium for learning. But not only that – it should be considered *an end in itself*, as it leaves significant indirect "imprints" (via meta-learning) on learners in terms of their self-perceptions and radius of action in their process of learning and becoming global democratic citizens.

Together with the idea of the open "dialogic" itself as part of a knowledge building process; the author envisions the processes of *imagination* and *creativity* in learning as highlighted to the extent that they may question and potentially suspend assumptions on a previous collaborative knowledge building process (Wegerif, 2016). There are two additional educational values of adapting the notion of digital dialogue. The first value being learning with the goal of *arguing-to-learn* approach, also named the argument-as-strategy approach. Here the underlying viewpoint is that conceptual understanding and learning emerge as a natural result of an argumentative intervention. The other value comes from the *learning-to-argue* approach, focusing on argumentation per se and on its educational benefits, especially in the limits of a specific curriculum context. Both values are democratic skills.

Consequently, from a design point of view, it seems essential to teach students *how to construct (new) knowledge together with others*, so that they can participate more fully and effectively in ongoing dialogues, than to teach them fixed knowledge or so-called facts. Therefore, the pedagogic aim is to engage students in sustained stretches of talk (dialogue), which enables speakers/writers and listeners to explore and build on their own and others' ideas – in the course of collaboratively producing NEW insight, while continuously respecting the quality of the argument.

Conceptual Design of Digital Dialogic Collaboration and Negotiation

How then may the dialogic D-CKB co-creative learning space be described? Which are the critical elements when designing an online learning architecture that, more closely, may support such ambitions?

Arguing that learning essentially involves elements of both *creativity* and *imagination* cultivated through engagement in negotiation of meaning (i.e. participation and reification) in D-CKB, some of the pedagogical design considerations in relation to the core curriculum include (Sorensen & Ó Murchú, 2006):

- Which elements in the process to structure and make procedures for on the basis of prediction?
- To what extent the design should depend on de-contextualised knowledge?
- How to balance student initiative/ownership and pedagogical authority?
- How to minimise teaching (the predicted) in order to maximise learning?
- How to maximise processes of negotiation of meaning enabled by interaction?
- How to broaden the scope of coverage without losing the depth of local engagement?
- To whom and in which ways does the design represent an opportunity to build an identity of participation?

Independently of which interpretation of the concept of collaborative learning is in focus (definition of learner perspective, number of individuals, or organisational methods), it is generally agreed upon that to ensure good quality learning, the *establishment of interactive dialogue* is essential (Bateson, 1976; Wenger, 1998). Whether it is a general epistemological approach to learning, a socio-constructivist, a sociocultural or a shared-cognitive – they all emphasise the essential role of interaction in learning.

The notion of D-CKB with its emphasis on meta-learning and L2L represents one such choice of "meta-pedagogy". Wegerif (2006b) captures the qualities of this choice in the following wording:

> This dialogic interpretative framework implies the need for a pedagogy of teaching dialogic, that is the ability to sustain more than one perspective simultaneously, as an end in itself and as the primary thinking skill upon

which all other thinking skills are derivative. This pedagogy can be described in terms of moving learners into the space of dialogue. Tools, including language and computer environments, can be used for opening up and maintaining dialogic spaces and for deepening and broadening dialogic spaces.

(Wegerif, 2006b, np)

The digital learning concept/model presented in the last part of this chapter is based entirely on the idea of "dialogic". It is intended to transcend borders of 1) time, 2) space, 3) cultures (pedagogic view on the role of dialogue in learning), 4) disciplines and 5) roles (participants: students and teachers). In terms of quality criteria, the learning developed through this model is intended to promote and enhance:

- Authenticity, empowerment and inclusion (diversity)
- Non-authoritarian approaches
- Participation and agency (involves "drawing on the resources of others and being a resource for others" (Edwards, 2011).
- Democratic dialogic attitudes
- Creativity
- A sense of the local–global
- Dialogue
- Collaborative dialogic meta-reflection/meta-learning promoting awareness and L2L.

According to Edwards (2011), and further emphasised by Sorensen and Brooks (2018), two underlying relational aspects of collaboration and negotiation are important:

The first is that each individual or team holds a specific expertise, and second, they combine both their core expertise and develop a relational expertise. This expertise stems from working across individual or team boundaries and is based on engaging with the knowledge of one's specialist practice as well as the ability to identify and respond to what others offer from their local systems of expertise.

(Edwards, 2011, p. 33)

Brown and Davis (2004) argue that a *shared culture* of an online community begins to develop as interaction starts evolving. In other words, the challenge we face as instructional designers and teachers when collaborating with participants in dialogic teaching and learning designs (which rest on the personal motivation among learners, born ontologically by our inquisitive and explorative nature as human beings), is the establishment of what we perceive as "online communities of practice" (Sorensen & Ó Murchú, 2006).

Figure 4.1 is intended to illustrate the main conceptual idea behind the D-CKB learning design approach:

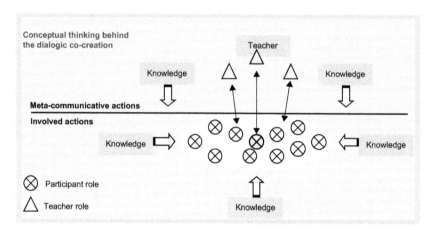

FIGURE 4.1 The conceptual understanding behind the D-CKB process.

The figure shows a student-centred, open negotiation process in which knowledge resources enter dynamically from all sides via the participants, the teacher(s) and a variety of other digital resources in a process, driven and motivated by participants and their individual knowledge (the latter is an important factor in adult education, where each of the participants constitutes an "expert" in their individual working context). It illustrates the dynamic interchange between teacher and learner roles. It also provides a rough indication of how much of the teacher's work challenges evolves at a meta-communicative level. In sum, the dialogic model possesses the following characteristics (Sorensen & Ó Murchú, 2006): it stimulates – "participation" and "engagement"; it is process oriented; it invites assessment of process; it denotes an open concept; it is participant oriented; it draws on student experiences; it is a lifelong model; it operationalises student experiences; it creates "participant" "ownership"; and it equals out teacher and learner roles.

Brown and Davis see the phenomenon of diversity and "culture shock" as an essential resource and ingredient for enhancing D-CKB (Brown & Davis, 2004). They suggest that it should be utilised directly in the establishment of online communities of practice (Brown & Davis, 2004).

If a set of learning objectives include engagement in D-CKB, relevant methods of assessment must incorporate an assertion of the quality of a D-CKB dialogue. This implies the need to more concretely stimulate a dialogue and, once dialogue appears, designers and instructors need to ensure that it actually evolves into a shared D-CKB process. Instructional designers and instructors need to stimulate the diverging D-CKB dialogue, at a meta-level, to ensure that convergence and synthesis are achieved. Moreover, this indicates a need for process-oriented assessment methods.

The collaborative dialogue space is where the democratic "play of learning" comes into existence through a tapestry of dialogue. The dialogue process allows for democratic attitudes of D-CKB to develop in learners through a learning architecture that invites meta-learning (awareness of learning through meta-fora), related to mutual exploration of issues, mutual examination of arguments, agreements and disagreements, mutual questioning of positions, dynamic inter-action, weaving of ideas, convergence of perspectives and synthesis of ideas. It also evokes meta-fora processes of reflection over the learning process, which are essential to develop and expand – in depth and in width (Bateson, 1976). The collaborative dialogue is where the strongest collaborative energy of a learning group manifests itself in the "Now", the instant of shared dynamic dialogue and strongest energy between participants:

> Nothing ever happened in the past; it happened in the Now. (…) The future is an imagined Now, a projection of the mind.
>
> (Tolle, 1999, pp. 41–42)

The collaborative dialogue space is the structuring centre of the teaching/learning process – the basic feature offered by the learning architecture:

> It is in the meanings we are able to negotiate through learning that we invest ourselves, and it is those meanings that are the source of energy required for learning.
>
> (Wenger, 1998, p. 266)

Meta-learning as a Vehicle for Cultivating Democratic Learning Attitudes

While at the same time submitting a pedagogical methodology and prac-tice – based fundamentally on digital dialogue and the sharing of learning values together globally in an online learning architecture, (e.g. a VLE) – the learners cultivate democratic skills, attitudes and intercultural perspectives on citizenship for the benefit of global prosperity. Through learning designs that methodologically are conducive to illustrating and promoting (through both example and content) democratic principles and values, we (the nations on our globe) are more likely to interact with each other with the goal of reach-ing agreements on global issues (Gibson, 2004).

The hypothesis of the author is that there exists this un-explored and there-fore not yet utilised space for meta-learning (i.e. higher-level learning), especially concerned with installing learner attitudes in learners in virtual learning envi-ronments (Figure 4.2).

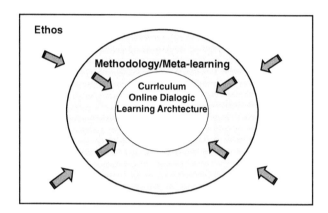

FIGURE 4.2 Dialogic collaborative knowledge building (D-CKB) promoting meta-learning and learning-to-learning.

Designers should move learners into a "space of dialogue", and *engagement in dialogue*, should be considered a medium for learning. The arguments goes even further, as it should be considered *an end in itself to dialogue*, because it is likely to leave *fruitful and significant "imprints"* (meta-learning) on learners in terms of their self-perceptions and radius of action in their process of becoming global democratic citizens. L2L is a meta-competence of higher order, orchestrating an articulated series of abilities and competencies with the ultimate goal to learn better, always and in any context, contributing in an empowered perspective to a better adaptation of the individual (or the group) to the socio-economic environment.

Figure 4.2 is intended to illustrate the author's understanding of learning and the overall role of the dialogic paradigm. It denotes my perception of the contexts in which our dialogic learning designs "through dialogue" are inserted. There is always an Ethos or a presupposed set of values – whether explicit or conscious – behind any online learning design. The latent values should become visible and explicit, as they influence the design decisions we as pedagogical designers make, and the pedagogical/instructional methodology we choose for teaching the core curriculum. For example, awareness and potential utilisation of meta-learning for promoting processes of L2L are methodological decisions, "submitted" the set of latent values. The core curriculum is important to build knowledge in a specific field, but following the dialogic view of moving learners away from a monologic notion in learning into the "space of dialogue", the core curriculum becomes even more vital via its role as a catalyst for the meta-learning of L2L.

The notion of D-CKB in the theoretical perspective of this chapter implies and emphasises the open "dialogic" itself as part of a collaborative knowledge building process. Within this concept the author envisions the processes of imagination and creativity as highlighted to the extent that they may question and potentially suspend assumptions on the previous collaborative knowledge build-ing process.

Experiences from using the D-CKB Model

The dialogic learning architecture has been implemented very successfully since 2000. It has developed over 20 years, hand in hand with its "context of use", MIL Master in ICT and Learning (MIL).[1] MIL is a two-year (part-time) education in ICT and learning with approximately 40–50 students pr. year group. It is struc-tured in three categories of studies: four modules (each consisting of three to four courses), one project work and one master thesis.

Many of the participants are highly qualified teachers at the high school level and some had extensive university education. And there were people from indus-try with high competence within their individual work areas.

The online course reported here lasted 5 weeks. It was divided into periods of reading and preparation (2 weeks) and debate (3 weeks). Goals of the course were that the participants through engaging in collaborative knowledge building were expected to acquire: 1) insight into the issues of quality in design and delivery of online learning, 2) meta-reflection on and understanding of the implication of teacher–learner roles, 3) meta-reflection on and understanding of the reflective, interactive and structuring potential of net-based learning processes and 4) self-reflective experience of one exemplary model, i.e. their own experience with the course they went through (while it was happening).

The participants were asked to distribute a set of roles among the members of their online group, on average consisting of four participants (Table 4.1). The roles were supposed to form, support and guide their later discussion and to give the participants a concrete point of departure in the discussion. In the small groups, some were presenters, some were moderators, etc. The description of the roles was clarified in the assignment. Both teacher and students agreed to commit themselves to attending the virtual learning space for a minimum of five times a week over the 3 weeks of debate. In the debate period, each of the groups was asked to present and prepare for different roles in the upcoming debate on a statement/problem identified in the small group and commonly agreed as rel-evant and possibly related to the literature (see table below). Moreover, they were asked to initiate, conduct and wrap up the succeeding online plenum discussion, which evolved from the problem identified by their group. In parallel with the discussions, the participants and the teacher were engaged in meta-reflections and meta-communication in a meta-forum, to reflect and discuss the experi-ences and processes of the participants, as they evolved in the three theme fora. The participants were graded on both quantity and quality of their contributions using a process-oriented assessment model (Sorensen & Takle, 2002), underlining the following set of assessment criteria

TABLE 4.1 D-Roles: Dialogic roles in small online groups, to be used for the plenum debate.

Dialogic roles	Description
Presenter	The task linked to the role of the presenter is to write a contribution (in the advised plenum forum of the small group) presenting a, potentially controversial, topic/problem statement for discussion. The statement should have a rationale with references to the course/theme literature, to the presenter's experiences, and to learning theoretical positions. The contribution should be approximately 20–30 lines.
Opponent	The task linked to the role of the opponent is to challenge – qualified and with serious arguments and references to literature – the views in the statement of the presenter. In other words, the opponent should pose a contrasting view rhetorically in a way that fosters further dialogue and discussion. **Note:** When the debate has kick-started and is evolving continuously, the opponent should stop opposing as a principle – and, instead, participate genuinely according to his/her own views and convictions (i.e. take the role of commentator).
Moderator	The task of the moderator is to support and weave the discussion started by his/her small group. The moderator encourages comments and reactions in relation to the statement made by the small group presenter, and challenges "lurkers" to comment. The moderator also keeps the discussion on a fruitful track and weaves to create communicative cohesion between the comments of the evolving dialogue. **Note:** The moderator has the final responsibility for summarising the debate elicited and posting this summary.
Commentator (all participants)	The task of a commentator is to comment generally on the ideas emerging from and presented by other participants, and to contribute in a qualified way to the collaborative knowledge building discussions. This role should be applied by each participant at all times in the plenum forum, so that each one contributes also to the discussions lead by other groups.

- Quantitative requirements included submitting at least five comments, give a certain number of comments to the contributions of others and a certain number of new initiatives, plus elicit a certain number of responses from others.
- Qualitative requirements included questions asked for clarity, comments that add new knowledge to the discussion, comments that provide relevant associations, comments that organise and promote argumentation and comments that synthesise previous points of view and point to new directions, conclusions and visions.

The framework above on D-Roles (Table 4.1) was implemented to stimulate both kick-start the "knitting together" and the "raising of dialogic awareness" (meta-learning). In order to ensure not only dialogicity and the establishment of interaction among participants in the period of debate, but also in retrospect be able to assess the level of dialogicity and the individual participants' dialogic behavior, the process-oriented assessment framework (Table 4.2) was implemented – first by Sorensen and Takle (2002), later modified by Sorensen and Ó Murchú (2006) (Table 4.2):

TABLE 4.2 A process-oriented assessment model (Sorensen & Takle, 2002).

	Dialogic Requirements (per participant)
Quantitative	submit **at least five** contributions, out of which two should be your own identifications, and three should be responses to your peers
Qualitative	contributions that ask for clarity; contributions that oppose; contributions adding new knowledge to the discussion; contributions of relevance; contributions that build on logical argumentation in relation to others; contributions that sum up and synthesise and take a new point of direction; etc. (open-ended list)

The assessment framework was implemented, both *prescriptively* for scaffolding the dialogic process and later, as a set of criteria, *for the purpose of assessment* of *dialogicity*.

Sorensen and Ó Murchú (2006) coined the term "dialogic tapestry" describing the texture and quality of the knowledge building process and negotiation of language games, which sprung and unfolded in "the power of the dialogic now".

Conclusion

This chapter has put forward for discussion a pedagogic design perspective based on a D-CKB model, that includes an overall ambition of concern for global prosperity. Wrapping up, there are a few points to revisit for future developments.

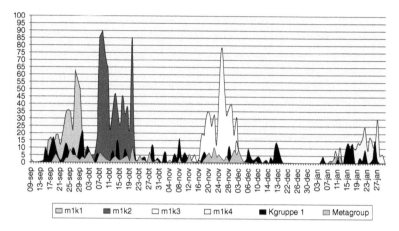

FIGURE 4.3 The digital, dialogic knowledge building interaction (D-CKB) of MIL, promoting meta-learning and learning-to-learn. The four fluctuations illustrate the four small courses on MIL module 1, that were designed from a pedagogical perspective of dialogic collaboration and meta-learning (Dirckinck-Holmfeld, Sorensen, & Ryberg, 2004).

It is important to remember that the overall principled goal of education is the making of *democratically oriented global citizens*. The author argues that inter-human interaction itself, i.e. student engagement in D-CKB, should be considered the medium for engagement in global, intercultural learning. More significantly, it should be considered the ultimate goal of education.

The model (Figure 4.4) envisions a methodology that incorporates, both 1) a strategic level of learning, 2) the micro-level of learning, and 3) the interdisciplinary meso-level of learning through interaction between participating agents. The

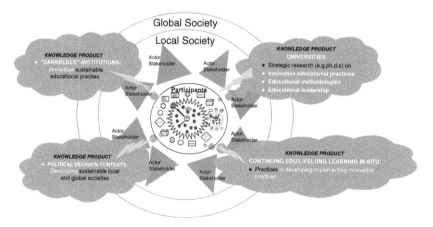

FIGURE 4.4 Transdisciplinary dialogic education and research (in education) – across stakeholders (Sorensen & Brooks, 2018).

model also envisions a network approach that interrelates both educational context and research context. The two contexts need to be able to work in environments for connecting and engaging in dialogue and collaboration across various types of divides. This truly invites the interactive, inter-connective, collaborative and reflective potential of digital technology to work for learning through co-creation and D-CKB – for creating an including networked society open to the emerging NEW data, processes and products of the future to emerge and for reifying a bridging of genuine collaborative learning processes across cultures.

The D-CKB model and its meta-fora allow for meta-perspectives (awareness through collaborative reflection) to develop and ensure learning to evolve at two levels: 1) learning of "the matter" at the involved dialogic level and 2) learning at the meta-reflective level (e.g. learner attitudes).

When cultivating democratically oriented global citizens, an ethos and commitment that denies suppression and hierarchies of authority and envision growth of global democracy and equality must be selective on choice of teaching styles and pedagogical methodology. Needed features like e.g. tolerance, mutuality, responsibility and a feeling of self-esteem (the belief that the individual voice makes a difference to mutuality) are for a large part promoted and mediated through educational systems; through the chosen instructional methodology (including teacher–learner roles) and its implementation in pedagogical designs.

It is relevant to add a final relevant affordance to the pedagogic vision about co-creation via digital technology. Pointing to digital networks, their potential for acting as vehicles for building digital learning contexts that further fundamental democratic, dialogic skills and generates empowering educational attitudes, is indisputable. Among those is an ability to listen to other "voices" in other dialogues than one's own. The ability to relate dialogically becomes a needed competence in an intercultural, globally oriented world.

From barely "minding gaps" in ways that support old educational power structures and paradigms, it is the hope of the author that the educational architects of our tomorrow will continue to identify fruitful *dialogic* marriages between digital technology and pedagogical co-creative methods and models. For D-CKB to work for the "building of bridges" over a variety of gaps, divides and imbalances among citizens of the Globe, we need to teach and master the method of "dialogic" in the service of mankind.

Note

1 MIL provides continuing education for working adults engaged in educational planning and integration of ICT in learning processes at schools and all types of educational institutions as well as employees with educational responsibilities in different types of organisations. Problem-Oriented Project Pedagogy (POPP) is the overall pedagogical approach. POPP (Sorensen & Murchú, 2004).

References

Bakhtin, M. M. (1981). *The Dialogic imagination: Four essays*. Michael Holquist Ed. Trans. Caryl Emerson and Michael Holquist. Austin and London: University of Texas Press.

Bateson, G. (1976). *Steps to an ecology of mind*. Chicago: The University of Chicago Press.

Brown, A., & Davis, N. (2004). Introduction. In A. Brown & N. Davis (Eds.), *Digital technology communities and education* (pp. 1–12). London: RoutledgeFarmer.

Dirckinck-Holmfeld, L., Sorensen, E. K. & Ryberg, T. (2004). E-Learning Communities and Collaborative Learning. EQUEL Position Paper (2004). Special Interest Group 3. Scientific Report, the EQUEL EU-project.

Edwards, A. (2011). Building common knowledge at the boundaries between professional practices: Relational agency and relational expertise in systems of distributed expertise, *International Journal of Educational Research*, *50*, pp. 33–39.

Gibson, I. W. (2004). Preparing School Leaders for New-Millennium Global Learning. In the online Journal, GlobalEducator.com, ISSN 1449-5082. Retrieved, February 8, 2006, from http://www.globaled.com/articles/IanGibson2004.pdf

Miyake, N., & Koschmann, T. D. (2002). Realizations of CSCL conversations: Technology transfer and the CSILE project. In T. Koschmann, R. Hall, & N. Miyake (Eds.), *CSCL 2: Carrying forward the conversation* (pp. 1–11). Mahwah, NJ: Lawrence Erlbaum.

Schön, D. A. (1987). *Educating the reflective practitioner*. San Francisco: Jossey-Bass Publishers

Sorensen, E. K., & Brooks, E. I. (2018). Interactivity, Game Creation, Design, Learning, and Innovation - 6th International Conference, ArtsIT 2017, and 2nd International Conference, DLI 2017, Proceedings: 6th International Conference, ArtsIT 2017, and Second International Conference, DLI 2017, Heraklion, Crete, Greece, October 30–31, 2017, Proceedings. Brooks, E., Brooks, A. L. & Vidakis, N. (eds.). Springer, p. 251-261 11 p. (Lecture Notes of the Institute for Computer Sciences, Social-Informatics and Telecommunications Engineering, LNICST, Vol. 229).

Sorensen, E. K., & Ó Murchú, D. (2004). Designing online learning communities of practice: A democratic perspective. *Jounal of Educational Multimedia (CJEM)*, *29*(3).

Sorensen, E. K., & Ó Murchú, D. (2006). Identifying an appropriate, pedagogical, networked architecture for online learning communities within higher and continuing education. In E. K. Sorensen & D. Ó Murchú (Eds.), *Enhancing learning through technology* (pp. 226–251). Hershey, PA: Idea Group Inc.

Sorensen E. K., & Takle, E. S. (2002). Collaborative knowledge building in web-based learning: Assessing the quality of dialogue. *The International Journal of E-Learning (IJEL)*, *1*(1), 28–32.

Tolle, E. (1999). *The power of the now*. London: Hodder & Stoughton.

Wegerif, R. (2006a). *Dialogic, educational and technology: Convergence in the space of learning*. New York: Springer-Verlag.

Wegerif, R. (2006b). A dialogic understanding of the relationship between CSCL and teaching thinking skills *ijcscl*. *1*(1), 143–157.

Wegerif, R. (2016). Applying dialogic theory to illuminate the relationship between literacy education and teaching thinking in the context of the Internet Age. International Perspectives on Dialogic Theory and Practice , edited by Sue Brindley, Mary Juzwik, and Alison Whitehurst. *L1-Educational Studies in Language and Literature*, *16*, 1–21. http://dx.doi.org/10.17239/L1ESLL-2016.16.02.07

Wenger, E. (1998). *Communities of practice. Learning, meaning and identity*. Cambridge, UK: Cambridge University Press.

PART 2

Inclusive Practices through Digital Technologies

Eva Brooks and Susanne Dau

Introduction: Inclusive Practices through Digital Technologies

This second part of the book emphasises a wider cultural understanding and respect for the individual and for human diversity. The challenges of digital technologies for the future imply decisions on what kind of life and society we want these technologies to sustain, e.g., how digital technologies can allow for individuals' full participation in societal matters. The different chapters unfold user diversity, covering a variation in their capabilities, needs and aspirations. The chapters discuss different target groups, such as children, higher education students and people with a variation of abilities. The chapters scrutinise barriers and opportunities for people to participate equally, confidently and independently in everyday activities. Each one of the chapters aim at obtaining a better understanding of in what ways the use and development of digital technologies in different contexts can improve inclusive practice.

Chapter 5, *Including interventions in educational settings*, by Hanne Voldborg Andersen, Elsebeth Korsgaard Sorensen and Rune Hagel Skaarup Jensen, is based on a research project called "ididact", which was carried out in Denmark during 2013–16. The authors elaborate on potentials of technology to support inclusion of learners with special educational needs in primary and lower secondary schools. In doing so, the chapter depicts ontological and epistemological values of learning, including individual potentialities, and pinpoints a dialogical approach as essential for learning. Hereby, the chapter examines how technology can support inclusion of vulnerable children that were challenged in school activities, relative to areas such as hyperactivity, impulsivity, social behaviour, comprehension and perception. The chapter thus offers a conceptual practice relevant input to the overall theme of inclusive practice through digital technologies.

The following chapter, *Designs for learning with adaptive games and Teachable Agents*, by Susanne Kjällander and Kristen Pilner Blair, aligns with the previous chapter's perspectives of collaboration and inclusion, by suggesting a didactic design, where both individuals and collaborative interactions are at play in digital as well as physical environments. This design aims at preventing preschool children's mathematical inequalities. The chapter is based on two randomised controlled intervention studies carried out in Sweden and USA, where adaptive math games were implemented in preschool settings. The game designs had a narrative structure and an implemented learning-by-teaching strategy. From a design theoretical perspective, game logs and empirical video data from the two intervention studies indicated that children between 4 and 5 years of age can benefit from using math games as a complement to math carried out with physical material. The outcomes furthermore showed that games possibly can be used (or designed) to encourage collaboration/prosocial behaviours in a way that reinforces early math concepts.

In Chapter 7, *Learning music by composing on iPads*, Bjørn-Terje Brandlien addresses another perspective of inclusion afforded by digital technologies. Based on a design theoretical approach forming a basis for an inclusive learning design in music, the chapter argues that iPad can enhance students' involvement and influence their agency. The chapter draws on a research project carried out in Norway, where secondary school students were involved in composing music by means of iPads, which can be considered as an orchestration of potential resources for transformation and representation of musical expressions. The study presented in the chapter is based on a microethnographic fieldwork including empirical data from observations and produced content on the iPads. In the chapter, the author emphasises the importance of letting students learn musical expressions by composing their own music. In such a context, students can bring in their own personal experiences and interests into play.

Chapter 8, *The zone of optimised motivation*, is authored by Anthony Lewis Brooks. In line with the earlier chapters in this part of the book, this chapter describes how Virtual Interactive Space (VIS) and Virtual Reality (VR) can support people's well-being and inclusion. The empirical study applies a design-based approach when investigating convergence of digital technologies in (re) habilitation contexts. The author explains how these technologies embrace a strategy for designing for accessibility and inclusion, entailing a technology in accordance with the user's idiosyncratic needs and desires, as well as to emerging communication between users. The outcomes of the study reveal a model, *Zone of Optimised Motivation* (ZOOM), and is suggested to support human intervention practices and empowering interaction involving users and facilitators during (re)habilitation activities. The ZOOM is thus suggested to afford a more inclusive and accessible rehabilitation using tailored VIS and VR.

All in all, the four chapters involve different technologies supporting inclusive practices in different environments targeting different groups of people, from young children to patients in rehabilitation. Together they bring new perspectives to inclusive practices and how technologies can afford and support such practices and situations. Technology is not seen as an aim in itself but purposefully used to facilitate and empower existing practices.

5

PROMISES AND PERILS

The Affordances of Technology for Promoting Inclusion of Learners in Educational Settings

Hanne Voldborg Andersen, Elsebeth Korsgaard Sorensen and Rune Hagel Skaarup Jensen

Promoting Learning and Inclusion

The United Nations states that people with disabilities have equal rights to education, and that all state parties are obliged to "enable persons with disabilities to learn life and social skills to facilitate their full and equal participation in education and as member of the community" (United Nations, 2006). However, when it comes to equal access and opportunities for participating and contributing in education it seems less simple. "Physically, placing disabled children in a class with non-disabled peers is not inclusion and will not ensure the accomplishment of both their academic and social goals" (Mavrou, 2012).

Education and learning may be about much more than cognition. It counts as well for development of a strong individual self and the experience of being connected to the world and the social community. Likewise, inclusion is much more than physical presence, but happens as a process of increasing participation: "Participation means learning alongside with others and collaborating with them in shared learning experiences. It requires active engagement with learning and having a say in how learning is experienced. More deeply, it is about being recognised, and accepted for oneself" (Booth & Ainscow, 2002 p. 3).

Following these perspectives on inclusion and learning, it seems necessary to clarify how to recognise the individual human being, how to understand co-existence and how to view the role of collaboration in shared learning experiences. Consequently, this section portrays the following ontological and epistemological values and perceptions of learning:

- A view on each human being as unique
- A view on co-existence and socialisation with the world
- A view on role of language and dialogue as essential for learning

A View on Each Human Being as Unique

This position implies a view of an individual as being unique (Kirkegaard, 1843; Sorensen & Andersen 2017a). Each learner is viewed to be unique and needs space and conditions in order to develop – based on his/her uniqueness – into a harmonious trusting human. It also implies a view on diversity as a resource.

A View on Co-existence and Socialisation with the World

This position encompasses a view on learning to co-exist with others, as an essential prerequisite for an individual to develop into a harmonious, trusting and emphatic human being, with an intention and ability to act, interact and learn with the world.

A View on Role of Language and Dialogue as Essential for Learning

This position includes the view that learning is regarded to be a social process that is mediated through linguistic interaction. The unique human being lives in a kind of "thrownness" (Heidegger, 1986) in relationships and interactions with other human beings. An individual gets socialised in an inter-human context, so to speak, socially and communicatively, in relation with other people. Thus, to be able to engage in collaboration, to learn to collaborate with and to listen to dialogue and negotiate democratically with fellow human beings seem an important skill to develop.

Our natural language and dialogues unfolding on any topic may be viewed as "a medium" for leaning (Sorensen & Andersen, 2017b). It supports the double optic and ying-yang relation between "hin enkelte" (individual) and co-existence (collaborative) in the learning process, and it underlines the need of being able to "listen to" and to "take the perspective of the other". It implies valuing the choir of shared voices in a democratic symphony and collaborative negotiation of meaning.

Instead of aiming at "reproducing" knowledge, a collaborative process allows for a continuous "shared construction of new knowledge" (Darsøe, 2011) through a dialectic commuting between involvement and reflection (Heidegger, 1986). Dialoguing is a method to become part of the "choir of voices", which gives birth to a polyphony of learning (Dysthe, 1997). The dialogic method is widely recognised as an important learning method and it becomes especially significant for the learners' development of empowerment (Dysthe, 1997).

In sum, we view these positions as essential prerequisites for any learner to learn and develop: Learning through being exposed to a kind of "double optic" or "ying-yang" challenge: an expectation to develop individually (as "hin enkelte"), and an expectation to develop socially (co-existing) and learning (collaborating) with others. To become included and (co-)exist in a global world calls for abilities and competencies to respectfully negotiate diversities and invite compromises, to dialogue with others, while respecting the voice and the value of the argument.

The Affordances of Technologies

Overall, there is tremendous promise of technologies for supporting learning in general education and learning processes; i.e. work for empowerment, at both the personal (individual) level and the general process of socialisation (involving collaboration and dialogue). According to Waller and Watkins (2013), digital technologies and tools also possess a potential for inclusion and, thus, may be viewed as valuable tools for such purposes, "particularly for people with disabilities, where technology can improve their quality of life, reduce social exclusion and increase participation" (WSIS, 2010).

Prototype test or explorative investigation of possible advantages and disadvantages of digital technologies characterises much research within the field of digital support for inclusive education. A literature review on assistive learning technologies for learners with special educational needs (Andersen & Jensen, 2019) identifies, as shown in Figure 5.1, seven categories of supportive technology-based interventions.

But the number of studies in each category is low and the number of participants few. Even though promising use of technologies was found, the small collection of studies leaves us with very mixed conclusions (Andersen & Jensen, 2019).

It may be assumed that the promised and identified potential of technology for learning and inclusion automatically promotes development of new pedagogical approaches and models for learning. Though, such assumptions seem not to have any evidence. Despite the onward march on digital technologies, the identification of pedagogical strategies for technology supported inclusion remains a challenge (Waller & Watkins, 2013). The pedagogical strategies and models, which utilise and operationalise the identified affordances, are lacking (Waller & Watkins, 2013).

Consequently, in order to be able to describe the promising potential of digital technologies, it seems to be relevant to distinguish between assessment of the

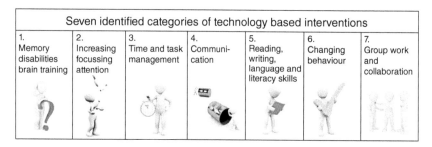

FIGURE 5.1 Categories of technology-based interventions for learners with special needs (Andersen & Jensen, 2019).

functions of technologies, viewed in isolation, and assessment of them in a "use situation". It is not the technological virtues, as it were, that are interesting, rather it is the function of digital technologies in each situation that is in focus. In essence, the potential revolves around their general functional ability to support and enhance learner participation, learner creation and learner collaboration in various learning processes (Conole et al., 2015). Dalsgaard and Sorensen (2008) have identified the communicative affordance of digital technology and networks as a strong and promising resource for teachers to employ in learning designs, provided the teachers, pedagogically and technologically, are able to utilise the potential.

Technology-based Interventions in Educational Settings

Such view on the function of digital technologies in a usage situation is investigated in the ididakt research program 2013–2016 (Andersen et al., 2016), when researchers in collaboration with 46 teachers investigate various kinds of technologies and develop technology rich pedagogical strategies for supporting inclusion of learners with special educational needs in primary and lower secondary schools. Interventions were conducted for more than 500 students in 26 classes. Fifty-six of them had special educational needs and were challenged in school activities regarding one or more of the following areas: memory, attention, persistence, hyperactivity, impulsivity, behaviour, emotions, social behaviour, comprehension and perception and language and communication.

The study identified five categories of technology-based interventions (Andersen & Sorensen 2016), which positively supported the learners with special educational needs to participate and contribute in teaching and learning:

1. Structure and overview
2. Shielding and focus
3. Differentiation and comprehension
4. Production and dissemination
5. Dialogue and collaboration

As illustrated in Figure 5.2, the study shows how these five categories contain valuable tools for both students, teachers and pedagogues when working for inclusion of all learners. The findings show significant improvement when it comes to students' attention, memory, concentration, persistence and hyperactivity, while no improvement regarding behaviour and social competencies is recognised (Andersen et al., 2016).

But the study shows as well how a certain technology's ability to interfere with, innovate and develop new practice is dependent on interaction of the following factors: the functionality of the technology, the pedagogical visions by the teachers and the organisational setting, in which the technology is to be implemented (Sorensen & Andersen, 2016).

	Used technologies	Learner experiences
Structure & Overview 	Visualisation Time and task management Templates Calendar Virtual portfolio Virtual Learning Platforms	The learners were with these tools empowered and independent, when the lessons and the tasks are planned with them and they are provided with structure and overview on what they are supposed to do.
Shielding & Focus 	Earmuff Sound Field Amplification Virtual presence Step-by-step guidance (where unnecessary information and disturbances are reduced)	These tools supported the learners to • be more calm, quiet and focused • increase attention and participation • better hear and understand instructions • keep concentrated
Differentiation & Comprehension 	Digital books Digital course materials Video content Digital rehearsing materials Learning games Technologies for reading and writing Individual or shared folders/sites with summaries	These technologies made it easier for the teachers to provide the learners with differentiated materials and enabled or assisted the learners to participate and contribute in the learning activities.
Production & Dissemination 	Process: Writing templates, video support, websites Product: Presentation tools, word processing tools, multimodality communication programs Communication: Writing support, Text2Speech, Speech2Text	These technologies enabled the learners to reify their knowledge, control their learning processes, experience ownership, independence and coping in task solving processes. The production was eased and risks minimized. Furthermore, they were supported to reflect on their own participation and contribution.
Dialogue & Collaboration 	Virtual Learning Environments, Learning platforms Dialogue Networking Production Co-creation Sharing	These technologies supported and scaffolded the learners to participate in dialogue, collaboration and co-creation. Learners with special needs were especially supported incollaborative knowledge processes, where they found inspiration and aid in shared documents and sites.

FIGURE 5.2 Used technologies and learner experiences for each of the five categories of interventions (Andersen & Sorensen, 2016).

Promises and Perils

Pedagogical Visions for Use of Technologies

While it can be difficult for teachers to have an influence on the functionality of technologies and the context in which they work, they to a greater extent have the power to define the pedagogical visions for their teaching practice. But it may be relevant for teachers and schools – as suggested by Andersen (2018) – to observe and question both the intended motive for using a certain technology-based intervention and the actual consequences for the learners involved. Would they recognise a focus on empowering learners to become stronger, more confident and controlling their lives and claiming their rights? Would they observe learning technologies applied for rehearsing specific skills, assisting learning processes or enabling learning which seem impossible without the technologies? Would they see technologies engaging and motivating the learners' participation and behaviour? Or would they identify technologies passivating the learners? (Andersen, 2018).

Intended versus Actual Effect

Examples from the ididakt research program not only illustrate how the same technology can be implemented to serve different purposes, but also elucidate the difference between the intended and the real effect (Sorensen & Andersen, 2016; Andersen et al., 2017).

A student was provided with a structuring application (MobilizeMe) in order to empower her to manage her own daily life. She explained how the program reminded her when it was time for her to leave for the school bus, do her homework, take her medicine, go to sport and do her home duties. It enabled her to manage these things independently and assisted her to split longer or complex tasks into several smaller manageable steps. But she exposed as well, that it was difficult for her to manage the application, as neither her teachers nor her parents were able to support her.

The same application was implemented in another context with other students to motivate and engage students to work persistently and concentrate in the lessons but seemed in reality to merely passivate the students to execute tasks in a specific order – scheduled and demanded by the teachers.

Perspectives on the Ididakt Framework

With the intention to develop a pedagogical framework for deployment of the five identified categories from the ididakt research, it was examined how the categories relate to each other. Ongoing iterations have introduced different perspectives, some of which will be portrayed and discussed in the following.

A Compensatory Framework?

The tools for structuring and shielding can be understood as basic resources adjustable to the specific need by the individual human being, while the tools for differentiating, production and collaboration may act as resources for the traditional learning activities in schools. Either illustrated as a hierarchical model (Figure 5.3 right side) or as a model, where specific needs must be covered before the learners can work from a common level zero (Figure 5.3 left side).

Such compensatory way of thinking was suggested, because students with ADHD or ASD were experienced as left behind in the classroom activities, if they were unable to structure and overview the tasks or stay focused due to outer disturbing stimulus. To be able, to act at the same level as their classmates, they had to be supported in these categories.

Teachers were recommended to provide learners with special alternative tasks, materials, methods and media: Does any individual student need further structuring and shielding support to be able to participate and contribute in the learning activities?

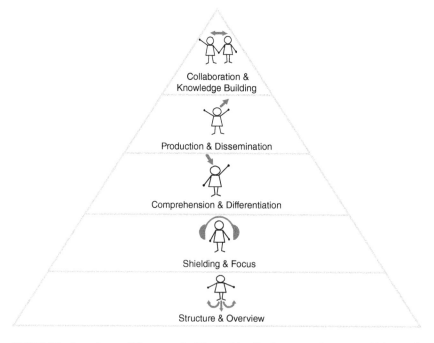

FIGURE 5.3 Iterations of framework: Hierarchic (Andersen & Sorensen, 2016) and common level zero (Andersen et al., 2016).

A Diversity Framework?

A later iteration (Andersen, 2018) relates the five categories to the three perspectives of inclusion in the IC3-model (Alenkær, 2010) and suggests as illustrated in Figure 5.4 shielding and structure to support the physical inclusion, differentiation and production to support the academic inclusion. It further suggests dialogue and collaboration to support the social inclusion. With such a pedagogical framework it would be appropriate to consider all learners as having individual strengths and needs and in that sense praise diversity.

Teachers are recommended to be aware of the five categories when planning and conducting learning activities for all students: Is the class provided with sufficient support to overview the tasks, to stay focused, to comprehend the content, to develop and to communicate their own understanding of the topic and, actively, participate in collaboration and dialogue with peers?

A Co-learning Framework

Even though the diversity framework to a great extent serves the vision of utilising technologies to promote inclusion of learners in educational settings, it can be claimed, that important parameters of quality in learning processes – like language, collaborative dialogues and collaborative knowledge building processes – are positioned too weakly. If language and dialogues are viewed as medium for learning,

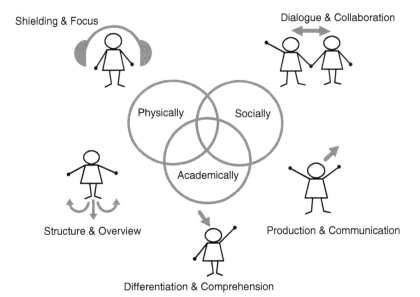

FIGURE 5.4 The categories of technology-based interventions related to the IC3 inclusion model (Andersen, 2018).

the space for activities where learners listen to and take the perspective of the other, express their individual perspectives and build new knowledge together must be central for the framework. Consequently, a new co-learning framework is suggested (Figure 5.5).

The co-learning framework suggest teachers to utilise digital technologies to support dialogue and collaboration in their design of learning activities: How can I provide all my students with a voice and involve all of them in shared construction of new knowledge in processes of co-creating, co-presenting and co-reflecting? Which structuring and shielding support will allow all of them to engage in such polyphonic learning environment? Which technologies promote differentiation, ease production and communication and, empower my students to open their minds, develop their thoughts and raise their voices?

Wider Perspectives

The co-learning framework aligns to a great extent with the Universal Design for Learning (UDL) framework, and rests on similar assumptions and values. UDL departs from the view that the primary barrier to fostering expert learners within instructional environments is that curricula are inflexible and adhere to the design philosophy of "one-size-fits-all" (Hall et al., 2012). All learners are unique. But some are different than mainstream. Such learners "in the margins" are vulnerable. Perhaps due to a special giftedness, or because they appear to be disadvantaged in comparison with mainstream. In addition, even learners who are identified as "mainstream" may not have their learning needs met, simply due to poor design of curricula.

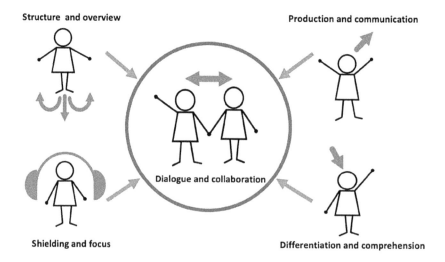

FIGURE 5.5 A co-learning framework to promote dialogue and collaboration.

In learning environments, such as schools and universities, individual variability is the norm, not the exception. When curricula are designed to meet the needs of an imaginary "average", they do not address the learner variability of reality.

To utilise technologies to promote inclusion of learners in educational setting we suggest accepting diversity (the uniqueness of the individual learner) as the norm and embrace learner variability. By allowing flexible goals, methods, materials and assessments, teachers can be empowered to meet the varied needs of students and praise their diversity. By encouraging teachers to create flexible designs, students can progress from where they are and not where we imagine them to be.

From our comprehensive research within the field of learning, inclusion and technology, it has become evident that the current amount of and easy access to technologies possess great opportunities for supporting and enabling inclusive learning and teaching. Though, these opportunities may not evolve from the technologies themselves, but need to be cultivated from the pedagogical visions.

From the context of investigation, we have experienced, how municipalities to a great extent are enthusiastic about new digital technologies and praise these brand-new learning resources – only for being switched on in the classroom. Simultaneously, we have observed how teachers in a top-down approach are provided with digital learning technologies, but no pedagogical support. Consequently, the functionality of the technologies seems to control the teaching practice and outperform both the teacher and the pedagogy.

To change this poor situation and let technologies serve the pedagogy instead of controlling it, it may be relevant with a critical and conscious view on the use of technologies in the schools, and a stronger focus on development of pedagogy in a digital age.

References

Alenkær, R. (2010). *Den inkluderende skole i praksis*. København: Frydenlund

Andersen, H.V., Sorensen, E. K., De Lopez, K. M. J., & Jensen, R. H. S. (2016). It-baseret inklusion af elever med udviklings- og opmærksomhedsproblemer i folkeskolen. (Nr. 1; s. 205). Aalborg Universitetsforlag. (accesed October 21, 2020) https://vbn.aau.dk/ws/portalfiles/portal/255984669/It_baseret_inklusion_af_elever_ONLINE.pdf

Andersen, H. V. (2018). Expanding Scenarios for Visible Learners: Innovative Designs of Including Technology-based Interventions for Learners with Developmental and Attention Difficulties in K1-K10 Practices. Aalborg Universitet.

Andersen, H. V., & Jensen, R. H. S. (2019). Assistive learning technologies for learners with ADHD and ASD. *Tidsskriftet Læring og Medier (LOM)*, 11(19). https://doi.org/10.7146/lom.v11i19.109755

Andersen, H.V., & Sorensen, E. K. (2016). Technology as a vehicle for inclusion of learners with attention deficits in mainstream schools. *European Journal of Open, Distance and E-Learning*. https://vbn.aau.dk/ws/portalfiles/portal/266894483/Barcelona_114_Andersen_Sorensen.pdf

Booth, T., & Ainscow, M. (2002). Index for inclusion—Developing learning and participation in schools. Centre for Studies on Inclusive Education (CSIE). http://www.eenet.org.uk/resources/docs/Index%20English.pdf

Conole, G., Klobučar, T., Rensing, C., Konert, J., & Lavoué, E. (Red.). (2015). *Design for Teaching and Learning in a Networked World: 10th European Conference on Technology Enhanced Learning, EC-TEL 2015*, Toledo, Spain, September 15–18, Proceedings (Bd. 9307). Springer International Publishing. https://doi.org/10.1007/978-3-319-24258-3

Dalsgaard, C., & Sorensen, E. K. (2008). A Typology for Web 2.0. *Proceedings of ECEL 2008. The 7th European Conference on e-Learning.* Agia Napa, Cyprus, 7–8 November.

Darsøe, L. (2011). *Innovationspædagogik: Kunsten at fremelske innovationskompetence.* Frederiksberg C: Samfundslitteratur.

Dysthe, O. (1997). *Det flerstemmige klasserum: Skrivning og samtale for at lære.* Aarhus: Klim.

Hall, T. E., Meyer, A., & Rose, D. H. (Eds.). (2012). *Universal design for learning in the classroom: practical applications.* New York: Guilford Press.

Heidegger, M. (1986). *Sein und Zeit.* Tübingen: Max Niemeyer Verlag.

Kirkegaard, S. A. (1843). *Enten—Eller.* København: C.A. Reitzel.

Mavrou, K. (2012). Examining peer acceptance in verbal and non-verbal interaction during computer-supported collaborative learning: Implications for inclusion. *International Journal of Inclusive Education, 16*(2), 119–138. https://doi.org/10.1080/13603111003671657

Sorensen, E. K., & Andersen, H. V. (2016). *Amplifying the process of inclusion through a genuine marriage between pedagogy and technology. Proceedings of the European Distance and E-Learning Network 2016 Annual Conference.* EDEN, Budapest.

Sorensen, E. K., & Andersen, H. V. (2017a). Solitude or co-existence – or learning-together-apart with digital dialogic technologies for kids with developmental and attention difficulties. *EAI Endorsed Transactions on Creative Technologies, 4*(12), 153157. https://doi.org/10.4108/eai.3-10-2017.153157

Sorensen, E. K., & Andersen, H. V. (2017b). Strengthening Inclusion of Learners With Attention Difficulties Through Interventions With Digital Technology In Processes of Production. *European Journal of Open, Distance and E-Learning, 20*(1), 45–60.

United Nations. (2006). Conventions on the rights of persons with disabilities. https://www.un.org/disabilities/documents/convention/convention_accessible_pdf.pdf

WSIS. (2010). Outecomes document. World Summit on the Information Society.

6

DESIGNS FOR LEARNING WITH ADAPTIVE GAMES AND TEACHABLE AGENTS

Susanne Kjällander and Kristen Pilner Blair

An unusual sight in a Swedish preschool: a group of children are spread out on the floor. They are cuddling close to each other in tiny papier mâché-dens behind a curtain, sitting alone on a colourful cushion or lying feet to feet on the big round carpet. But that is not what is unusual; what is unusual is that all of them are playing on their own digital tablet, wearing headphones. Despite this, children keep on communicating while playing the individual math game. They touch each other's shoulders, point at each other's screens and often shout out loud while playing: "Yes, I've got five treasures now!", "There you go little birdie, your mum is on the second floor"! or "Come on bumble bee, go faster: only four steps left"! At the same time, but on the other side of the world, some American children are playing the same kind of game, also individually, but sitting in a small group of about five children at a table during preschool "station time" – but this is not such an unusual sight. They help the characters in the game to make an old Wild West town prosperous again, by helping them, e.g. mend chairs by choosing the right chair leg or help a chef estimate how much food he should cook to feed his customers. In both the Swedish and American preschools, children are playing a specific kind of digital game, where the aim is not to win themselves, but to use the math they are learning to teach the characters in the game and help them achieve their goals.

Introduction

Digitalisation in education begun some time ago, both in Swedish and American preschools, but teaching materials for younger children tend to lag. In this chapter, we will, by illustrative empirical examples from two different research projects, discuss the potentials of implementing adaptive math games with Teachable Agents (TAs) in preschools and illustrate how preschoolers are engaging with math towards pro-social ends. These games bring benefits – some more affective and some more cognitive. But there are also some concerns that must be addressed, e.g. if, and in that case how, this kind of didactic design could be implemented in preschools that are aiming at more collaborative learning processes. We will describe one particular type of adaptive digital game design, called a TA, that aims to support preschool aged learners' developing math competency, while also promoting positive collaborative behaviours, such as helping, teaching and reflecting. We believe that this may be a particularly strong way to support young children's math learning and their beliefs about themselves as math learners, by positioning them as experts who are using math to help others. We will cast light on how adaptive games and TAs can be introduced, implemented and used in education and discuss potentials as well as constraints. We also discuss more generally how adaptive games could possibly be used or designed to encourage collaboration/pro-social behaviours in a way that reinforces the math concepts. This is something that, as far as we know, has not been studied before.

Aristotle some thousand years ago was said to have claimed that: "*Teaching is the highest form of understanding*". Likewise, philosopher Lucius Seneca stated, "*We learn by teaching*", but little did any of them know that their didactic thoughts would be combined with Artificial Intelligence (AI) and designed into digital games and used by preschoolers on digital tablets. There are potentials of using AI in designing digital learning for preschool students learning with something called "Teachable Agents" (TAs). A TA (Blair, Schwartz, Biswas, & Leelawong, 2007) is a character that students are supposed to teach what they have just learned, e.g. how to count to five (Haake, Anderberg, Husain, & Gulz, 2015). Children teach the agent to help it solve problems, such as getting a baby bird back to its correct nest. We will discuss the interaction between a child and TA character, and we will especially focus on what signs of learning – affective (attitudes towards math) and cognitive (uptake of feedback) – can be seen in the interaction between the child and the TA. Questions asked are, e.g.: How can preschool students learn early math by interacting with a TA in an adaptive digital game? How can the potential power of collaboration be used more in individual digital math games in preschool?

Earlier Research Related to Digital Math in Preschool

According to EU Horizon 2020 (Becker et al., 2017), adaptive teaching materials are progressing, and so are designs for learning that make use of gamification. In the following, relevant earlier research is presented.

Earlier Research on Digital Games in Preschool Contexts

Mobile technologies, such as digital tablets, are currently transforming existing educational practice in preschool as well as in school. On the positive side, prior research indicates that digital learning environments can be a foundation for the emergence of creative, innovative, explorative, playful and out-of-the-box educational practices (Kjällander, 2019). Additionally, with respect to early mathematics, research has found that digital games can support formative learning processes which may contribute to the development and advancement of early math skills (Husain, Gulz, & Haake, 2015).

A Swedish research institute has, out of 85 studies worldwide, found ten relevant experimental research studies where students in preschool have used digital games in math concluding in a few statements, that are relevant to this article. First, it seems to be beneficial if the game and how they work around the game encourage conversation between students and preschool teachers since students can be stimulated to use mathematical concepts and terms – especially if they get to talk about the specific assignment, sharing ideas and talking about solutions and explanations. Also, the possibility to ask for help on the math content is highlighted whether children are working cooperatively or individually in a community (Swedish Institute for Educational Research, 2018). Research (Gomes, Falcão, & Tedesco, 2018) targeting the age group of preschool children, also indicate that digital games possess important elements for learning such as cumulative challenges, fast and individual feedback along with the visualisation of the consequences of misunderstandings (Ginsburg, Jamalian, & Creighan, 2013). In a study like the one presented here, Lourenco, Bonny, and Schwartz (2016) studied how preschoolers were trained numerical skills with an adaptive game and came to the result that the game enhanced numeral skills, especially more advanced skills, such as spatial representation and mental calculation, in preschoolers from different socio-economic backgrounds with different math competences.

Digital games can support learning academic skills among preschool children, but are they aligned with socio-emotional learning goals of preschool? Well, according to researchers Plowman and McPake (2013), who have been doing research on the technology use of 3–4-year-olds in their homes, there are many myths about young children and technology, one of them being that technology prevent social interaction between children since children are lured to spend time with technology rather than with their families. They suggest that this is unwarranted, at least for 3–4-year-olds, since they, perhaps did watch TV or other digital media, but most often interspersed with other activities such as play, dressing up or acting out scenes and often discussing what they saw with siblings and parents – thus, media afford children to ask questions about the world and discuss it with their families. Also, young children are prompted to communicate with others, despite time or place differences as they are provided intriguing possibilities for their communicative skills. The researchers finish by stating that "...*used thoughtfully, technology can enhance rather than hinder social interaction.*" (Plowman & McPake, 2013, p. 29). So, what about preschool – does technology use hinder social interaction? Earlier research suggest that games enable social learning (Phillips & Popović, 2012) and research (Kjällander, 2011; Kjällander & Moinian, 2014) also present that children, although not told to cooperate on a digital device, most often try to cooperate anyhow.

Earlier Research on Learning by Teaching in Digital Environments

"The learning by teaching" paradigm has been used successfully with older learners in a variety of contexts, e.g.science and mathematics (Biswas, Leelawong, Schwartz, Vye, and The Teachable Agents Group at Vanderbilt, 2005; Chase, Chin, Oppezzo, & Schwartz, 2009). There are several components of TAs that help lead to the learning benefits, which have been described previously (see Blair, 2013). Here, we discuss two characteristics that we hypothesise are particularly relevant to early mathematics learning. First, the TA provides affordances for the child to become emotionally engaged in his/her digital tutee's learning in the game. Children not only notice and correct their tutee's mistakes (and thus their own understanding), but also learn for themselves (Chase et al., 2009). By positioning the child as the teacher, helping other characters use math to solve problems, TAs may improve young children's self-efficacy (or beliefs about their potential to succeed) in mathematics, something that has been shown with elementary school-aged children (Tärning, 2018). Second, TAs can provide adaptive and individualised challenges and feedback to the child. Some apps for children are adaptive and provide feedback when children answer wrong or right, but not a lot of game apps provide children with constructive, multimodal feedback and support (Blair, 2013; Tärning, 2018). Assessment feedback should, according to Black and Wiliam (2009) be corrective, specific and timely, something that can be made easier with digital tools. Because TAs are embedded in a game context, and learners can see the TA going through its reasoning process as it solves challenges, it presents the opportunity to provide rich, contextualised feedback and help children be more reflective about whether their quantitative answers make sense.

Earlier Research on Attitudes, Self-efficacy and Learning in Mathematics

It is often believed that how skilled you are in math depend on whether you think of yourself or position yourself as a "math-person" or not. Palmer (2010) has shown that young girls, e.g. less often position themselves as knowledgeable in math, with the consequence that they have, and receive, lower expectations on their achievements in math later. Similarly, researchers discovered that having a female math teacher with math anxiety increased preschool and school girls' belief that boys are better than girls in math and the girls' performance declined (Beilock, Gunderson, Ramirez, & Levine, 2010). Recently, Stanford neuro researchers (Chen et al., 2018) have, in a study with 240 elementary school students, where they, among other methods used MRI, found that a child's positive attitude to math predicts their math achievement. They found that a math interest and self-perceived ability in math were related to enhanced memory and more effective problem-solving capacities. This study is the first to reveal what many teachers have always felt: that there are neurocognitive mechanisms by which positive attitude impacts both young student's learning and their academic achievement.

For elementary school-aged students, it has been shown that teaching an agent, especially one that is seen as needing a lot of help, increases not only the student's achievement in mathematics, but also their self-efficacy in mathematics, particularly those with low self-efficacy (Tärning, 2018). Additionally, because children see the characters using the math they are being taught to solve problems in the game world, this can help children see math as a useful tool in their own everyday lives, something that has been shown to carryover from the digital environments to classroom play activities (Gulz, Kjällander, Frankenberg, & Haake, 2020).

Studies have documented that there is an effect on general learning and motivation when students are using educational digital games (Ke, 2008), but other research (Neumann, 2018) indicates that an intervention will give results on what trained in the intervention – transfer effects are uncommon. Pareto, Haake, Lindström, Sjödén, and Gulz (2012) have found that an effective design strategy for learning and motivation in digital games is one that allows for combinations of both collaborative and competitive play, a design strategy that is not commonly implemented in adaptive individual games. Instead, in this chapter we take stance on adaptive games that are non-competitive. We will here discuss how students work in a digital game with affection for all characters in general (wanting to help) and with their TA specifically (wanting to teach). A recent research overview (Drigas, Kokkalia, & Lytras, 2018) concludes that digital resources are tools that can foster collaborative co-learning in preschool-aged children. They also suggest that preschool education in terms of co-learning in digital learning environments (in special education) needs more research.

Designs for Learning: A Tool to Understand Interaction between a Child and a Teachable Agent

To help determine if TAs are supporting children's learning and behaviours in the ways hypothesised, we use a theoretical framework called Designs for Learning (Selander, 2008; Kress, 2010; Selander & Kress, 2010).

This theoretical perspective draws on transdisciplinary work between didactics and digitalisation (Selander, 2008; Selander & Kress, 2010), just as this chapter does. A research interest from this perspective can be observable interaction in the interface between the digital device and the child. Digital resources are seen as meaning-making, actional, visual and linguistic resources (Kress & Leeuwen, 2001) that the child can use to communicate and learn. Interaction occurs in different modes, such as symbols, sounds and colours, and all these modes hold possibilities for meaning-making (Kress, 2010; Selander, 2008). Digital tablets and adaptive games can afford students to work with realistic multimodal representations of the world around them (Shaffer, 2006).

To meet the demands of a post-modern society, it is no longer obvious how learning shall be organised. Guidelines or school norms do not tell teachers about what specific teaching material or apps for math to use, instead pedagogues are supposed to make these choices themselves; as a result, they are active in forming the school of today (Selander, 2009) – together with their students. In preschool, e.g. teaching material can be chosen due to what is free to download, or on children's own experiences and interests. Two aspects of design are relevant (Selander & Kress, 2010): Design *for* learning (here the intervention design, the game design and the teachers' implementation of the game) and Design *in* learning (how students create their learning paths in the game).

Orchestration describes the process of how the teachers (in intervention studies together with researchers) select and assemble the material which is given a shape through the process of design (Kress, 2010) and which can be viewed as a matter of choice in relation to the setting (Kress & Leeuwen, 2001), here the use of adaptive games. The ensemble of different modes can become meaningful to the child (Kress, 2010) who makes meaning transforming information to their own representations of new knowledge. An important notion in this perspective is affordance (Selander & Kress, 2010), which can be explained as the semiotic potential/limitation for representation in a mode. According to Kress (2010), a digital resource such as a tablet provides possibilities for both hardware and software affordances. What the child recognises as an affordance depends on the child's needs, interests and the specific situation at hand (Leeuwen van, 2005). Here the notion of prompt is important too, as it explains an invitation to interaction (Kress, 2010), such as a question from the TA. This notion refers to how a TA can express as well as elicit emotions, something that the researchers Zhao, Ailiya, and Shen (2012) highlight as crucial for students' learning. Emotions are thought to deeply influence the interactive experience between TAs and students (Brave & Nass, 2003) and can for example be expressed in the TA's facial expressions and voice.

Researchers, teachers and students are didactic designers (Selander, 2008; Holm Sørensen, Audon, & Tweddell Levinsen, 2010) forming the game to be something slightly different from the original. Transformation as didactic design starts with the teacher's imagining of the task; knowledge of both the resources available to perform the task and knowledge of the students and their capacities. Design in learning, on the other hand, starts with the child's imagining of the formation and creating his or her learning path. Students' learning is understood as a trajectory of sign-making, designing activities within a framing.

Teachers and students choose between sets of semiotic resources when bringing modes and media together to direct focus and attention at something and represent their understanding, such as talking to the TA or clicking at different number representations.

Two Empirical Examples from Sweden and the USA

We present two types of empirical material from preschool children interacting with TA-based digital math games – video documentation and game log, which we will discuss from a Designs for Learning perspective. Both types of material were produced while children were playing the games, and both reflect different types of uptake and transformation of the game content by the children in support of math learning. In the first example, video analysis shows how children are interacting with the teaching and helping narrative of the game. In the second example, log data is combined with pre-post interviews of math learning from outside the game to determine how children are learning and approaching feedback within the game. Combined, the analyses examine both affective and math learning elements of the game.

Preschool Research Projects in Sweden and USA

The Swedish research project at Stockholm University: "*Enhancing Preschool Children's Attention, Language and Communication Skills*", led by Lenz-Taguchi and financed by the Swedish National Research Council (Vetenskapsrådet), is the largest randomised controlled trial in Swedish preschool. The American research project, *Critter Corral*, was made at the AAA-lab at the Graduate School of Education, Stanford University. Both projects involved developing and implementing a digital adaptive math game in preschool classes with children ages 4–5. The Swedish project (Gerholm et al., 2018) was implemented and taught by about 30 preschool teachers who used an adaptive game with about 100 preschool children in ten municipal preschools every morning during 6 weeks. The American project was carried out in a large, urban school district. Over 2 years of studies, approximately 300 children played a game three times per week (15–20 minutes each time) for 5 to 10 weeks, with matched game-play and control classrooms. Ethical guidelines for research with human beings (www.vr.se) was thoroughly followed and the Swedish project has been granted ethical clearance by the regional Ethics Committee at the Karolinska Institute (www.epn.se/Stockholm/). Guardians, teachers and children have through the project's all different stages been given information and consent has been given in a continuous process. Special notice has been paid to children's oral and bodily consent by means of gestures and questions as such. The American study was approved by and followed the guidelines set out by the human subjects research institutional review board. In the Swedish project, a range of different empirical research material has been produced, but only the video recordings of teachers and children's interaction with the adaptive game and fieldnotes will here be presented and used. In the American project, video data was not collected, as the researchers did not have permission to capture children on video. Before and after playing, children completed an one-on-one interview-based assessment of early number concepts, and logging data captured children's moves within the digital game.

Designs *for* and *in* Learning with Magical Garden and Critter Corral

In the following empirical examples, we can see how preschool students engage in digital math games, often due to their own interests, designing their own learning paths.

Magical Garden – An Adaptive Game with Teachable Agents

Magical Garden is a math game aimed at preschool students in the age of 4–6 (Haake et al., 2015) developed by Lund and Linköping Universities [3], Sweden, with support from Stanford University [4], USA. According to the game developers, goals and objectives are to enhance children's early math learning (i.e. number sense, order, addition and subtraction). The theoretical base for Magical Garden, with constructive feedback, is inspired by scaffolding in a Vygotskian tradition (Vygotsky, 1978) and game design is in line with general Swedish pedagogical preschool values (Haake et al., 2015; Kjällander & Frankenberg, 2018).

The TAs are visualised as three different animals; a panda, a mouse and a hedgehog that are supposed to help other characters (Figure 6.1). There are a number of sub-games in Magical Garden plus a garden where the players grow plants with

FIGURE 6.1 The Teachable Agents – TA Panders, Mille and Igis (Digital Game Magical Garden produced by The Education Technology Group at Lund and Linköping Universities, Sweden.[1]

their TAs. All worlds have the same kind of rules and feedback provided similarly, always specific and timely, and often corrective (Black & Wiliam, 2009). They all have the theme of some character in need of help to get food or to accomplish a duty, help that shall be provided by the child, making the child understand math as a useful tool to solve everyday problems. This theme is clearly important to pre-school students who engage emotionally in the game and are motivated to help and to teach his/her TA so that the TA can help in its turn. The game design/rules (Prensky, 2001) can be described in eight steps: 1) The child is asked to help with a problem and must wait for instructions. (A voice tells the child what to do: for example, helping lost baby birds to find their parents in a tree after being blown off by a storm). 2) The child is trying different solutions. (Clicking at different number representations at the lower part of the screen, such as four dots, four lines, the numberfour, a hand holding up four fingers and so on). 3) The player passes the task and solves the problem. (The baby bird goes up in the elevator and finds its parent, with laughter and hugs or it ends up in another bird nest, with a funny noise and question marks as result and if the answer is wrong the bird gives feedback like: I live a little higher up!). 4) TA turns up on screen and asks if it can watch. (The TA watch the child playing). 5) TA thinks and gives a suggestion to a solution. (A thought bubble with another number representation is visible and the TA says: Am I thinking right now?) 6) The child accepts the solution or helps the TA to understand and find the right answer. (The TA has different facial expressions on being wrong or right and tries again, supported by the child.) 7) When the TA and the child have helped the baby birds for a while they are rewarded with waterdrops, getting the same amount of water irrespectively of how many right answers they have got. 8) The child uses the waterdrops to grow plants in the garden. This is didactically designed as the rewarding part of the game.

There is an intention to provide the game to all preschoolers during their last year in preschool, to prevent mathematical inequalities among children before they start school.

Critter Corral – An Adaptive Game in a Wild West Town

The game Critter Corral is developed and tested by researchers at Stanford University, USA, and implemented in California. It helps children build founda-tional number concepts through play. Many of the design principles employed in Magical Garden and Critter Corral are the same. A flexible understanding of number goes beyond simply knowing the counting sequence, and includes cardi-nality, relative magnitude, estimation, numeral identification, 1:1 correspondence and set composition/decomposition (Purpura & Lonigan, 2013). Building on the ideas of Robbie Case and his colleagues, the games in Critter Corral attempt to help students integrate different conceptions and representations of number (Griffin, Case, & Siegler, 1994). For example, across games, "3" is represented as three objects, a length of three, tapping three times, the digit three and the third item in the counting sequence. The spatial structure of the number line is utilised throughout to facilitate this integration.

There are five sub-games in Critter Corral. The games represent different businesses, and the learner's task is to help each of the businesses to return Critter Corral to the booming Wild West town it once was. In all games, the learner's task is to help the character create a 1:1 correspondence with a target amount. For example, Figure 6.2 shows the restaurant game, where the learner's job is to help the chef cook the right amount of food so every customer will have a meal.

The other four games in the app follow similar play patterns. For example, in a theatre game, the learner sees a chair that is missing one leg and chooses which size leg will fix it. If the learner chooses the correct leg size, it fits the chair and fixes it so the characters can sit and watch a show. In the delivery game, the player needs to help the monkey go the right number of spaces to deliver a present to a waiting customer.

Critter Corral employs many of the features of TAs. Learners are telling the character they are helping what to do, e.g., they get to see the result when the character does what the child has told it to do. This is a light version of a TA, with a narrative focused on helping.

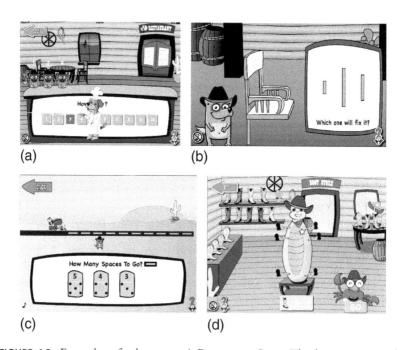

(a) (b)

(c) (d)

FIGURE 6.2 Examples of sub-games: a) Restaurant Game. The learner counts the customers and tells the chef how much food to cook. b) Theatre game. The learner decides which leg will fix the chair. c) Delivery game. The learner helps the monkey know how many spaces to go to deliver the present to the customer. d) Boot game. The learner shows the clerk how many shoes to bring out.

Two Empirical Examples from Two Continents

Two empirical examples will be presented here: i) Sweden: example of how four-year-old children's emotions, friendship and the urge to help each other and the TA holds potentials for mathematical learning, self-esteem and collaboration ii) United States of America: example of preschool students reflecting and self-correcting their own mistakes after interacting with rich, contextualised forms of feedback.

Swedish Example: Collaboration and Interaction in Magical Garden

In a pilot before the Swedish study, Magical Garden was implemented and ana-lysed together with another adaptive game (Kjällander & Frankenberg, 2018). Something that was appreciated with Magical Garden in the pilot, was that children did not compare how skilled they were, comparing gained stars and accomplished levels, as Magical Garden is designed to put the pedagogy of "learning-by-teaching" into practice (Haake et al., 2015). Magical Garden was therefore understood, by teachers and children, as more aligned with the Swedish preschool philosophy, although the individual aspect of the game is understood as somewhat of a clash. Also, children were prompted to help different characters in the game, a prompt that could have narrative as the following:

BUMBLEBEE: My eyesight gets worse every day. How should I find the flower with nectar? Is anybody there? [Bumblebee appeals to the player]. Be a star and show me the right flower. First decide how far I shall fly. Tap the correct number to show me how far it is.

CHAMELEON: Nice to sleep! Is it an ant over there? Oups, fail! That tastes like tree! I need help to aim. You there, [appeals to the player], select the button that matches what you were counting on. Thanks!

Recurring through the 6-week-interventions on the ten units is the urge for cooperation between children, although this is not afforded or prompted by the game design. They want to sit next to each other, touching shoulders or feet and they call on each other's attention to what the TA looks like, what plants they are growing or how an animal sounds – despite that they are always using headphones. After each session of Magical Garden many preschoolers want to tell and teach their friends about what they have done during the session and here mathematical concepts are repeated and signs of learning can be visualised. At many of the preschools, this kind of reflection also becomes a standard procedure, something that is not originally in the intervention design, but a result of teachers listening to children's suggestions and transforming their didactic design accord-ingly – often with the twist of drawing on early math and challenging students by mathematical questions in this reflection. At one preschool all children were asked to mention two good things and something that could have been better after playing the game (cf. "*Two stars and a wish*"). The different worlds in the game is randomised by the game, but some preschool students try to manipulate the game to enter the same world simultaneously and play together. On succeeding they talk more and louder to each other, interacting by pointing at each other's screens: clearly satisfied with their move. Here, they do not seem to notice that they are on different levels of difficulty – even if one child is counting plus and minus in the area of 1–4 while another is practicing 5–9.

In one filmed occasion, two preschool students make mistakes on purpose, to slow the game down, for a third child to be able to catch up so that they can play "together". This design in learning have been posed by earlier research as well (Kjällander, 2019) with different agendas such as to challenge the game, to fool the game, to provoke the teachers or to explore the multimodality of the game. So, preschool students tend to sometimes give the wrong answers on purpose, but it does not have to be to challenge and explore the game (or to fool the TA). It can also be, as revealed in children's interviews in another study (Ternblad, Haake, Anderberg, & Gulz, 2018), that they wanted the TA to "*learn from its own mistakes*". The game developers had not had this kind of meta-level of teaching in mind when designing the game, but the preschoolers, as young as they are, designed this possibility into the game.

In another filmed sequence one child says that she will "Skip the watering!" – which is the rewarding element in the game (where children can use the water they have earned to grow plants in their garden). She does this to be able to enter the same world as her peer. At a few of the preschools, teachers have been trying to make children catch up with Magical Garden in the afternoon, outside the class game session, if a child has been absent, but without succeeding. It is obvious in the focus groups with teachers, as well as in the filmed material of children that the social framing means a lot for children's motivation.

FIGURE 6.3 A child is playing the Bird rescue game in Magical Garden, learning mathematical order 1–4. Photo: Susanne Kjällander.

The following empirical example was chosen since it reveals the emotional, yet mathematical, interaction between a child and a TA (Figure 6.3).

Charlie, a 4-year-old, sits on a cushion on a preschool floor, surrounded by ten other preschoolers, all with a headset, individually playing a digital tablet. Charlie is playing Magical Garden, training the numbers of 1–4 in the world "The bird rescue", making use of different number representations that is supposed to correspond to the correct level (1–4) of branches in a tree, to which a sad baby bird shall be brought back to its parent, by means of an elevator that stops at different branches/levels.

09.05: Charlie counts on fingers, clicking at the different number representations on the colourful screen. The child's mathematical answer, represented by levels (1–4), has been corrected several times by the constructive formative feedback of a bird character in the game, and now the child counts to the right level (1) and the answer is correct: level one: "*Yeeey, mmmmm, I looooove birds!*" Charlie gestures and laughs loudly while the baby bird cuddles up next to its parent.

09.20: The child keeps playing and then says to the TA, that has been chosen and personally designed by the child, a blue panda called Panders: "*You have to look if bird points like this – or like this!*" Charlie holds two and then three fingers up in the air to teach Panders.

09.33: While the bird is gesticulating the child says: "*One. It pointed. That's how you do when you point at something. Like bird.*" …

09.45: The baby bird says: "*Could you help me to get home?*"

09.51: With a frowning face expression, the TA Panders says: "*Is it this one?*" simultaneously as a thought bubble with one line, representing the number one is visible above Panders head. The child keeps on talking to his TA Panders and says: "*Yes! That's the one. Now you will see!*" …

09.59: "*Hm. Hm. Hm.*" The child counts with a humming sound and a nod, imitating the bird elevator's movement between levels and the sound, repeating it to the TA who is "thinking" about a number. "*I told you! I showed you!*" The TA begins to smile. Both the TA and the child are smiling, waving their arms in the air. … The bird rescue finishes with the TA saying: "*What a good teacher you are!*" The child smiles and keep on playing.

Gomes et al. (2018) suggest, based on their own research on other games, that important elements for learning, such as cumulative challenges where the exercises adapts to children's new knowledge along with fast and individual feedback presented multimodally in frowns, smiles and sounds offer potential for learning. Several conversations are going on here, between child–TA; child–bird; TA–bird; and child–another child. The example reveals how we can understand pro-social, affective affordances provided in the digital interface and potential signs of learning in math. For example, numbers are represented multimodally by Charlie who is counting by clicking, humming, gesticulating with fingers and nodding and the

FIGURE 6.4 A child is considering the TA:s answer in the game Magicla Garden, as visualized in the thought bubble. Photo: Susanne Kjällander.

TAs mimic questions and thinking bubbles as well as the bird's gestures seem to be understood as prompts since the child chooses to act on them (Figure 6.4). Research by Gomes et al. (2018) show that multimodal visualisation of the consequences of mathematical representations afford and support children's learning. Magical Garden is not the first adaptive game that have been shown to train numerical skills and spatial representation among preschool children (see, e.g. Lourenco et al., 2016), but in this specific game also the narrative with the realistic multimodal representation, as highlighted by, e.g. Shaffer (2006) and the social aspect of wanting to rescue the baby bird makes meaning to the child.

American Example: Feedback and Self-correction in Critter Corral

The American example takes a different approach to the Swedish example, using pre-post interviews of children's math knowledge and game play logs of students' interactions to examine how children are learning in the game. The development of Critter Corral has been an exploration into maximising the informativeness of feedback in a pro-social context. In this context, the game can provide feedback that shows the quantitative implications of an answer as the child is trying to help the character. It shows learners how far off an answer is (e.g. a chef cooks too much or too little food for the number of customers) and gives the learner the opportunity to correct the character's mistakes (and thus their own). This approach is in contrast to most feedback in digital learning games, which only indicates whether the child is correct or incorrect but does not take advantage of other affordances of multimodal environments (Schwartz, Tsang, & Blair, 2016).

The study examined how math learning interacted with the way feedback was provided to children in the game. Children were randomly assigned to play Critter Corral under one of two feedback conditions. Half of the children played with the type of feedback described above. If children answered incorrectly, they

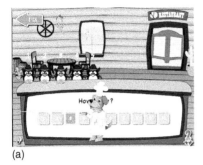

(a)   (b)

FIGURE 6.5 Two examples of implication feedback in the game Critter Corral, developed in the reaserch group AAA-lab at the Graduate School of Education Stanford University, USA[2]. In A).the child has (incorrectly) told the chef there are three customers, so he cooks three fish. Some customers are left without food. The child will then have the opportunity to add fish to help the chef correct the mistake. In B) the child has chosen a chair let that is too long to fit the chair. The child sees the outcome, presented with related size vocabulary "too long", and has the opportunity to choose another chair leg to fix it.

saw how far off the answer was from the correct answer (e.g. chef did not cook enough food and chair leg was too long). We call this the implication feedback condition, because children see the quantitative implications of their responses in the results of the character's behaviours. The other half played under more traditional feedback conditions, common in games for young students (Blair, 2013). In this condition, after an incorrect response, such as telling the chef to cook too little food, children received an error sound and a shaking of the incorrect choice indicating they had made an error, and they were prompted to try again. After three incorrect responses, they were shown the correct answer. All other elements of the game were the same between conditions. The only difference was in the feedback when children answered incorrectly. Children either saw the quantitative implications of their incorrect response (too many, not enough) and tried to fix it, or they simply received an error message indicating the answer was incorrect and tried again (Figure 6.5).

Collapsing across both feedback conditions, preschool children learned more when they were interacting with the game than when they were not, based on pre-post interview-based assessment results (Blair, Pfaffman, Cutumisu, Hallinen, & Schwartz, 2015). As seen in Figure 6.6, preschool children made about 10% greater gains during the time they were playing the game.

Though we found overall learning gains for playing the game, we did not find consistent differences between the two feedback conditions in our outside-the-game assessment measures. However, using the logs of students' actions to consider what students were doing within the game, we saw suggestions that the implication feedback may help children to learn to self-correct compared to the more traditional feedback. A follow-up study, which was conducted with a new cohort of students

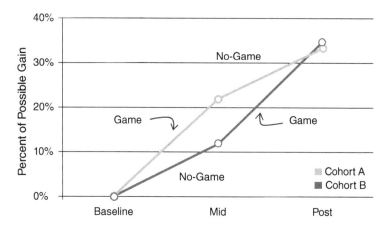

FIGURE 6.6 Gains on assessments conducted outside of the game, based on whether children were playing the game during a time frame or not playing. Cohort A consisted of seven classes that played the game for 5 weeks in the classroom from the baseline to mid-assessment time frames. Cohort B (a matched set of seven classes) did not play during this time. After the mid-assessment, the cohorts switched, and Cohort A stopped playing, while Cohort B started playing the game for 5 weeks, at which point all children completed the post-assessment.

in the same district, included embedded assessment questions within the game that all students answered at regular intervals. Some of the questions included an opportunity to self-correct. In one type of problem, a set of balloons was shown on one side of the screen. The child's task was to create another set of balloons that matched the number of balloons in the first set. They did this by dragging balloons to a target area. In some cases, a cloud rolled in while the child was working and hid the first set of balloons. The child thus had to create the second set from memory, which was a challenging task. Once the child made her answer, the cloud was removed, and she could see the original set of balloons again. The child was given the opportunity to adjust her answer if she desired, now that she could see the original set again. In the terms of designs for learning, this served as the prompt from the game and was the same for all children. However, how children responded to this prompt depended on how they had gotten used to seeing and correcting mistakes through the feedback in the other parts of gameplay. Children in both feedback conditions were about equally accurate in their initial guesses. However, once the cloud was removed and children had the opportunity to self-correct, there was a trend for children in the implication feedback condition to do so more often and in a way that made their answer more accurate (children self-corrected to improve their responses 34% of possible times in the implication feedback condition compared to 20% in the traditional feedback condition, $p = .08$, *two-tailed Fisher's exact test*).

Having been in the condition with richer feedback, seeing the quantitative implications of the character's answers and helping the character correct its mistakes based on those outcomes, children in the implication feedback condition trended towards being more likely to reflect on their answers and positively correct their own mistakes when given the opportunity.

Digital Games and Teachable Agents' Support in Early Math – And Possibilities for Collaboration

A recent international research overview on digital games in preschool shows that it is, also with only a few sessions/weeks for a number of weeks, possible to achieve good results (Swedish Institute for Educational Research, 2018). Here we will give examples related to that statement. Using video, assessment and game-log data, we have examined how two adaptive digital games involving TAs can support preschool learner's mathematics learning, as well as engage them in positive interactions with the technology and each other around mathematics. In the first empirical example, the speech and body language of the child of focus suggests elation in being able to teach the character math and help it solve the problem and return the baby bird to its home – and while doing that the child is simultaneously representing numbers physically and digitally with fingers and numbers. In the second example, log files of children's interactions showed that after helping the game's characters correct their mistakes, children become more likely to notice and correct their own mistakes.

While the TA multimodally express emotions, they take on a role as a naive learner in a believable manner. Earlier research (Zhao et al., 2012) illustrates how TA's expressions encourage students to concentrate while teaching. If it is, as we think, important to focus and be able to position oneself as a person that knows math, these kinds of individual digital games can be helpful, since the student will teach someone else, that does not know as much math: the TA (see, e.g. Tärning, 2018).

Researchers (Phillips & Popović, 2012) claim that games can be powerful for social learning and research has shown that digital resources can enhance social communication (Plowman & McPake, 2013), something that happened in our study as well where preschool students found many ways to be social with each other. We could also see how the social aspects of the game often provided intrinsic motivation. This has been clearly visualised in other research with older students who are keen on training and teaching their TA (e.g. Chase et al., 2009), and also in the examples in this chapter where the children really want to help the panda, mouse, hedgehog or other animal to understand math (although, sometimes they just want to fool them). Children seem to be happy while they are learning math, they laugh and smile. In the example, we can see a child imitating the TA's body language when he/she finally gets the right answer and a compliment about his/her teaching.

However, this social learning element could be even further emphasised. If we think gamification has something to offer math, we could also state that gaming and playing are often enjoyed together with friends. In the Swedish context, the preschool philosophy aims at collaborative explorative learning, and a designed individual math-game like this, was new and unfamiliar to teachers and children. In fact, children almost instinctively began to find alternative ways to collaborate while engaging in Magical Garden – something that occurs because gaming here is framed within the setting of formal education. This opens for a discussion about how collaborativeness can be designed into games or at least into the activity. This is also a key concept for the success of using digital games in preschool, according to a recent international research overview (Swedish Institute for Educational Research, 2018). Just as Pareto et al. (2012) we could observe how children on their own initiative invented and designed their own learning paths to be able to collaborate in ways beyond what the game was designed for. Teachers and children sometimes also work collaboratively with the game content outside the screen (Gulz et al., 2020) and this obviously holds potentials for collaboration. So, there is some work to do on designing for collaborative learning in adaptive games for preschool students. Here we briefly suggest some possible designs for collaborative learning framed by the existing adaptive game:

- A game world/level where the child must invite a peer to solve the problem
- Production of representations that encourage teachers and children to extend the digital interface into the physical environment and keep on working with early math with physical material, as illustrated in Gulz et al. (2020)
- The possibility for children to pedagogically document some math related contents their TA has learned, during the session and present this to the whole class
- Game elements where each child/agent solves a part of a challenge, and multiple children come together to complete the whole challenge

In Sweden, most digital teaching materials have been designed as book-in-a-box, instead of using the potentials of multimodal technology, robotics or AI. Likewise, in the United States, researchers (Phillips & Popović, 2012) have found that there is seldom overlap between the education market and the commercial game market, meaning that game developers so far have not had the incentive in the educational market, that is often run by textbook publishers. Thus, math has been a subject where students work individually in their math books, something we do not need to repeat now that we have the possibility to use adaptive digital tools. We propose that by using the affordances of digital learning environments and advances in AI, we can develop adaptive individualised learning tools that are also social and collaborative in nature.

Future Perspective on Teachable Agents and Adaptive Games

We want to finish in a concluding discussion of how adaptive games and TAs in different countries and settings can have potentials for future education. A contemporary input to the discussion has to do with potentials of individual and collective designs for learning with adaptive games.

In this chapter we have suggested a few reasons why we think that digital adaptive games such as Critter Coral and Magical Garden can serve as a complement, next to other learning resources and physical material in the preschool environment – possibly for half an hour play each morning, or a few sessions per week during about half a term since this dosage has proved to give good results in children's early math (Swedish Institute for Educational Research, 2018). Further research will show us the impacts, challenges and constraints with using digital tools in education of young children. So far there are no overarching proofs that screen activity is negative, but obviously we do not want children to experience the entire school (nor the whole day) through a screen. One must always put the question on what the children would have done instead, if they were not playing a math game on the digital tablet. Had they been working individually in a math book or had they been collectively solving a math problem posed by cones, sticks and stones in the fresh air in the woods? We think that all these different didactic designs have a place in preschool and we suggest a combination of many mathematical designs for learning, out of which adaptive games with TAs could be one tool in the toolbox of instructional strategies.

A concern is, that although preschool teachers use math in their everyday lives, many of them do not appreciate themselves as being skilled in math (Palmer, 2010) – preschool teachers often position themselves as a person that does not know math (even if they do) and many of them claimed that they chose their profession due to their lack of self-esteem in math. If a game and teaching with a game in preschool is well-designed, a game can, according to a research overview (Swedish Institute for Educational Research, 2018) support preschool children's early math. This is claimed to be especially relevant if preschool teachers are not so experienced in mathematical activities. Here lies a possible problem, because if teachers have low self-efficacy in math they might think that it is better to outsource math to digital resources, meaning that they might lose insight and interest in the preschool students' mathematical exploration, progression and knowledge representation. Earlier research (Hattie, 2014) illustrates the need and possibilities of digital tools for teachers to be able to follow children's individual learning processes and representations in a digital interface. A new research project in Swedish preschools (Gulz et al., 2020) will address this possible problem and give some insight in the future about how digital learning environments can support preschool teachers in their mathematics instruction.

Acknowledgements

The Magical Garden study was undertaken as part of the intervention study Enhancing Preschool Children's Attention, Language and Communication Skills,[3] financed by the Swedish National Research Council. The Critter Corral study was funded by a grant from the Knut and Alice Wallenberg foundation. We want to additionally thank "Riksbankens Jubileumsfond", The Swedish Foundation for Research in the Humanities and Social Sciences" (www.rj.se) and Marianne and Marcus Wallenberg Foundation for making this article possible.

Notes

1 https://www.lucs.lu.se/etg/
2 https://aaalab.stanford.edu/
3 This study was undertaken as part of the intervention study Enhancing Preschool Children's Attention, Language and Communication Skills, financed by the Swedish National Research Council (Vetenskapsrådet) by Lenz Taguchi, Gerholm, Kjällander, Frankenberg, Palmer, Kallionen and Tonér, Stockholm University, Sweden.

References

Becker, S. A., Cummins, M., Davis, A., Freeman, A., Hall, C. G., & Ananthanarayanan, V. (2017). *NMC horizon report: 2017 higher education edition* (pp. 1–60). The New Media Consortium.

Beilock, S. L., Gunderson, E. A., Ramirez, G., & Levine, S. C. (2010). Female teachers' math anxiety affects girls' math achievement. *Proceedings of the National Academy of Sciences*, *107*(5), 1860–1863.

Biswas, G., Leelawong, K., Schwartz, D., Vye, N., & The Teachable Agents Group at Vanderbilt. (2005). Learning by teaching: A new agent paradigm for educational software. *Applied Artificial Intelligence*, *19*(3–4), 363–392.

Black, P., & Wiliam, D. (2009). Developing the theory of formative assessment. *Educational Assessment, Evaluation and Accountability (formerly: Journal of Personnel Evaluation in Education)*, *21*(1), 5–31.

Blair, K. P. (2013, June). *Learning in critter corral: evaluating three kinds of feedback in a preschool math app*. In *Proceedings of the 12th International Conference on Interaction Design and Children* (pp. 372–375). ACM, Paris.

Blair, C., McKinnon, R. D. & The Family Project Investigators (2016). Moderating effects of executive functions and the teacher-child relationship on the development of mathematics ability in kindergarden. *Learing and Instruction*, *41* (x) 85–93.

Blair, K. P., Pfaffman, J., Cutumisu, M., Hallinen, N., & Schwartz, D. (2015, April). *Testing the effectiveness of iPad math game: lessons learned from running a multi-classroom Study*. In *Proceedings of the 33rd Annual ACM Conference Extended Abstracts on Human Factors in Computing Systems*(pp. 727–734). ACM, Seoul.

Blair, K., Schwartz, D. L., Biswas, G., & Leelawong, K. (2007). Pedagogical agents for learning by teaching: Teachable agents. *Educational Technology*, *47*(1), 56–61.

Brave, S., & Nass, C. (2003). Emotion in human-computer-interaction. In J.A. Jacko & A. Sears (Eds.), *The human-computer interaction handbook* (pp. 81–96). Mahvah, NJ: Erlbaum.

Chase, C., Chin, D., Oppezzo, M., Schwartz, D. (2009) Teachable agents and the protégé effect: increasing the effort towards learning. *Journal of Science Education and Technology* *18*, 334–352.

Chen, L., Bae, S. R., Battista, C., Qin, S., Chen, T., Evans, T. M., & Menon, V. (2018). Positive Attitude Toward Math Supports Early Academic Success: Behavioral Evidence and Neurocognitive Mechanisms. *Psychological Science*. doi: 10.1177/0956797617735528.

Drigas A., Kokkalia G., & Lytras M.. (2018). ICT and collaborative co-learning in pre-school children who face memory difficulties. Computers In Human Behavior [serial online]. October 1, 2015;51(Part B):645–651. Available from: ScienceDirect, Ipswich, MA. Accessed March 30, 2018.

Gerholm, T., Hörberg, T., Tonér, S., Kallioinen, P., Frankenberg, S., Kjällander, S., Palmer, A., & Taguchi, H. L. (2018). A protocol for a three-arm cluster randomized controlled superiority trial investigating the effects of two pedagogical methodologies in Swedish preschool settings on language and communication, executive functions, auditive selective attention, socioemotional skills and early maths skills. *BMC Psychology, 6*(1), 29. doi: 10.1186/s40359-018-0239-y(OY)

Ginsburg, H. P., Jamalian, A., & Creighan, S. (2013). Cognitive guidelines for the design and evaluation of early mathematics software: The example of MathemAntics. In L. English & J. Mulligan (Eds.), *Reconceptualizing early mathematics learning* (pp. 83–120). Dordrecht, The Netherlands: Springer.

Gomes, T. C. S., Falcão, T. P., & Tedesco, P. C. D. A. R. (2018). Exploring an approach based on digital games for teaching programming concepts to young children. *International Journal of Child-Computer Interaction, 16*, 77–84.

Griffin, S. A., Case, R., & Siegler, R. S. (1994). *Rightstart: Providing the central conceptual pre-requisites for first formal learning of arithmetic to students at risk for school failure.* Cambridge: The MIT Press.

Gulz, A., Kjällander, S., Frankenberg, S., & Haake, M. (2020). Early Math in a Preschool Context: Spontaneous extension of the digital into the physical. *IxD&A–Interaction Design and Architecture (s) Journal*, 44, 129–154.

Haake, M., Anderberg, E., Husain, L., & Gulz, A. (2015). *No Child Behind nor Singled out? – Adaptive Instruction Combined with Inclusive Pedagogy in Early Math Software.* Volume 9112 of the series Lecture Notes in Computer Science pp. 612–615 17th International Conference on Artificial Intelligence in Education (AIED). Madrid.

Hattie, J. (2014). *Synligt lärande: en syntes av mer än 800 metaanalyser om vad som påverkar elevers skolresultat.* Stockholm: Natur & kultur

Holm Sørensen, B., Audon, L. & Tweddell Levinsen, K. (2010). *Skole 2.0. Didaktiske bidrag.* Århus: Forlaget Klim.

Husain, L., Gulz, A., & Haake, M. (2015). Supporting early math-rationales and require-ments for high quality software. *Journal of Computers in Mathematics and Science Teaching, 34*(4), 409–429.

Ke, F. (2008). Alternative goal structures for computer game-based learning. *International Journal of Computer Supported Collaborative Learning, 3*(4), 429–445.

Kjällander, S. (2011). Designs for learning in an extended digital environment. Case studies of social interaction in the social science classroom. (Doctoral dissertation. Institutionen för pedagogik och didaktik, Stockholm University.)

Kjällander, S. (2019). Forskningsperspektiv på digitala verktyg i förskolan. In: S. Kjällander & B. Riddersporre. *Digitalisering i en förskola på vetenskaplig grund.* Stockholm: Natur & Kultur

Kjällander, S., & Frankenberg, S. (2018). How to design a digital individual learn-ing RCT-study in the context of Swedish preschool. In Special Issue: Co Ed. Nind, M & Hall, K. Research methods for pedagogy and innovation: Seeing the hidden and hard to know. International Journal of Research & Method in Education. doi: 10.1080/1743727X.2018.1470161 (Green OA)

Kjällander, S., & Moinian, F. (2014). Digital tablets and applications in preschool everyday practices, Preschoolers' creative challenges of didactic designs. *Designs for Learning* 7(1).

Kress, G. (2010). *Multimodality: A social semiotic approach to contemporary communication*. London/New York: Routledge.

Kress, G., & van Leeuwen, T. (2001). *Multimodal discourse: The modes and media of contemporary communication*. London: Arnold

Leeuwen van, T. (2005). *Introducing social semiotics*. London & New York: Routledge

Lourenco, S. F., Bonny, J. W., & Schwartz, B. L. (2016). Children and adults use physical size and numerical alliances in third-party judgments of dominance. *Frontiers in psychology*, *6*, 2050.

Neumann, M. M. (2018). Using tablets and apps to enhance emergent literacy skills in young children. *Early Childhood Research Quarterly*, *42*, 239–246.

Palmer, A. (2010). Att bli matematisk: Matematisk subjektivitet och genus i lärarutbildningen för de yngre åldrarna (Doctoral dissertation, Pedagogiska institutionen, Stockholms universitet).

Pareto, L., Haake, M., Lindström, P., Sjödén, B., & Gulz, A. (2012). A teachable-agent-based game affording collaboration and competition: evaluating math comprehension and motivation. *Educational Technology Research and Development*, 60(5), 723–751.

Phillips, V., & Popović, Z. (2012). More than child's play: Games have potential learning and assessment tools. *Phi Delta Kappan*, *94*(2), 26–30.

Plowman, L., & McPake, J. (2013). Seven myths about young children and technology, *Childhood Education*, *89*(1), 27–33. doi:10.1080/00094056.2013.757490

Prensky, M. (2001). Fun, play and games: What makes games engaging. *Digital Game-based Learning*, *5*(1), 5–31.

Purpura, D., & Lonigan, C. (2013). Informal Numeracy Skills: The structure and relations among numbering, relations, and arithmetic operations in preschool. *American Educational Research Journal*, *50*, 178–209.

Schwartz, D. L., Tsang, J. T., Blair, K. P. (2016). *The ABCs of how we learn: 26 scientifically proven approaches, how they work, and when to use them*. New York, NY: W. W. Norton & Company

Selander, S. (2008). Tecken för lärande – tecken på lärande. Ett designteoretiskt perspektiv. In S. Selander & A.-L. Rostvall (red.) *Design för lärande* (pp. 28–43). Stockholm: Norstedts Akademiska Förlag.

Selander, S. (2009). Didaktisk Design. In S. Selander & E. Svärdemo-Åberg (red.) *Didaktisk design i digital miljö – nya möjligheter för lärande*. Stockholm: Liber.

Selander, S. & Kress, G. (2010). *Design för lärande: Ett multimodalt perspektiv*. Stockholm: Norstedts Akademiska Förlag.

Shaffer, D. W. (2006). *How computer games help children learn*. New York: Palgrave Macmillan.

Swedish Institute for Educational Research (2018). *Digitala lärresurser i matematikundervisningen. Delrapport förskola*. Stockholm: Skolforskningsinstitutets systematiska översikter.

Tärning, B. (2018). Design of Teachable Agents and feedback in educational software (Doctoral Dissertation), Lund University.

Ternblad, E. M., Haake, M., Anderberg, E., & Gulz, A. (2018, June). *Do preschoolers 'Game the System'? A case study of children's intelligent (mis) use of a teachable agent based play-&-learn game in mathematics*. In *International Conference on Artificial Intelligence in Education* (pp. 557–569). Cham: Springer.

Vygotsky, L. S. (1978). *Socio-cultural theory*. Mind in society.

Zhao, G., Ailiya, B., & Shen, Z. (2012). Learning-by-teaching: Designing teachable agents with intrinsic motivation. *Educational Technology & Society*, *15* (4), 62–74.

7

LEARNING MUSIC BY COMPOSING ON IPADS

Bjørn-Terje Bandlien

Introduction

In this chapter, I explore how iPad technology in a design theoretical perspective can give basis for inclusive learning designs in the music subject. This means that both learning and inclusion are in focus at the same time, through a design theoretical view of music learning and teaching with the use of iPad. The chapter is based on a research project where secondary school students composed music weekly with GarageBand on iPad for more than two months, and where I was present as a participating observer and also collected the students' sub-products after each teaching session.

Traditionally, music education in Norway has often been conducted in such a way that the teacher quite heavily directs all the learning activity – either as individual teaching of playing musical instruments or as more collective processes such as choral singing, collective listening to music or theoretical discussion of music. This teaching has been strongly influenced by normative understandings of music and learning, grounded in master-apprentice tradition and musical canon. The master-apprentice tradition and music-cultural canonisation of repertory and music knowledge carry on the understandings and values of a collective memory, but can at the same time also exclude students who do not fit in with the conventional preferences of the professional tradition.

Based on this, I explore a music pedagogical learning design that breaks with the traditional patterns of strong teacher management. Instead of practicing music, music creation is focused, instead of dissemination of knowledge, students' engagement and active creation of their own knowledge are supported and instead of purely individual *or* collective teaching, a hybrid of individualised activities within a classroom with many students is attempted.

In the following, I will give a brief overview of what existing research says about iPad and design theory from an inclusive music pedagogical perspective.

iPad and Design Theory in Music Education Research

iPad is a relatively new digital technology, and music education research on iPad is sparse. Nevertheless, this research contains several examples of argumentation that highlight iPad as a technology with the potential to contribute to an inclusive music didactic design where a mass of students with a multitude of preconditions, preconceptions, interests and aversions is offered the opportunity for musical learning and engagement.

Several research contributions indicate that student agency can be enhanced in music education where the iPad technology is central (Brown, Stewart, Hansen, & Stewart, 2014; Juntunen, 2017; Bandlien, 2019). This assumption is further reinforced by several research contributions examining the iPad as a new musical instrument (Randles, 2013; Williams, 2014; Verrico & Reese, 2016; Park, 2017). Some key points in these contributions are the ability of the technology to open up for artistic freedom through new, innovative physical and tactile playing techniques and expressions, as well as great artistic freedom because no normative iPad music tradition exists. Also within a context of special education, something of the same is highlighted. Devito (2017, pp. 410–411) emphasises how iPad can contribute to changing what it means to play – that iPad can simplify hand–eye coordination when playing, while at the same time contribute to changing what it means to be musical. Vanderlinde (2017, p. 440) writes: "To be able to produce and express musical ideas in a way that is socially normative and personally meaningful is empowering". The notion that the technology contributes to the simplification of otherwise difficult musical activities is reflected in much of the literature, regardless of the context. Reese, Bicheler, and Robinson (2016) argue that the iPad can help remove barriers that may hinder students' musical performance, and through this support students in their belief in their own abilities – also called *self-efficacy* (Bandura, 1997).

In addition to these research contributions' emphasis of iPad as a tool for inclusion, I also highlight design theory (Selander & Kress, 2012; Selander, 2017) as a foundation for an inclusive music pedagogical practice. A design-theoretical view of music and music education is based on a multimodal understanding of music and sound, and as situated communication, as opposed to music as objects of inherent value (Bandlien, 2019; Kempe & West, 2010). From this, it can be argued for a democratic, anti-authoritarian understanding of music and of what *musicality* entails, and that the digital revolution helps to change the content and knowledge of the music subject by blurring the differences between composition, orchestration, arrangement, production, exercise and distribution.

Sounding Music in a Multimodal Perspective

From a design-theoretical point of view, music as meaningful sounding material can be regarded as a multimodal complex (Bandlien, 2019). This means that music is regarded as communication, and that structures of auditory, tactile and visual signs and sign structures in both a temporal and a spatial dimension constitute material substance in musical communication. With these material resources, and also through social construction, the complex aesthetics of music are shaped with the power to touch people on sensual, emotional, cognitive and existential levels with communicative content that exceed the boundaries of language.

Consequently, considering music as a multimodal complex also means recognising that music involves a large complex of different forms of knowledge, which are combined in musical activity. Degrees of understanding or precision in using the time dimension, space dimension, auditory representations, the influence of bodily movements on sound and pitch on a wide variety of different instruments and sound sources are just a few of all the various possible sign structures – modes – that are processed through different kinds of knowledge while dealing with music. By combining multiple musical modes, complexity is increased. With these few examples mentioned, we can finally begin to understand what enormously multifaceted knowledge content follows musical activity.

From a multimodal perspective (Selander, 2017) on music, the music educator's basic question is: "How can students develop knowledge to deal with the complex sign structures of music"?

The School and the Students

Traditionally, the question of how music is taught in formal contexts such as primary and secondary school, high school, music and art schools and higher education has often been answered through principles of collective scaffolding and mediating assistance in a proximal development zone (Vygotsky, 1978) or through adaptation in the form of simplification. By such an approach, the teacher largely shapes the professional learning content, while the social game the student is part of has a great impact. In such a situation, the influence of the individual student on their own knowledge development may be weakened, and the student's motivation and interest may come under pressure.

In higher education and in music and art schools, there has been a tradition of individual teaching on an instrument. In this way, these educational arenas have shown clear signs of recognising the importance of individual learning. The focus has been quite directly on the individually precise and individually independent treatment of musical sign structures in the form of body movements, sensation and co-ordination. It may seem that music and art schools and higher education have largely acknowledged that the complexity and precision of music requires a lot on an individual level. However, as in elementary school, the teacher has largely had power over which learning content is chosen, while the social focus may have been less than in elementary school.

Pupils, regardless of school system, come to the classroom with their individual preconditions, prior knowledge, interests and aversions – various existing understandings of, and preferences for, musical sign structures. Pupils come with different types and degrees of musicality related to rhythm and time, to tones and harmonics, to sensitivity to dynamics, to intonation or sound processing. They have different skills or lack of skills on different instruments or in note reading. Pupils also often have strong personal relationships – negative as well as positive – to specific musical expressions. In an inclusive learning design, in my opinion, all these facets must be allowed. Otherwise, the design is not inclusive, but rather exclusive as it can prevent students from grasping and mastering musical sign structures and engaging affectively in the musical expressions they communicate.

If the informal learning arena is recognised as the background for the activity in school, this means that the learning design takes into account a variety of musical preferences and understandings. In addition, the recognition of students as existing individuals with their own desires and expressive needs means that the learning design takes into account unexpected, unplanned, musical communication. Depending on the diversity of the specific class or among the students of the individual teacher, this may sound like an insurmountable educational task. However, I would argue that the task is very feasible if the pedagogical attitude changes from a teacher-driven design to a design where the students themselves contribute to the learning design on a similar level as the teacher. Design theory (Selander, 2017) as didactic theory makes this possible by starting from what are potential resources (p. 149) for student learning and how students can transform these into new representations of knowledge, rather than limiting learning activity to preprogrammed ideas about what students should learn. A very effective way of doing this is by letting students shape and communicate – musically – their own musical expressions, by composing their own music. In such a context, students composing on iPad can mean that the personal experiences and intentions of the students have value and meaning, and that the adult authorities are downgraded to more equal learning partners, encouraging students to create and innovate their own understandings, solutions and expressions of the knowledge and the challenges they face in their efforts transforming potential resources.

In the next section, I will discuss the compositing processes of two very different 8th grade students, Abdul and Anna, who side by side in the same class, did a piece of musical learning through composing with GarageBand on iPad. The stories are constructed from observations, conversations and student products in a microethnographic fieldwork where I followed the students' composition with GarageBand on iPad during secondary school weekly music lessons for more than 2 months.

Abdul

Abdul compared himself to his brother and father who were musicians. He told me that his brother was a rapper and that his father had been a DJ. He did not, however, think that his own musical abilities were particularly strong, but nevertheless became satisfied with what he eventually produced. Abdul wanted to try on a particular genre he had a relationship with listening to: *Gangsta rap*. Gangsta rap is often associated with stressed environments within lower social classes in the United States and is characterised by providing close perspectives on controversial topics such as violence, drugs and prostitution. Famous rappers associated with the style include Ice Cube, Dr Dre, Ice T, Snoop Dog, Eminem and 50 Cent. Abdul chose to use parts of the lyrics from the rap song "Livsstilen" by the Swedish group 24K. (https://youtu.be/7noO0QaOICs).[1]

In the first session, Abdul recorded drum rhythms and synth sounds that he left without changing throughout the second and third sessions. The accompaniment he made was characterised by a lot of drums and some synth bass. The accompaniment was very symmetrically arranged in periods of eight and eight beats. In the first session he had obviously also experimented with some more synth sounds, but on these he had turned down the volume (Figure 7.1).[2]

When I talked to him along the way in the second and third sessions, he was always busy practicing rapping, which was soon to be recorded, but the recordings after the sessions showed that nothing was even recorded. He stated that he needed to practice, because it was difficult to learn the whole rap and manage to perform it in a satisfying way.

FIGURE 7.1   Abdul after the first session. https://youtu.be/TC4fVDtb_k8.

FIGURE 7.2 Abdul's finished and complete product. https://youtu.be/0JwQJ8H48qc.

Nevertheless, during the last teaching session, he acknowledged that he had to complete the work and recorded the rap (Figure 7.2).

In connection with the recording of the rap, Abdul felt the need to change something in the connection between the rap and the accompaniment. While not completely satisfied, he had faith in being able to fix it by editing the recorded accompaniment. After finally having recorded the rap and found that he would accept the vocal recording, he began to change the accompaniment that so far had been left in peace through three sessions. In the end result there is nevertheless still unclear rhythmic connection between the accompaniment and the rap (Figure 7.2), but both the rap (Figure 7.3) and the accompaniment (Figure 7.4) are by themselves characterised by fairly clear and orderly music style features. The videos related to Figures 7.3 and 7.4 show the rap for itself and accompaniment for itself, respectively. Although the rhythmic relationship between rap and accompaniment is unclear, it is worth noting that Abdul had the accompaniment he had made on his earphones while recording the rap. In the rap, Abdul largely used fixed pitches and rhythmic groupings of syllables. The actual pronunciation of the words more often gave almost equal weight to several syllables than the usual spoken language would entail. Abdul often kept almost the same tone throughout a whole text phrase, but switched pitch between some phrases. Several phrases start with a rising melodic movement, and some phrases have a slight melodic dip in the falling direction towards the end. In this way, the vocal performance of Abdul bears a rather clear mark of being a transformed representation of the vocal expressions of 24K (https://youtu.be/7noO0QaOICs).

Figure 7.5 shows the orderly form with periods of eight or four beats in Abdul's accompaniment visually through the screenshot of the edit window. The different parts of the accompaniment are distinguished by the different characterising

FIGURE 7.3 Abdul, only vocal https://youtu.be/sBSne6rZAk4.

FIGURE 7.4 Abdul, only accompaniment https://youtu.be/NYOK3cm_Dz4.

elements that occur at the start of each party (indicated by arrows in the illustration on the following page).

Abdul's accompaniment keeps more distance to the production of 24K. However, the sound of the dry bass drum can be recognised as similar. Abdul's accompaniment is strongly influenced by the dry bass drum that is played a lot and constitutes a fairly continuous aggressive rhythm. 24K, however, used the bass drum somewhat less. Abdul's instrument range is also otherwise characterised by bass. The deepest of all the bass sounds, which were also used throughout the composition, is another more synthetic and lower bass drum sound, where the tone, which is very deep in the first place, drops through its sounding time down

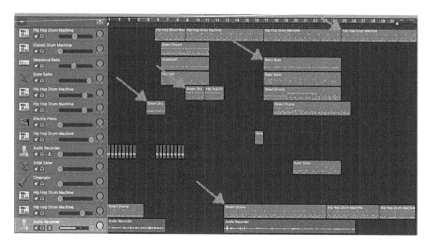

FIGURE 7.5 Abdul's composition. The arrows point to where new characteristic material is introduced every fourth or eighth beat.

to barely audible register. Abdul told along the way that the feeling of bass was important.

In a design theoretical perspective, Abdul transformed and represented his understanding of the features that belong to the stylistic expression he was trying to make. Both the way he has built the accompaniment of the composition in a clear and orderly form and the way he has represented the vocal rap style are representations of Abdul's musical and genre understandings, as he strived to create music related to musical styles that he knew from a listener's perspective. The most difficult thing for Abdul was to combine the rap and the accompaniment – in the multimodal sense: layout (Kress, 2010, pp. 88–92).

The story that follows is about Anna who had had some formal musical education in the municipal music and art school. She made a melody based on a chord progression that she put together before the melody.

Anna

Anna perceived herself as musical, something she had also heard from others, including her teachers. In the retrospective interview, she said that she often listened to music in her spare time, and attended the music and art school for to learn how to play the piano. In addition, she played guitar in her spare time. Songs that she listened to, she used to find out on her own how to play on guitar. She described the music she liked: "pop music, maybe a little in the direction of country". She cited Taylor Swift, Ed Shearan, Coldplay and Megan Trainer as examples.

The first session was Anna away from school. During the second session, she made two recordings. One recording consisted of four parts: A A B B with an

FIGURE 7.6 Anna's recording number 1 https://youtu.be/PJKwmE7GE78.

arpeggiated acoustic guitar autocomp. The chord progression for part A went over eight bars with two bars for each chord like this: Em-Em-Am-Am-G-G-D-D. The chord progression for part B went over eight bars with two bars for each chord like this: Am-Am-C-C-G-G-D-D. In the B part, she added a track with a hihat sound on every quarter note played by a drum machine (Figure 7.6).

The second recording used the same chord base and structure, but was done without the use of a metronome, and the chords were played manually on the touch screen by pressing the chord symbol so that each time the guitar chord should sound in unison without any automated accompaniment pattern. She

FIGURE 7.7 Anna's recording number 2 https://youtu.be/RdN4Wmh6xoM.

played the chords according to a fixed rhythm pattern that consisted of two punctured quarters and a clean quarter for each beat. The hihat in the B part complemented the pattern: punctured quarter, quarter, eighth and quarter. The B part was played only once in this recording. In addition, she had made a C part with other chords, where the chords changed faster so that each beat had two chords. The chords in the C section were: Em, A, C and G (Figure 7.7).

In the third teaching session Anna came to a crossroad and made a choice. She decided to use the recording with the automatically arpeggiated guitar accompaniment for further work, while she just as well deleted the recording with the manually played rhythm guitar accompaniment. Furthermore, Anna used the third teaching session to experiment with melody playing on the piano.

In the fourth teaching session, Anna, who played piano at the music and art school, decided that the melody of the composition should be played on a traditional piano with keys. She wanted to record the sound of this piano through the microphone in an audio track.

As she began working on the tune, she became aware that she wanted an intro to the tune. However, she had not thought of this when recording the accompaniment. It was as if she was thinking: "Wait a minute, shouldn't there have been an intro here?" The need for an intro, she first became aware of when she got the melody of the composition into her perspective. Anna easily solved this by simply using the first bar of the prerecorded accompaniment as an intro. However, this change had a decisive impact on a deep aesthetic and creative level, with far-reaching consequences for the further composition. By making the first beat an intro, she moved the musical form balance throughout the composition. Instead of Em-Em-Am-Am-G-G-D-D, it now became Em-Am-Am-G-G-D-D-Em (2nd time Am finally), and instead of Am-Am-C-C-G-G-D-D it became Am-C-C-G-G-D-D-Am (2nd time Em finally). This displacement of musical form elements was crucial to how the tune could be developed. Particularly at the transition between the two parts, something musically surprising happened, because she somehow lacked a beat and ended the round on a new chord (Am) that led elsewhere the second time. This seems to have further led her to form the melody in another harmonious landscape in the B part, where the melody tones rest more often on dissonant tones than in the more consonant A part.

When she came to the final chord in the second repetition of the B part, a similar problem arose again: The B part accompaniment ends with the chord D, which is dominant to the tonic chord (E minor) parallel: G major. Based on traditional tonal music understanding, this implies a strong signal of further movement towards G or Em – or in other words, that D was not a chord to land the composition on.

So what could Anna do with her missing a chord to end the composition on? Anna chose to reintroduce the previously deleted C part. This C part thus became a separate concluding part of Anna's composition, which allowed her to finish on the chord G major and the tone G. This means that her entire composition moves from going in E minor to ending in G major. However, this

FIGURE 7.8   Anna's finished composition https://youtu.be/HLasU4JFATo.

modulation is done in the traditional tonal way, using the basic chords of the G-major key (G, C, D) through the B part (Figure 7.8).

The recording was done with a mix of resources and working methods that Anna had access to. In addition to using a traditional piano for sound recording via the microphone of the iPad, she used both on-screen manual play, auto-accompaniment features and the use of automatic rhythm features in GarageBand. When using the traditional piano Anna's prior knowledge as a pianist was crucial.

Anna's composition bears witness to several forms of musical understanding. Through her composition, Anna showed that she knew and controlled culturally established tonality relationships with associated tones, rhythms and rhythmic foundations. She developed and varied melodic motifs, harmonic tensions and a formal musical structure with tension rising and dissolving. Anna's harmonic treatment of the melody is quite complicated and testifies that her musical ear was trained within a (broad) western music tradition. In the retrospective interview I conducted after the composition, she stated that she had been looking for notes that would fit the chosen chords. In practice, she found consonant chord tones on heavy beats in the A part and dissonant chordless tones on heavy beat in the B part. However, all the notes, including the dissonant ones, belong to the same key. In this way, the dissonance seems to be controlled by a traditional Western music understanding that includes both Western art music tradition, African American and popular musical styles.

Abdul's and Anna's Construction, Transformation and Representation of Knowledge

The stories of Abdul's and Anna's compositional processes are, from a design theoretical perspective, also stories of learning, because they transformed potential resources to new representations several times in a row. Abdul and Anna had very different musical preconditions and interests, but they both grasped the potential resources that they had at their disposal. They made individual choices about what resources they would use and how those resources could be transformed. In several ways, it is clear how the musical prerequisites, prior knowledge, interests and aversions of the students guided the learning activity into areas that the two students could individually engage in. The way I see it, this genuine and deep commitment to musical materiality and the associated communicative meaning is crucial for musical learning to take place. Pupils need to transform the semiotic resources of music over and over again, thus becoming more and more familiar in the sign worlds they operate. This basic and transformative work does not take place through instruction of the teacher. As I see it, important differences between a didactic design based on instruction and a didactic design based on construction lie in the differences between receptive and expressive understandings. As different semiotic modalities are diverse at an ontological level (Kress, 2017, p. 44), instruction that requires transduction from a receptive to an expressive sign system cannot serve its purpose without the student knowing the semiotic modalities transduced between from before. In other words, construction comes before instruction.

Although the teacher and assistants were able to support and answer questions, Abdul's, Anna's and their fellow students' learning activities were not based on instruction. The didactic design allowed them to explore the potential resources and construct understandings without having to consider any instruction on what kind of knowledge they should focus on or what that knowledge might entail. In such a learning design, it is up to the students to explore what music consists of, how music is built, how technology works, how visual representations are interpreted and what they perceive as an appropriate method of composing. During the exploratory work, the students merged their socially constructed musical understandings with the resources made available in technology – resources that are also socially constructed. They explored opportunities and transformed semiotic resources into new representations. In this way, they constructed, transformed and represented their understandings in response to the invitation to exploratory music creation.

Composition with GarageBand on iPad – An Inclusive Didactic Design

The Design Theoretical Learning Sequence (Selander, 2017, p. 150) suggests how inclusive learning activity can be designed. Based on certain institutional patterns and intentions, and with the iPad and GarageBand as an orchestration of potential semiotic resources, learning activities in which the resources are transformed and presented can be staged. In the transformation process, the interests and affective reflections of each student have an impact on how the potential resources are utilised and transformed. The strengthening of the student's agency in this way is important in an inclusive perspective, because it means that the students' various assumptions and identities are allowed as resources and not as obstacles.

Both Juntunen (2017) and Brown et al. (2014) highlights the ability of iPad technology to enhance student agency. However, I would like to point out that the didactic design is of great importance. Pupils' agency is strengthened by exploring the world themselves. If the teacher, the institutional patterns or the goals of the didactic design, in the opposite way, suggest that the technology is used to require students to take specific actions in measurable assignments, the students' agency in their learning processes will be weakened. The key to empowering students' agency lies in freeing students to explore the material and socially constructed resources available in technology. In such a didactic design, students are educated that *their* interests, meaning and affective experiences are important and have meaning and value, regardless of normative boundaries. In this context, it is also interesting with the increasing number of research contributions that in various ways highlight the iPad as a new musical instrument without any normative tradition (Randles, 2013; Williams, 2014; Verrico & Reese, 2016; Devito, 2017; Park, 2017; Vanderlinde, 2017) and that iPad technology can help simplify otherwise difficult music-related activities (Reese et al., 2016). In these perspectives precisely are the opportunity to create new understandings that cover a greater breadth, thus opening up to strengthen the agency of a greater breadth of students.

In today's educational policy situation, such didactic argumentation is prone to meet resistance in relation to demands for measurability in assessment practice. It is difficult to rank student performance normatively – as the school has developed a tradition for – when students are free to give different answers to a task. However, specifically in the art field, there is, in my opinion, a fundamental need for learning activity to contain an element of openness and uncertainty associated with creativity and aesthetics. If this is removed from the subject, contact with the artistic meaning content on which the subject is based is lost. In this case a different kind of assessment practice is needed than those who are concerned about objective measurability. Such a practice can be based on the design theoretical idea of "signs of learning" (Selander, 2017, pp. 151–152), in that the difference between two representations of knowledge, given one after another,

implies signs of learning. In such cases objective assessment criteria are not necessarily meaningful. The assessment criteria can be found in the individual process
of learning art creation and expression.

Notes

1 The URL for this reference changes rapidly. The best advice is to search for the title
 on YouTube.
2 A QR-reader for any mobile device can be downloaded for free from your app store.

References

Bandlien, B-.T. (2019). Ungdomsskoleelvers komponering med GarageBand på iPad: En
 musikkdidaktisk studie av performative stopp-punkter i et kritisk designteoretisk perspektiv [Secondary school students' composing with GarageBand on iPad: A music
 educational study of performative stop-moments in a design theoretical perspective].
 (Doctoral thesis). Norwegian university of science and technology. Trondheim.
Bandura, A. (1997). *Self-efficacy: The exercise of control*. New York, NY: Freeman.
Brown, A. R., Stewart, D., Hansen, A. & Stewart, A. (2014). Making meaningful musical experiences accessible using the iPad. In D. Keller, V. Lazzarini &
 M. S. Pimenta (Eds.), *Ubiquitous music* (pp. 65–81). Cham: Springer. https://doi.
 org/10.1007/978-3-319-11152-0
Devito, D. (2017). Technology and music collaboration for people with significant dis-
 abilities. In S. A. Ruthmann & R. Mantie (Eds.), *The Oxford handbook of technology and
 music education* (pp. 405–412). New York, NY: Oxford University Press.
Juntunen, M.-L. (2017). Using socio-digital technology to enhance participation and
 creative engagement in a lower secondary music classroom. *Nordisk Musikkpedagogisk
 Forskning, 18*, 47–74.
Kempe, A., & West, T. (2010). *Design för lärande i musik*. Stockholm: Norstedts.
Kress, G. (2010). *Multimodality: A social semiotic approach to contemporary communication*.
 London: Routledge.
Kress, G. (2017). Semiotic work: Design, transformation, transduction. In E. Insulander, S.
 Kjällander, F. Lindstrand, & A. Åkerfeldt (Eds.), *Didaktik i omvandlingens tid: Text, repre-
 sentation och design* (pp. 39–51). Stockholm: Liber.
Park, T. H. (2017). Instrument technology: Bones, tones, phones, and beyond. In A. King,
 E. Himonides, & A. Ruthmann (Eds.), *The Routledge companion to music technology and
 education* (pp. 15–22). New York, NY: Routledge.
Randles, C. (2013). Being an iPadist. *General Music Today, 27*(1), 48–51. https://doi.
 org/10.1177/1048371313496786
Reese, J. A. Bicheler, R. & Robinson, C. (2016). Field experiences using iPads: Impact
 of experience on preservice teachers' beliefs. *Journal of Music Teacher Education, 26*(1),
 96–111. https://doi.org/10.1177/1057083715616441
Selander, S. (2017). *Didaktiken efter Vygotskij: Design för lärande*. Stockholm: Liber.
Selander, S., & Kress, G. (2012). *Läringsdesign: I et multimodalt perspektiv*. Frederiksberg:
 Frydenlund.

Vanderlinde, D. (2017). Possibilities for inclusion with music technologies. In S. A. Ruthmann & R. Mantie (Eds.), *The Oxford handbook of technology and music education* (pp. 439–445). New York, NY: Oxford University Press.

Verrico, K. & Reese, J. (2016). University musicians' experiences in an iPad ensemble: A phenomenological case study. *Journal of Music, Technology & Education, 9*(3), 315–328. https://doi.org/10.1386/jmte.9.3.315_1

Vygotsky, L. (1978). *Mind in Society: The development of higher psychological processes.* Cambridge, MA: Harvard University Press.

Williams, D. A. (2014). Another perspective: The iPad is a real musical instrument. *Music Educators Journal, 101*(1), 93–98. https://doi.org/10.1177/0027432114540476

8

THE ZONE OF OPTIMISED MOTIVATION (ZOOM)

Anthony Lewis Brooks

Now we're at the threshold of the next revolution in user-computer inter-action: a technology that will take the user through the screen into the world 'inside' the computer – a world in which the user can interact with three dimensional objects whose fidelity will grow as computing power increases and display technology increases. This virtual world can be what-ever the designer makes it.

(John Walker quoted in Pimentel & Teixeira, 1995, p. 78)

Introduction and Background/History

What's in a Name?

SoundScapes was selected as title for the body of research that is behind the sub-ject of this chapter due to the feedback stimuli in the second phase of the work (1990s) moving beyond auditory stimuli (music, sounds and effects) –as imple-mented in earlier phase when the body of work was titled HANDI-MIDI. By incorporating wider multimedia than sonic feedback – including visuals, robotic devices, lighting apparatus, Virtual Reality (VR), Vibroacoustics [haptic feedback] and more – the inclusive design research of specific user-computer interaction could select input apparatus and feedback media stimulus (or stimuli when syn-chronous modalities are mapped). Earlier author publications inform on usage of these specific feedback. Herein, inclusive design-based research is termed in respect of the approach investigating selection and/or convergence of digital technologies such as within sensor-based Virtual Interactive Space (VIS), VR and more, in creating immersive interactive environments that are tailored to users (individuals or communities). This flexible, modular and selection approach was conceived to best-address tailoring different preferences, needs and desires of users to achieve an adapted individual interactive experience as best-fit to optimal patient-experience and session/programme goals. Increased accessibility, inclusion and improved therapist experiences were also targeted via this approach. Such adaptive tailored interactions with selected direct feedback of interactive stimuli were found to motivate differently according to users. This is analogised aligned with Gardner's (1983) "Theory of Multiple Intelligences" that emphasises human individual *differences* – thus SoundScapes targeted maximum flexibility, modularity and as best as possible being open to adapt and tailor the interactive environments according to informed or perceived needs, preferences and desires of participants/patients.

This approach to design aligns with present and future stages of evolution in the health sector, i.e. Health 4.0 and 5.0, where, respectively, keywords of *digitisation* and *personalisation* relate (Kowalkiewicz, 2017). During the years of research each session and programme was analysed under a hermeneutic action research strategy as a segmented learning process towards developing the methodology and method as posited herein. A focus was on optimising user-experience (in and of the session) and outcome. This is stated where "user" has wide referral to, e.g. patient/participant, carer/therapist/facilitator and family and friends towards benefit and potential transfer to actual daily living (ADL) including home-based self-driven intervention and compliance to programme.

In line with Walker (in Pimentel & Teixeira, 1995, p. 78), who reflected on pre-21st century VR *–see under-abstract quote –* current advances in VR and associated technologies align by offering new opportunities for designers across disciplines towards increased adoption of digital technologies into emergent practices whereby human endeavours are supplemented and potentially optimised. This is a strategy emergent from applied research, design and intervention by creators in close consultation with discipline professionals. Such is the framework and history of SoundScapes where inclusive design, as posited herein, has focused upon research field work and close consultation with end-users and those closest to them in order to optimise system accessibility, inclusion and tailoring. However, beyond the posited technology systemic solution – i.e. solely apparatus, this work ongoingly emphasises a need for systematic "methodology" for optimising intervention, analysis and evaluation of using such technology. This posited as a learnt methodology requiring a defined emergent model from the research to guide in-action (within intervention activities in sessions) and on-action (objective analysis post-session of activities targeting subsequent system refinement within an iterative inclusive design framework in "treatment" programmes for each patient). In this way the emergent model is posited as "method".

Inspirations for the synthesised model grew from luminary literatures such as Schön's reflective practitioner (1983) – *in-action* and *on-action* referring to in-session and on-session (intervention); Vygotsky's Zone of Proximal Development (ZPD –Vygotsky, 1978; Wertsch, 1985) in context of intervention where, typically, the facilitator acts as the "more knowledgeable other" however it is argued how digital systems, when used such as in SoundScapes, the technology is posited supporting as a "masterful other", which is herein predicted to increase prevalence as Artificial Intelligence and Machine Learning progressively evolve to contextually impact. Additionally, Bruner's scaffolding theory (Bruner, 1990) on meaningful actions and support by an "other" is contextually adapted related to constructivism, which aligns to scalloped learning and Microdevelopment (Yan, 1998; Yan & Fischer, 2002). Related earlier detail on the model origination, development and evolution, is available under link to publications.

Project – History of Contribution to Model

An early version of this posited framework was first titled "Communication method and apparatus" – a text (poorly) detailing the concept to realise seven published patents from 2000 through 2005 alongside national and international projects that funded the patent publications (see details on next pages). The national project based upon SoundScapes was funded by the Danish government and titled "Humanics" – (*Human Interactive Communication System*s). The research was hosted at the "Center for Hjerneskade" (CFH – *Center for Rehabilitation of Brain Injury* in English) for approximately 6 years (1996–2002) in both Aarhus and Copenhagen. The CFH specialises in neuropsychological, linguistic and physical challenges resulting from acquired brain injury and offers training and rehabilitation for adults and children with brain injury where rehabilitation programmes all contain dynamic, intensive and focused training, which aim to aid individuals with brain injury into employment or educational pursuits and a productive life style – both teaching and research are conducted at CFH (cf https://cfh.ku.dk/english).

The first of the international projects based upon SoundScapes was namely one titled "Twi-aysi" – *The World Is As You See It* (https://www.bristol.ac.uk/Twi-aysi), which was funded as a future probe by The European Network for Intelligent Information Interfaces (https://www.i3net.org) under the programme Experimental School Environments (ESEs). ESE's focus was on funding projects that explored new child-centred paradigms for learning, through novel IT-based devices, artefacts and environments. The second project, resulting out of the successes from the Twi-aysi future probe – was separately funded by the European Commission (not specifically i3net), and titled "CAREHERE" – *Creating Aesthetic Resonant Environments for Handicapped, Elderly and REhabilitation* (https://www.bristol.ac.uk/carehere). Partners in the European project CAREHERE were Sweden, United Kingdom, Italy and Denmark. During this period the SoundScapes concept and research was recipient of *the European 1999 EUREKA award for Applied Multimedia* and subsequently it was awarded *the 2006 Vanførefonden Danish research prize*.

The next section elaborates on this concept, the research and the ongoing process of inclusive design that led to emergent practice, methodology and the resultant model/method that is focus of this text.

Designing Accessibility, Inclusion and Tailoring

The concept behind this body of work grew from tacit knowledge from years of exposure to handicapped individuals and communities. Concept development followed years of field research on how different individuals needed different set-ups of sensing apparatus, while also having specific preferences and desires relative to how they responded differently to selected stimuli modalities. Thus, SoundScapes needed to fill a void in what was available in the field to address preferences of interaction/interface, aligned to learning, information processing and subsequent responsive feedback. Such designs were evident, needed following discussions and evaluations from families, carers, therapists and other expert healthcare professionals. Thus, the inclusive design approach was not specific but rather a "forever learning" strategy gained from included participants and those closest (family, friends, carers, etc.) to inform on a best-fit scenario for the various aspects of intervention. The original bespoke system additionally adopted commercial apparatus that was "re-designed" (adapted) for use in context of such needs to again widen the systemic and methodology flexibility to maximise access and inclusion.

Following consultations with movement disorder experts at Rochester University hospital in USA, an intervention goal in the work was defined as targeting to achieve human afferent efferent neural feedback loop closure through the feed-forward human input being optimally mapped to preferred feedback stimuli. This, such that a pleasurable experience was attained where the participant was further motivated and empowered to continue interactions towards developing creativity, imagination and expression, through interactive environments. These environments were subject of improvisations under the developing methodology and method model – however, under this emergent model the improvisations were also needing to be systematically approached within a structure of planned presets per user profile.

Aesthetic Resonance was a catalyst of the early work which subsequently evolved as a core of the emergent model presented herein, which was built upon developed apparatus and method targeting *inter-subjective* as well as *intra-subjective* impact from emergent practices. Introducing *inter-subjective* perspectives is to bring in various communicational relationships between parties (artist/designer, patient, system, facilitator, audience, carer, family, friends, etc.) – similarly, *intra-subjective* aspects (i.e. considerations of what happens internally to the artist/designer, patient, facilitator, etc.,) are not discussed herein as these aspects of the research are too involved to further discuss in this brief text, which has different focus – also as these aspects of the work are elaborated elsewhere within publications (including doctorate thesis) listed under a university profile (footnote 2).

Exposure – from global to local societal impact and sustainability informing inclusive design.

Soundscapes was a self-funded entity that was able to be presented around various countries in the world under Corporate Social Responsibility (CSR) support predominantly by IBM (Denmark/Scandinavia/United States/Worldwide) since approximately 1992. This invaluable sponsorship was alongside support from other leading corporations, who were exposed to the research via field work, show-cases and exhibitions: For example, the annual Health & Rehab Scandinavia (see https://www.health-rehab.dk) were among those who sponsored exhibition space over many years, which led to increased interest from various healthcare profes-sionals, as well as visiting companies and corporate representatives. A definition of CSR is how companies contribute to social, environmental and economic sus-tainability, while simultaneously addressing their potential adverse impacts on the agreed international principles on social, environmental and economic sustainabil-ity. SoundScapes was justified sponsorship under such a framework towards societal impact and sustainability that was considered innovative and positively disruptive (i.e. from IBM and other industrial documentations and expert evaluations).

Through the various sponsorships received to present SoundScapes in various countries a wider cultural perspective grew that informed the inclusive design in the research. For example, "Virtual Interactive Space (V.I.S.) as a movement capture interface tool giving multimedia feedback for treatment and analysis" was presented at "Bridging Cultures" – program of the 13th International Congress of the World Confederation for Physical Therapy, Yokohama, Japan, May 23–28, 1999. This was part of an IBM-sponsored world tour where the research was exposed to a wide array of end-users (e.g. various, across the span of dysfunction, age-range and situations), their families, friends, their health-carers/therapists/leadership/experts etc. It was also presented under IBM (and others) sponsorship at the Olympics/Paralympic Games events in Atlanta, USA in 1996 and Sydney, Australia in 2000 – including its scientific congress – again gaining data from various nationalities exploring the "invention".

Each separate instance of exposure to various dysfunctional individuals/com-munities (both professional and public) proved to be a learning experience incre-menting specific inclusive design elements towards the overall inclusive design. This process was how a modular flexible system, an emergent practise, method-ology, and model/method for intervention, analysis and evaluation was realised. It is considered timely, in this text, to acknowledge the many supporting inputs received from individuals and communities over many years that are too many to name – hopefully they read this and know who they are.

This chapter's focus, as stated earlier in the text, is to further present the emer-gent model (method under methodology) that resulted from the SoundScapes body of research and its achievements. Further identifying the topic and relating emergent practice and needed contemporary model aligned to new ideas and designs is how Microsoft (MS) posit "Inclusive Design is a methodology, born out of digital environments, that enables and draws on the full range of human diversity. Most importantly, this means including and learning from people with a range of perspectives". Additionally, stating that "Exclusion happens when we solve problems using our own biases. As Microsoft designers, we seek out those exclusions, and use them as opportunities to create new ideas and inclusive designs". It is considered apt to include a reference to the game industry as around the turn of the century approaches were made to leading platform producers informing how a targeting of adaptable, accessible and inclusive games, i.e. accessible to all (including developers to programmes), could be beneficial for handicapped in line with this research.

The next section introduces the emergent model (that includes an inclusive design approach aligned to MS's), which, in this text, is posited to provoke and promote critique input towards ongoing improvement of the model under an iterative process.

Emergent Model – Background and Related Impact via Patents

SoundScapes originated from a family history of being born into a family having severely disabled members where exposure resulted in a tacit knowledge informing creativity, invention and authorship. The "*Zone of Optimised Motivation (ZOOM)*" model emerged from the SoundScapes body of research with a goal of supporting systematic human intervention practices (facilitator > participant/patient/client…) when using a sensor-based systemic digital technology created environment that empowered interactions by a human participant/patient. A model need was determined from the early phases of fieldworks in the research towards developing means of supporting preparation and optimal use of a modular sensing system within a (re)habilitation session. Furthermore, the model needed to be useable for analysis and refinement of both system and intervention under an iterative strategy. As mentioned, this research led to develop the methodology and patented "method" aligned with selectable apparatus (e.g. see family of patents US6893407B1; EP1279092B1; AU5822101A; and WO2001086406A1;) and further "process and device" (e.g. patent DE60115876T2) –these being also background for further patents, e.g. US20060166620A1 and US20060158515A1 claimed by a third party distantly associated to SoundScapes' earlier research.

In creating and developing a methodology including method, apparatus, process and device, each session is considered as one of many that are designed for being sequentially conducted under a treatment programme. Each session builds upon previous to increment knowledge, skills and competences. The "system" under discussion is that which has developed from research and has been referred to as a Virtual Interactive Space (VIS); Virtual Information Space (VIS); or simply by third-party therapists as a computer feedback system (see Hagedorn & Holm, 2010).

It was also envisioned that such a model embedded within an algorithm of a future digital technology system can one day be fully self-contained without the need for an in-attendance therapist through the system having innate Artificial Intelligence and Machine Learning to be self-optimising towards realising a best-fit to patient-experience. This posited future embedded emergent model is baseline of how the optimisation will function to be autonomous for the patient/participant.

An aspect of this future design is towards supporting management of medical professionals' time due to the increased burden that the health industry is seeing – especially in regards with longer living and increased aged in society. An overview of the current emergent model as baseline to support professional practices follows.

ZOOM – The Emergent Model "Zone of Optimised Motivation"

The research developed an emergent model for in-action intervention that is aligned to an on-action evaluation model: In-action refers to reflecting in the session activities in real-time (as they happen – thus an innate facilitator model): On-action reflects on the session (i.e. post-session towards objective analysis and refinement by the team) – e.g. see Schön's reflective practitioner (Schön, 1983).

The concept is to advance the (re)habilitation intervention (sessions within a treatment programme) though its systematic strategy on use of the technology in an appropriate and optimal way to motivate engagement, compliance and best-experience. To do this a profound understanding of (1) the technologies involved – both feed-forward and feedback, (2) the methods of implementation towards optimised changes and outcome, (3) the adaption means to tailor for each individual's preference, desire, need, etc., as well as (4) the timing factor of change decisions are required. In addition, through initially researching with a therapist/care-worker who knows the participant/end-user very well, design of the start-sessions is informed that begins a treatment programme of sessions.

For the therapist to gain knowledge and familiarity with the system, hands-on via role play self-led training is advised with one or more peers. This is training where each therapist acts out a role as a client/patient through already acquired knowledge of the "patient/persona" and then changing to be session facilitator where their peer is "patient/persona". The term "patient/persona" refers to an actual known client (like experienced therapists) or a fictional one (e.g. in educational setting). The "patient/persona" knowledge should be considering functional abilities and dysfunction, preferences and needs for stimuli. This gives hand-on system practise. As facilitator the need is to work through system presets to optimise intervention where change decisions are determined by client/patient responses (typically behavioural representations or utterances).

Typically, is that session interactions between participant and facilitator begins with a set of presets that can easily, without (or with minimal) inter-subjective disconnection (e.g. loosing eye-contact), be adjusted according to progress matching task challenge to ability/skill/function. While this matching sounds simplistic it is posited as a challenge for the facilitator to gauge the situation until interaction activity begins. During the interactions the facilitator interprets behavioural representations of the participant in order to ascertain if matching is evident (i.e. challenge to skill competence is represented through behaviour) and whether a preset change is required to increase engagement via improved matching. In this case, concepts of Flow, Agency, Efficacy and Aesthetic Resonance are related from the facilitator's knowledge of these entities and his/her knowledge, skill and competence of operating the digital technology system alongside skill inherent to interpreting patient/participant's reactions to given challenges/tasks within the interactive environment.

Moments of preset change associate to Yan's concept of Scalloped Learning (Yan, 1998) where the change can challenge the participant in incrementally raising his/her activity accordingly fitting the adapted matching that targets development. Just as a facilitator can provide a scaffold to support the activity within the VIS, it can be speculated whether the participant requires a certain level of ability in order to use what is referred to as "bridging" – i.e. a level of performance to search and work out in order to attain the next incremental level. "Microdevelopment", described by Yan and Fischer (2002), as dynamic variations in cognitive development, is posited as associated and linked to physical development, and is thus a main component of the emergent model.

The re-design of presets offered in a session is ongoing as each session informs the next through analysis and further inclusive design in what has been termed a recursive reflective process. Scalloped Learning and Microdevelopment are but two of the theoretical frameworks of inspiration that led to the emergent model (see elsewhere in this text for more that have influenced the construct).

Aesthetic Resonance

In concluding the introduction of the ZOOM model in this context it is worth repeating that design and analysis/evaluation of intervention sessions was conducted with therapists who knew each patient through traditional exchanges in context to a healthcare, well-being, and/or life quality situation. Relatedly, Aesthetic Resonance – achieved through use of the apparatus and method was defined in SoundScapes research as a situation where the response to an intent is so immediate and aesthetically pleasing as to make one forget the physical movement (and often effort) involved in the conveying of the intention. For further on Aesthetic Resonance see also Ellis (1997); Hagman (2010); Camurri et al. (2003); and Ellis (2004). In the case of the research presented herein, the emergent therapist intervention model titled ZOOM – has as its core catalyst Aesthetic Resonance. An outcome of this work is to posit how *Aesthetic Resonance* (or *Aesthetic Resonant Environments* – as environments created to target Aesthetic Resonance), offer potentials for others to research further either in similar contexts or in different disciplines. In closing, this text the next penultimate section summarises the background justifying model need from field research towards provoking critique and reflection in order to improve.

Model Need – Justification Through Field Research

A commission was received at the end of the 1990s that included creating a designated *SoundScapes Room* and system built upon the prototype system used in earlier research. The commission design was that each of four institutes would send two end-users (typically *Profound Multiple Learning Disabled*) and two female carers/therapists to the central institute in the city (four institutes were under "*Voksenhandicap og Udviklingsenheden, Socialforvaltningen, Århus Kommune*"). The central institute being where the field study sessions throughout the preceding (approximately five) years in thrice-weekly sessions with initial bespoke proto-type system had been researched as (re)habilitation sessions experienced as fun, social, playful, and creative rather than solely as therapy that can be mundane, boring and tedious – thus compliance can often be a problem.

The goal of the commission reflected the positive expert evaluations of the interventions over the years and subsequent outcomes for end-users reported by their carers/therapists. Commissioning was agreed for each institute to eventually invest in their own system and a designated SoundScapes room. Typical procedure upon arrival at the central institute was that one carer/therapist and one end-user would begin a session in the SoundScapes room whilst the other carer/therapist and end-user would wait in a near-by coffee-room. Once the first carer/therapist and end-user had completed the sessions they changed over with the second carer/therapist and end-user conducting sessions in the SoundScapes room whilst the initial pairing waited in the coffee room. All four institutions had similar "pairings" of carers/therapists and end-users. Monthly evaluations with the SoundScapes methodology and apparatus creator were included in the commission.

The emergent model presented herein was deemed necessary as a reflection following the monthly evaluations between the author and the eight therapists/care-givers (i.e. the two therapists/care-givers from each institute) as it became evident that there was not a systematic intervention strategy in place by any of the institutes for their professional staff.

A finding was in how, at the time, most of the all-female therapists/care-givers were uncomfortable with the digital technology. This was problematic due to that these people were the interface for the patient to the system and they were the decider of preset change towards optimising motivation, engagement and thus patient-experience. As far as is known, following cessation of the funded period of commission (approximately 2000) the core system was relocated and established at a different institute in Aarhus Kommune – one of the four originally commissioning.

This relocation was apparently due to internal dispute and no further funding to involve the author/creator in educating use of the system. It is not known how much the system was used following relocation.

Two-decades later it can be speculated how things have changed so that digital technology use is more pervasive/ubiquitous/omnipresent and more "user-friendly" such that attitudes of discomfort, as found in research reports by carers/

therapists in this work, are likely lessened to open for increased possibilities to explore such systems in (re)habilitation, learning, and beyond. As such, this ZOOM emergent model (and its ongoing improvements) is considered relevant for future systems incorporating Artificial Intelligence, Machine Learning, and similar developments alongside the existing digital technologies that may support carers/therapists in optimising and prioritising their precious time whilst simultaneously optimising patient-experiences of (re)habilitation intervention thus motivating compliance and self-driven activities of benefit.

Conclusions

SoundScapes is the title of a body of research that originated from a youth interacting and "inventing" with family members who had profound physical dysfunction. Tacit knowledge from these early interactions, where improvised and adaptive means of empowering improved access and autonomous control, led, decades later, to conceiving technological apparatus and method that supported traditional therapeutic intervention, training and thus associated learning. Years of field research followed that made clear, through assessing third-party use of the apparatus and method, a need for an implementation systematic strategy to support professionals who were educated in traditional (re)habilitation intervention. Thus, the ZOOM emergent model that developed from within the author's iterative research process – of inclusive design, practiced fieldwork, recursive analysis and evaluation reflections, – which is focus of this text contribution, towards improved use of digital interactive sensor-based technologies to realise optimal motivation related to the concept of Aesthetic Resonance and associated inspirational theories as presented herein. Relatedly, problem definition and discipline, as well as concept and method formation in this work, are continuously challenged by idiosyncratic aspects such as individual differences – this is something that is attempted addressed by the adaption and tailoring of SoundScapes apparatus and methodology.

Attesting to this computer-feedback digital technology enhanced (re)habilitation strategy targeting fun and playful interactions and its positive use within the field, third-party/independent therapists Hagedorn and Holm (2010) reported from their randomised intervention study comparing effects of traditional physical training and visual computer feedback training (i.e. a system [Personics] developed from the author's earlier bespoke system) in frail elderly patients that

> the computer feed-back training group showed a marked improvement that was up to 400% in the training specific performance. CONCLUSION: Elderly frail patients were able to increase muscle strength and physical endurance. A limited improvement was seen in the static balance tests. The computer feedback group showed a remarkable increase in training specific performance. Clinical Rehabilitation Impact.
>
> (Hagedorn & Holm, 2010)

Closing, this text is to suggest that scientific research problem definition and discipline have been presented alongside concept, methodology and method formulation resulting from inclusive design and emergent practice. These having been furthered in conditions that have often not been optimal in which research due to alienation as SoundScapes has been considered ahead of its time and the aligned reluctance of adoption of digital technology into a care situation. However, results convey the story and summarising is to posit that in this work a systematic model for intervention (such as ZOOM) can benefit optimisation of use of digital interactive technologies towards realising an optimal patient-experience and compliance to treatment programme, as well as potential transfer to ADL and home-based self-driven training. While this is a more bottom-up approach compared to other contemporary patient-experience strategies across the healthcare field it is considered a significant contribution.

References

Bruner, J. (1990). *Acts of meaning*. Harvard University Press.

Camurri, A., Mazzarino, B., Volpe, G., Morasso, P., Priano, F., & Re, C. (2003). Application of multimedia techniques in the physical rehabilitation of Parkinson's patients, *Journal of Visualization and Computer Animation*, *14*(5): 269–278.

Ellis, P. (1997). The Music of Sound: A new approach for children with severe and profound and multiple learning difficulties, *British Journal of Music Education*, *14*(2): 173–186.

Ellis, P. (2004). Caress – an endearing touch. In *Developing new technologies for young children* (pp. 113–137). Trentham Books.

Gardner, H. (1983). *Frames of mind: The theory of multiple intelligences*. Basic Books.

Hagedorn, D. K., & Holm, E. (2010) Effects of traditional physical training and visual computer feedback training in frail elderly patients. A randomized intervention study, *European Journal of Physical and Rehabilitation Medicine*, *46*(2), 159–168

Hagman, G. (2010). *The artist's mind*. Routledge.

Kowalkiewicz, M. (2017). *Health 5.0: the emergence of digital wellness*. https://medium.com/qut-cde/health-5-0-the-emergence-of-digital-wellness-b21fdff635b9

Pimentel, K., & Teixeira, K. (1995). *Virtual reality: Through the new looking glass*. McGraw-Hill.

Schön, D. (1983). *The reflective practitioner*. Basic Books.

Vygotsky, L. (1978). *Mind and society*. Harvard University.

Wertsch, J. (1985). *Vygotsky and the social formation of mind*. Harvard University.

Yan, Z. (1998). *Measuring microdevelopment of understanding the VMS-SAS structure: A developmental scale pilot*. Harvard University.

Yan, Z., & Fischer, K. (2002). Always under construction: Dynamic variations in adult cognitive microdevelopment. *Human Development*, *45*, 141–160.

PART 3

Empowering Participation

Susanne Dau and Staffan Selander

Introduction: New Technologies – New Practices

This part of the book addresses some vital aspects of the development of new technologies for innovative designs aiming at empowering participation. It builds on the theoretical perspectives presented in Part One, and on the perspectives in Part Two, addressing participative digital technologies and inclusive designs. New landscapes for collaborative learning, and practices, are constantly created anew. However, there is a need to underline the importance of a reflective mind concerning a future, open and democratic society.

New and innovative designs are developed not only out of individual interests, but also delimited by social norms and institutional framings, as well as by wider political, technological and economic conditions and ambitions. However, this does not mean that framings only are diminishing practices. They can also initiate new practices by directing them in certain ways. One example is the demand for 21st-century skills/competences, launched for the school system by OECD, focusing on such aspects as creative thinking and collaborative learning, democratic processes and individual responsibility, in order to prepare children and youngsters for a future, hybrid society. This also relates to new, communicative patterns on social media and new competencies to engage in digital games and simulations, and also in programming, something which most possible will develop into new learning environments. Professionals involved in contemporary design processes will thus be encouraged to continuously, and open-minded, discuss innovative processes and new practices in terms of purposes, criteria for best practice, end users' need, and not first and foremost from the views of political control or skimpy economic interest.

Part Three offers multi-layered perspectives on various design principles and design processes, with an intention to reveal different perspectives and reflections for future practices. The chapters include descriptions and examples of different types of technological solutions and new practices, and they include examples of different target groups' involvement with technology. These chapters address especially game elements, virtual realities, makerspaces and robotics, and they map out a complexity of practices and innovative design for empowering practice and learner-centred agency, interest-driven engagement and playful learning. The theoretical perspectives range from epistemological basics derived from cultural studies, social-constructivism, pragmatism, multimodal social semiotics and designs for learning and more. These chapters also include different consideration for future practice and research. For instance, examples of how transformative potentials, ethics in situ discussions and research design co-operation matters in the processes involved. In summary, it can be said that Part Three offers a sketch of new emerging practices, design methods and principles for research.

Both Chapter 9 on *Reflective and innovative learning designs inspired by gaming principles* by Gyldendahl Jensen and Dau and Chapter 10 *When the game breaks down, the stories begin* by Tretow-Fish and Hanghøj, draw attention to the gaming and game principles for learning. Gyldendahl and Dau reveals how game principles can be rethought for mediating reflection in higher education, and Tretow-Fish and Hanghøj explores how pervasive games enable players to frame and reframe their experience of the world in secondary upper education. The latter one look into two case studies and they conclude that pervasive games and reframing of players' experience can scaffold reflection and dialogue and support engagement.

The game idea is also present in the Chapter 11, *Virtual Reality Learning Experiences about Dementia* by Møller and Löchtefeld. The authors show how virtual reality (VR) could be used by informal caregivers in learning about dementia. These three chapters together thus present different levels of practice and different settings and different elements for future design where games are included. They also extend the idea of simply applying predetermined games for educational use, as they investigate the purpose relevance and how it is possible to make appropriate use of the designs applied for the target groups and in the concrete learning environment.

The next three chapters in Part Three (12–14) entail work with programming or robots from different perspectives. In Chapter 12 *Children's programming of robots by designing fairy tales*, Brook and Sjöberg look at children's interaction and creativity when programming. The authors describe how children can engage in programming of robots afforded by fairy tales, stressing that the playful process enhance imagination and creativity by way of emotional and imaginative interactions. In Chapter 13 *The transformative potential of school-based makerspaces: Novel designs in educational practice,* Kumpulainen and Kajamaa investigates the potentials of makerspace and the empowerment of student's skills to work with makerspaces, based on the investigation of the implementation of makerspaces in schools and how these teachers adapted their work to a makerspace setting. The chapter thus brings central perspectives to educational design of makerspaces and the empowerment of students' 21st century skills.

In the following Chapter 14 *Whiteboxing "bits n bots": How "flawed" and emerging technologies can facilitate computational play and learning,* Brogaard and Fredskilde argue for computational play and "whiteboxing" as central elements in children's work with educational robots, 3D printers and Lego. Finally, in Chapter 15 *Designing virtual cases for learning and assessment,* Uno Fors shows how the construction of digital cases for education could entail both learning and evaluation aspects, and also how students could collaborate to solve these cases.

All in all, these case studies and examples show a rich variety of emerging practices in relation to leaning in different settings. We hope that these examples and discussions also will inspire to continuous educational efforts to extend computational thinking and new participative designs in a hybrid society.

9

REFLECTIVE AND INNOVATIVE LEARNING DESIGNS INSPIRED BY GAMING PRINCIPLES

Camilla Gyldendahl Jensen and Susanne Dau

Introduction to Game Design Principles

Applying game design efficiently in a learning environment is often by the teachers experienced with difficulties as existing games do not meet the substantive requirements for the educational situation regarding both the learning process and acquisition of knowledge (Egenfeldt-Nielsen, Smith, & Tosca, 2019; Melero & Hernández-Leo, 2014; Qian & Clark, 2016). Particularly in higher education, there is a need for new specific models for how academic activities can be enhanced through the use of game design or gamification. Also, learning situations have an individual expression with many variables related to the qualifications of participants, content and context, as well as the learning outcomes.

This approach provides an opportunity to look at commercial computer games in the genre of "Massive Multi Online Role Playing Game" (MMORPG), where research previously has shown that users through the gameplay develop a number of generic skills that are not readily connected to the game's narrative intentions (Ang, Zaphiris, & Mahmood, 2007; Chang & Lin, 2014; Chen, 2010; De Souza, e Silva, & Roazzi, 2010; Golub, 2010; Hou, 2012; McCreery, Schrader, & Krach, 2011; Sourmelis, Ioannou, & Zaphiris, 2017; Suznjevic & Matijasevic, 2010). MMORPG is defined as a network-based and virtual universe where people located in different geographic locations interact with each other in real-time. MMORPG is considered in the literature as one type of computer games, that have explicit incorporation of a designed intense learning process (Jensen & Sorensen, 2017). As Squire (2006) argues: "*The most intense social learning is found in massively multiplayer games, where players interact with thousands of other players in real time over the Internet*" (Squire, 2006, p. 23). A literature review by Sourmelis et al. (2017) reveals that several studies indicate that MMORPG activities can facilitate the development of particular academic competencies among users, thereby supporting the development of 21st-century skills. For instance, they write: "*...can instigate players to analyze new situations, interact with people that don't really know, solve problems, think strategically, and collaborate effectively, all of which are essential skills for the knowledge workers of the 21st-century workspace*" (Sourmelis et al., 2017). Many of the existing studies of gamification used in an educational context are based on a linear narrative supported by simplistic gaming principles, such as reward systems like levels and badges (Egenfeldt-Nielsen, Smith, & Tosca, 2019; Melero & Hernández-Leo, 2014; Qian & Clark, 2016).

Future visions (Egenfeldt-Nielsen, Smith, & Tosca, 2019; Melero & Hernández-Leo, 2014; Qian & Clark, 2016) of gamification focus around a design strategy where the combination of a wide range of gaming principles interacting in a complex system can benefit learning in higher education. Particularly the principles of MMORPG (Ang et al., 2007; De Souza et al., 2010; Golub, 2010; Hou, 2012; Chang & Lin, 2014; Chen, 2010; McCreery et al., 2011; Sourmelis et al., 2017; Suznjevic & Matijasevic, 2010) are a great source of inspiration as it moves the focus from thinking about **content** towards thinking **how** the content should be taught. In other words, instead of seeing gamification as a method for learning a particular curriculum, it can be a way of changing the conditions in teaching situations, so learning **is** possible. Successful utilisation of the concept of gamification as design methodologies for learning requires a particular focus on what behaviour we want to promote and how do the games create individual learning sequences or personal learning trajectories. Thinking in play structures and the dynamics of game designs, allows the educator to organise and work systematically with different combinations of **knowledge acquisition, reflection, progression** and **development of ideas** regarding achieving specific learning outcome. It is, therefore, interesting to look into how gamification can be designed, based on a vision of students experiencing the freedom to form their individual learning processes. This freedom is what sets the direction of the game and thus becomes the narrative. It can, therefore, be argued that the game design has to contain far more different types of multimodal activities that can be randomly combined while motivating students to work in depth through different pace strategies – it is not just about winning the game. Particularly the two concepts **Crafting** and **Farming**, known from MMORPG, provide interesting perspectives regarding rethinking how gamification in the future can support explorative and innovative forms of learning. Both terms will be elaborated further in this article.

The new interest in using game-principle in educational context entails to a reassessment of the teacher's role as initiating the learning process. Game design as a teaching platform thus changes the teacher's responsibility and role into being far more organising and frame generating. Game-based learning as the overall educational design, therefore, implies both new challenges and opportunities for the creation of reflective, explorative and practice-based processes when the focal point suddenly is focused on Quests and Levels, Missions, Crafting and Farming through personal trajectories of narratives.

Based on a theoretical discussion of relevant literature supported by empirical data, the article will examine how the use of game-oriented learning affect students' learning when working with academic disciplines in a higher education context. A particular focus will be on exploration of the vision behind game design as a predefined **Exemplary Process** against the desire for reflective and interdisciplinary teaching practices where students independently take responsibility for their process. This paradox paves the way for a critical look at the future vision of game-oriented learning regarding facilitating and scaffolding reflective, explorative and innovative learning processes. Also, the question of whether academic learning activities can be implemented in a game design is mentioned to be fundamentally based on the idea of an "Exemplary Process".

The article will initially unfold why game design based on predetermined narrative contains a learning paradox. Followed by an elaboration about how traditionally and predefined Quest system can be challenged through game principles known from MMORPG. Dewey's (1997, 1998, 2013) ontological understanding of learning will be the theoretical position of the argumentation. The next section will present a model for how gamification can address academic disciplines through a rethinking of Quest systems, with a particular focus on the concepts Crafting and Farming.

The Dilemma of Game-oriented Learning in Education

The use of game-oriented learning in the classroom is increasingly common in higher education as a suggestion for one of the future educational tools. A literature review by Qian and Clark (2016), however, indicates that a significant proportion of the games developed for educational purposes do not adequately support reflective, explorative and innovative learning activities. They conclude that; "*Many educational games are simple designs that are narrowly focused on academic content, target low-level literacy, provide drill and practice methods similar to worksheets, and stress memorization of facts*". One of the reasons is that game-oriented learning is typically based on a mechanical built, where only the internal design grammar is the focal point (Jensen & Sorensen, 2017; Qian & Clark, 2016). This thinking gives education a one-sided focus on the acquisition of curricula and skills, which does not adequately create the necessary learning activities that support reflection and thereby depth learning (Jensen & Sorensen, 2017; Qian & Clark, 2016).

A perspective on this problem seems to be the idea of game-oriented learning being built around a predetermined narrative, rather than something that is created along the way, by the students' own stories and personal learning trajectories (see Figure 9.1). In 2006, Squire described how several researchers and teachers had criticised the game-oriented learning concept for not providing students with complex learning as the "hidden curriculum" stored in the fictional story is not recognisable (Squire, 2006).

MMORPG is not built around a single narrative but consists of complex Quest strings and diverse activities that merge into an extensive sophisticated system where players choose which Quest or events they want to pursue and thus build their own stories and sub-stories. Also, MMORPG is designed in a way where the gaming activities take a long time to complete as they are built around hard and tough challenges (Gee, 2003; Egenfeldt-Nielsen, Smith, & Tosca, 2019; Nardi, 2010). Nardi (2010) uses Dewey's definition of *"Aesthetic experience"* (Dewey, 2005) to explain the game design behind an MMORPG. *"Aesthetic experience"* can be defined as active participation towards a final goal, which at the same time also is experienced as satisfaction through interacting with a variety of different activities. Dewey also speaks about *"successive phases that are an emphasis of the varied colors of aesthetic experiences"* where activities can be seen as sequential structures (Dewey, 2005).

These sequential structures of Quest lines maintain the user at a given level for a more extended period, as the game design requires curiosity and exploration rather than a single focus on winning. It, therefore, makes sense to incorporate this thinking into game-oriented learning, as curiosity and exploration are the means to make the students immersive in the professional substance. It can be argued that the complex structure of MMORPGs through series of unique Quests at each new level is what creates an *"Aesthetic experience"* and the possibility of getting in-depth with the content as a result (Jensen, 2016).

In particular, the Crafting or Farming principles known from MMORPGs can help students immerse themselves in a specific topic, and thereby maintaining themselves in a more reflective and analytical learning process. Much of the game activities in MMORPG is, therefore, all about crafting new items and players, consequently, spending many hours collecting material, also called farming. The principles of Crafting or Farming forms a complexity of both the creation, reflection and ideological development of new knowledge (items) in the game, rather than pushing towards a goal as a result. The fundamental principle behind Crafting and Farming is all about slowing the game down and keeping the gamers busy. Nardi (2010) highlights the paradox that players accept the boredom of farming as it fulfils the need of collecting items that contribute to solving complex tasks later on. Furthermore, Crafting and Farming stimulate both social communication and collaboration concerning preparing a joint action through the use of Missions (Gee, 2003; Jensen, 2016; Nardi, 2010).

Educational games should instead consist of multimodal activities that are arbitrarily combined based on students' personal exploration and reflection processes. Thus, it is possible to challenge the predefined teacher led instructions (Dewey, 1997). If game designs are built on simple Quest strings that aim to bring the student through particular narratives based on the acquisition of a specific curriculum, there is a risk that learning outcomes will remain reduced. Instead, it must be about allowing the student to work with intermediate actions and activities that require findings, objects or ideas as a prerequisite for achieving a more distant goal. Here the idea of Crafting and Farming is interesting, as it allows for actively supporting data collection, knowledge creation, brainstorms, development of ideas, e.g. Serious of Quest based on the idea of Crafting and Farming activities thereby becoming a way of controlling a far-reaching goal through sequences of explorations and reflections that tie it all together. Dewey describes it so;

> The question of methodology in connection with the formation of reflexive thinking is a matter of establishing the conditions that can arouse and control the curiosity, to create coherence in the perceived things, a context that will later promote the flow of spontaneous thoughts and lead them to the formulation of issues and purposes that promote the connection in the flow of thought.
>
> (Dewey, 1997, p. 54)

Accordingly, the Quest system can support and facilitate conscious activities consisting of different ways of working through systemic thinking that creates sequences of explorations pointing to a final goal. Reflective, explorative and innovative processes imply a form of coherence and continuity of an organised mindset with the right balance and distribution of the three dimensions of thoughts – ease and speed, scale and variation, as well as depth.

Thus, this means that learning processes contain flexibility and diversity in the manner of which the curriculum is treated and processed while there is a clear and definite direction towards a goal. The acquisition of the academic disciplines, therefore, contrasts with a mechanical and routine uniformity or, as Dewey describes it, the movement of a grasshopper (Dewey, 1997, 1998, 2013). Hence, there is a need for addressing the curriculum from several angles, including gathering of data and knowledge, evaluation, and assessment, asking questions, discussions and argumentation. This position of learning means that if gamification is to support the acquisition of academic disciplines, the gaming principles must contain the necessary flexibility and diversity in activities that constitute the game design, e.g. regarding Quest system. Thus, it is limited to think in simple Quest strings based on a predefined "exemplary process" and narrative.

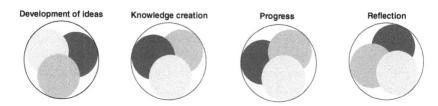

FIGURE 9.1 An interpretation of Dewey's understanding of the three dimensions of thoughts.

Game-oriented Learning Informed by "Crafting and Farming"

By Dewey's understanding of learning, it is meaningful to consider gamification as a learning design that consists of different types of activities that mediate and support the student's learning. It involves a shift from an understanding of gamification as a predefined narrative that is built around specific content, towards seeing it as generic tools and methods that can stimulate and facilitate a learning process. Combining Dewey's three dimensions of thoughts creates four different categories of activities (see Figure 9.2) that represent disciplines characterising an academic process:

Progression – Low variation of Thought + Fast Thought + Superficial Thought.

Knowledge acquisition – Big variation of Thought + Deep thought + Slow thought.

Development of ideas – Fast Thought + Superficial Thought + Big variation of Thought.

Reflection – Deep thought + Slow thought + Low variation of Thought.

When these four categories are incorporated into a traditional game design that typically consists of elements such as levels, achievements and missions and Quests, it opens up for a puzzling mindset where precisely the possibilities of combination contribute to a depth in the learning process. In addition, the idea of an exemplary process is expelled, as it is no longer the narrative that constitutes the game structure. A student describes the experience by using gamification as a facilitating tool as follows:

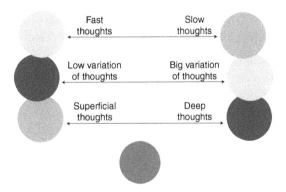

FIGURE 9.2 A combination of the three dimensions of thoughts into four Quest categories.

> I really think it's a good help and we made some activities we would not have made otherwise. And we described a lot of content we normally would not have described so well. It helped us with what we really need to consider.

The students follow their personal and unique problem formulations but are supported along the way by activities that challenge the learning process on several levels, including pushing it and obstructions. Each activity triggers points that allow new levels and thereby, new activities. A student describes here how he experienced a link between getting help in managing the learning process while being motivated by the competition element:

> I also think it was cool enough. It was as the game got us through it (red. The curriculum) to start with, and then we learned what was needed and beyond. We could compete with the others (red. Project groups), and we thought that was cool.

This approach to gamification implies for the students a constant shift of positions created by the game activities, combined with one particular direction that leads them towards the final goals of their projesct.

The four categories have several parallels to the previously mentioned gaming principles; Crafting and Farming. Thus, it can be argued that the combination of the two concepts and their interrelationships creates the necessary complexity to develop reflective, explorative and innovative skills of the student.

The categories "**Knowledge acquisition**" and "**Development of ideas**" focus on activities aimed at collecting new elements, knowledge, angles and observations, e.g. that can challenge the curriculum – in a game context, this is called "Farming". The collected parts do not in themselves have any value and therefore needs to be combined or used for developing new knowledge or solutions for the project. The "Development of ideas" category thus creates fast and superficial thoughts while the category of "Knowledge acquisition" consists of more slow and thorough workflows.

Farming – **Knowledge acquisition** (slow) and **Development of ideas** (fast).

The categories "**Progression**" and "**Reflection**", however, concern activities aimed at linking and combining the collected elements, knowledge, angles and observations, e.g. –in a game context, this is called "Crafting". The "Progression" category is the quick method of concluding and making decisions based on the existing knowledge base and ideas of the project, while the category "reflection" consists of slow and thorough activities that discuss and put perspective to the curriculum.

Crafting – **Progression** (fast) and **Reflection** (slow).

The following sections exemplify each of the four categories and are also substantiated by empirical statements from students who have used gamification as a scaffolding method in connection with project-based learning. In this context, the students participating in the empirical studies were characterised by not having an immediate interest in working with academic disciplines. The use of gamification is therefore based on an idea of changing the conditions in the learning environment so learning can take place through the presence of an external motivation factor.

Quest – Progression

The category of "**Progress**" contains Quest activities that through the principle of crafting aim to orient students' process towards reaching a final goal. These activities are characterised by rapid thoughts that train students to make competent decisions based on their existing knowledge base, development of ideas and reflection. A student describes how the group through the use of gamification got a systematic approach to making the best choices for their project;

> There were arguments other than "I like" that. These arguments were used when we found the architectural form of the building because we had made some analyses and knew what that meant for the different concepts. So, it was so easy to decide because there was no such thing as "what do you think" something we should discuss.

The activities of the category "Progress" help students to focus and create an indirect motivation and sense of feeling that the project is taking shape and direction without losing its depth. Another important argument is the fragmentation of the process into smaller parts or learning sequences. Consequently, the student does not necessarily need to have a full overview of their entire learning process. Also, the complexity of activities increases as new levels are achieved. A student describes it thus; "*The higher level we reached, the larger and better tools we got somehow*".

Quest – Development of Ideas

The category of "**Development of Ideas**" contains Quest activities that through the principle of "farming" aim to focus on innovative use of the curriculum. A prerequisite for being able to work innovatively with a particular topic is a systematic process of fast thinking processes triggered by external inspiration or stimulus. The quality of the creative process is often dependent on the number of new ideas and angles to a problem. It is therefore crucial that the process has a speed that does not consider the usefulness, relevance, rendering or quality of the ideas along the way. It is essential to use different types of idea-generating tools, to stimulate the flow of creative thoughts. The students described here how gamification contributed to being inspired to use tools they previously would have opted for; "*Normally we would not have played with LEGO blocks … No (swearing), we would not have found the time to do that*". Gamification provides a natural opportunity to incorporate fun-failure as a way to launch a fast generation of ideas. During a fixed timeframe student brainstorm relevant concepts and words for their project and thus "farm" new potential topics, directions or ideas that subsequently can challenge their project. In the following example, a student describes how fun-failure thinking influenced their idea generation process;

> We did that downstairs in the auditorium where we were to write the 50 ideas. What we think would be cool […], and then we had a time frame to brainstorm in, and if we did not reach it, we should start over again. I think we had to do that two or three times […] Well, it meant that the second time you did it, the ideas were stronger. That is, if we had 35 ideas for the first time, Well, out of the 35th, maybe only 30 of them came back where the last five were made were new. It was never like, we had 30, and it was the same 30 that came up again, it was constantly slightly rotated. I also think without knowing it for sure, but I think that the ideas we stored in round two might be the ideas that actually meant something to us. So, the ideas were giving more and more meaning as they arose on the board […] It gave some good points of view on the building, at least, how it should be.

The analysis thus reveals that the use of gaming principles creates what Dewey calls a "systematic process of fast thinking processes triggered by external inspiration or stimulus". It creates situations where the students have the opportunity to define the quality or the direction of their work through the generation of new ideas.

Quest – Knowledge Acquisition

The category of "**Knowledge acquisition**" contains Quest activities that through the principle of "crafting" initiates and facilitates students doing analysis, studies, exploration and innovation as well as literacy. The activities are characterised by being a time-consuming performance that draws the pace out of the process. The structured and organised acquisition of knowledge through the use of gamification ensures the necessary depth of mind needed to get a sufficient learning process. A student describes how they experienced being rewarded for working in-depth with their project;

> So, you are rewarded for going in-depth, so you get a quick reward for going into depth with something that you may not have spent much time on before. So, it is not up to you to pull yourselves together. Okay, now I have some problem-based learning to do, and now I have to learn this. So it is more like creating a quick reward for what you do.

In addition, the activities present the students to new fields of study and theories that put potential obstruction for their process and challenge them to seek new and unknown solutions. A student describes how they through exploration became acquainted with a subject area they in a traditional learning environment would have skipped;

> Yes, I think there were things we had to explore. So, there were a time when we had him, Jan Gehl (a theorist within architecture), we would never have seen it (the red movie) if it were not.... It actually turned out to be one of the most important elements for us.

The above quote illustrates how the topic affords academic outcome and how gamification challenges them to seek new and unknown solutions that would not have explored without the principles of farming knowledge.

Quest – Reflection

The category of "**reflection**" contains Quest activities that through the principle of "crafting" are focusing on identified themes being handled through an in-depth and slow process that allows reflection processes along the way. The activities in this category have the particular purpose of creating reflection based on the project's analytical contexts as well as theory links. A student thus describes how reflection activities helped the group to gain a better understanding of the necessity and importance of their analysis work;

> It offered me a lot, and I also think we gained a better understanding of why it is crucial for analysing things and not just rush towards the finish and get a result. But actually, just giving it an extra thought about why we have done it like this.

Also, the activities contribute to an increased understanding of academic content. The students describe how gamification activities supported reflections of relevant concerns of the project by written materials;

> So, it is a way to get the control, those who make the game, they can control that you do some writing. Because it is 110% for sure, I had not sat down and written some reflection if I had not got 100 points for it.

Quests that includes reflection activities also aim to initiate metacognition partly related to how gamification as a method supports the learning process and partly whether the intended goal is achieved.

Conclusions

The articles represent an idea of using a model for how gamification through the inspiration of game-principle known from "Massive Multi Online Role-Playing Games (MMORPG)" can inspire the design of new teaching concepts and representations of the academic and therefore challenge existing normativity within higher education. Here the theoretical discussion points to the fact that learning game's effectiveness seems to be depending on the Quest systems' ability to support and facilitate conscious activities consisting of different ways of working through systemic thinking that creates sequences of explorations pointing to a final goal. We conclude that games can inspire a mediation of reflective, explorative and innovative learning in higher education through the idea of Crafting and Farming. It provides an understanding for how reflective, explorative and innovative processes can create coherence and organised mindset with the right balance and distribution of the three dimensions of thoughts – ease and speed, scale and variation, as well as depth. If game-based learning is going to have an impact on students' development of reflective, explorative and innovative competencies, then it is crucial that the game design supports the intended learning processes through a holistic design strategy. There is, therefore, a particular need for empirical research for how game mechanisms can inspire the creation of new innovative representations of the academic in a meaningful way with the experienced freedom to challenge the presented content.

References

Ang, C. S., Zaphiris, P., & Mahmood, S.. "A model of cognitive loads in massively multiplayer online role-playing games." *Interacting with Computers 19*(2) (2007): 167–179.

Chang, S. M., & Lin, S. S. (2014). Team knowledge with motivation in a successful MMORPG game team: A case study. *Computers & Education, 73*, 129–140.

Chen, M. (2010). *Leet noobs: Expertise and collaboration in a World of Warcraft player group as distributed sociomaterial practice* (Doctoral dissertation, University of Washington Graduate School).

De Souza, B. C., e Silva, L. X. D. L., & Roazzi, A. (2010). MMORPGS and cognitive performance: A study with 1280 Brazilian high school students. *Computers in Human Behavior, 26*(6), 1564–1573.

Deterding, S. (2012). Gamification: designing for motivation. *Interactions, 19*(4), 14–17.

Dewey, J. (1997). *How we think.* York, NY: Courier Corporation.

Dewey, J. (1998). *Experience and education.* Kappa Delta Pi.

Dewey, J. (2005). *Art as experience.* Penguin.

Egenfeldt-Nielsen, S., Smith, J. H., & Tosca, S. P. (2019). *Understanding video games: The essential introduction.* Routledge.

Gee, J. P. (2003). What video games have to teach us about learning and literacy. *Computers in Entertainment (CIE), ACM Computers in Entertainment, 1*(1), 20–20.

Golub, A. (2010). Being in the world (of warcraft): Raiding, realism, and knowledge production in a massively multiplayer online game. *Anthropological Quarterly*, 83(1), 17–45.

Hainey, T., Connolly, T. M., Boyle, E. A., Wilson, A., & Razak, A. (2016). A systematic literature review of games-based learning empirical evidence in primary education. *Computers & Education*, 102, 202–223.

Hamari, J., Koivisto, J., & Sarsa, H. (2014, January). *Does gamification work?--a Literature review of empirical studies on gamification*. In *System Sciences (HICSS), 2014 47th Hawaii International Conference on* (pp. 3025–3034). IEEE.

Hou, H. T. (2012). Exploring the behavioral patterns of learners in an educational massively multiple online role-playing game (MMORPG). *Computers & Education*, 58(4), 1225–1233.

Jensen, C. G. (2016). *Gamification of innovation processes by bringing World of Warcraft into the real world*. In *EDUlearn16* (pp. 59–68). IATED.

Jensen, C. G., & Sorensen, E. (2017). *Maintaining collaborative democratic and dialogue-based learning processes in virtual and game-based learning environments*. In *10th annual International Conference of Education, Research and Innovation* (pp. 1797–1805).

McCreery, M. P., Schrader, P. G., & Krach, S. K. (2011). Navigating massively multiplayer online games: Evaluating 21st century skills for learning within virtual environments. *Journal of Educational Computing Research*, 44(4), 473–493.

McGonigal, J. (2011). *Reality is broken: Why games make us better and how they can change the world*. Penguin.

Melero, J., & Hernández-Leo, D. (2014). A Model for the Design of Puzzle-based Games Including Virtual and Physical Objects. *Educational Technology & Society*, 17(3), 192–207.

Nardi, B. (2010). *My life as a night elf priest: An anthropological account of World of Warcraft*. University of Michigan Press.

Novak, K. (2017). It takes a guild-social metacognition and collaborative creation of a learning organization. In *Integrating an awareness of selfhood and society into virtual learning* (pp. 198–224). IGI Global.

Poels, K., Ijsselsteijn, W. A., & Dekort, Y. (2015). World of Warcraft, the aftermath: How game elements transfer into perceptions, associations and (day) dreams in the everyday life of massively multiplayer online role-playing game players. *New Media & Society*, 17(7), 1137–1153.

Qian, M., & Clark, K. R. (2016). Game-based Learning and 21st century skills: A review of recent research. *Computers in Human Behavior*, 63, 50–58.

Riva, M. (2000). The need for a socio-cultural perspective in the implementation of virtual environments. *Springer London, Virtual Reality*, 5, 32–38.

Sourmelis, T., Ioannou, A., & Zaphiris, P. (2017). Massively Multiplayer Online Role Playing Games (MMORPGs) and the 21st century skills: A comprehensive research review from 2010 to 2016. *Computers in Human Behavior*, 67, 41–48.

Squire, K. (2006). From content to context: Videogames as designed experience. *Educational Researcher*, 35(8), 19–29.

Suznjevic, M., & Matijasevic, M. (2010). Why MMORPG players do what they do: relating motivations to action categories. *International Journal of Advanced Media and Communication*, 4(4), 405–424.

10

WHEN THE GAME BREAKS DOWN, THE STORIES BEGIN

Tobias Alexander Bang Tretow-Fish and Thorkild Hanghøj

Introduction

Games can be understood as narrative worlds that allow players to make their own choices in order to explore different storylines. Because the narrative aspect of games, and especially video games, is often emphasised by game theorists (e.g. Jenkins, 2004), there is a tendency to primarily understand game narratives in relation to the ways in which specific narratives are embedded in a game's design. However, in this chapter, we wish to argue that it is important to pay closer attention to how players create their *own* narratives, both individually and in collaboration with other players, in relation to their game experiences. In short, we are less interested in the options and meanings of specifically designed game narratives than in understanding players' own emerging narratives. We believe these emerging narratives can provide important learning opportunities for both game designers and educators who are using games in educational contexts as well as empowering the participation of players and designers in playing and designing games.

Our study is centred on the pervasive game format: a relatively open-ended game type that provides an ambiguous game space. Such an ambiguous game space creates many potential variations in the ways in which a given pervasive game can be played and interpreted. This ambiguity may create frustration among players who are inexperienced with pervasive games, but the ambiguity also offers many creative possibilities for players to construct new narratives around the game. Even though the players' narratives will be framed by a given pervasive game's design, which will provide specific premises, goals and narrative cues for participation in the game, the players' narratives will only be partially related to these intended game narratives. Because pervasive games let players construct their own narratives, which may or may not resonate with the designed game narratives, pervasive games provide a greater sense of agency than many other game types. In this way, pervasive games can engage with players' shifting perspectives as they move between a state of immersion in a game experience (in-game) and viewing and reflecting on the game experience from an outsider's perspective (off-game).

Given this flexibility in the narrative of pervasive games, we pose the following question: How can the design and use of pervasive games enable players to construct new narratives by framing and reframing their game experiences in relation to the intended game narrative? In answering this question, we wish to show how players' narratives create potential for the continuous redesign of pervasive games. In this sense, pervasive games are never finished, but are potentially always open to further redesign. Moreover, we wish to show how "broken" game experiences – e.g. when players are unable to engage in a pervasive game or when players make a game crash by pushing the boundaries of the game system – also involve learning potential for everyone from players to game designers and facilitators. In order to demonstrate these theories and answer our posed question, below we present two case studies on two different types of pervasive games, namely the Alternate Reality Game (ARG) *Hedeheksen* and the educational mixed-media pervasive game *Tough Road*.

What Defines Pervasive Games?

Pervasive games are games that challenge and even break down the boundaries between the ordinary world and the play world (Montola et al., 2009). This can be done in three separate dimensions: the *spatial*, the *temporal* and the *social*. If players question the boundaries of a game in any one of these dimensions then a game qualifies as a pervasive game. In this way, pervasive games exceed our understanding of more traditional game formats that have clearly defined boundaries, such as board games or video games, where game activities primarily take place on the delineated surfaces of a board or a screen. A game does not necessarily need digital technology to qualify as a pervasive game. However, many pervasive games do involve some form of digital technology, such as mobile phones or computer simulations, often in combination with activities in a physical game space. Schmitz, Klemke, and Specht (2012) point out that this definition is so broad that the term pervasive games can include quite a broad family of games: anything from treasure hunts to ARGs, smart street sports and massively multiplayer mobile games. Because of this, the category of pervasive game includes a vast array of sub-genres, many of which only exist as short-lived events and become fairly unknown to mainstream audiences.

For the purposes of this chapter, we wish to focus on two types of pervasive games: Alternative Reality Games (ARGs) and educational pervasive games. Both game types, but especially ARGs, have a connection with role-playing games, where the element of acting out different roles is a central aspect of the game. ARGs are networked narratives of interactivity: they use the real world as their platform and transmedia storytelling to deliver their narratives. The narratives of ARGs are highly influenced by players' ideas and actions as they play. Kittl and Petrovic (2008) found that in ARGs the need for players to be socially adaptable to meet the challenges of the environment of their ARGs is especially important. In educational pervasive games, it is important that the educational aspect is interwoven throughout the game so the players experience a valid learning process (Ardito et al., 2011).

Both educational games and ARGs require effort from the players in establishing and maintaining game boundaries. Watson (2012) connects the need of player adaptability to the strategic and responsive curation of the development process of the game. Because of the complexity involved in pervasive games, a collaborative design effort between players, game facilitators and designers is necessary when creating and playing pervasive games. Studies of pervasive games highlight the importance of collaboration both as a key aspect of player behaviour (Evans, Flintham, & Martindale, 2014) and as a necessity when designing games that can support players' social roles (Bonsignore, Hansen, Kraus, Visconti, & Fraistat, 2016). Several game theorists further emphasise how pervasive games can inspire players to actively engage in problem-solving, knowledge sharing and the co-creative process of building new knowledge (Gurzick et al., 2011; Muscat, 2013).

Theoretical Perspectives

In order to explore the narrative aspects of playing pervasive games, we draw inspiration from three complementary theoretical perspectives, which we will describe in the following sections: Goffman's frame analysis, Bruner's narrative theory and Dewey's pragmatist theory of inquiry.

Framing Game Experiences

One of the defining characteristics of pervasive games is that they allow players to play with the meaning of the game situation itself: What marks the temporal, social and physical boundaries of the game world? In non-pervasive games, there is a clear distinction between being in-game and being off-game – i.e. between being a character in the game and being a player playing the game. In contrast, switching between different modes of interaction is a central aspect of playing a pervasive game. This means that the pervasive aspects of a pervasive game may make it difficult for players to determine when a player is in-game or off-game.

In order to describe the layered meanings of pervasive games, we will follow Goffman's (1974) understanding of social situations as involving different interactional *frames*. According to Goffman, we reside in a number of different social worlds and these worlds are finite. When we move between these worlds, e.g. move from discussing events in our everyday life to acting as detectives in a witchcraft murder mystery, we juggle different frames (or worlds) of meaning. These worlds are shared with other people and are therefore social worlds constituted by frames of experience. A frame is a "situational definition constructed in accord with organising principles that governs both the events themselves and participants' experiences of these events" (Goffman, 1974, pp. 10–11). This definition makes frame analysis ideal both for a descriptive analysis of how we interact socially and as a tool for designing games with a constructed prescriptive intent, e.g. designing games for educational purposes.

Elaborating on Goffman's theory, Fine (1983) argues that meaning-making in the tabletop role-playing game *Dungeon & Dragons* typically involves three different frames:

1. The primary frame – or the real world – where gaming is but one of many activities that are available. In this frame there is no dependency on other frames.
2. The game context, where players act as *players* and where they interact in a context governed by a complicated set of rules different to those of the real world. Players know of their characters and move them around in the game world according to the rules not of their primary frame (the real world) but according to the conventions of the game.
3. The gaming world, where players not only move identifiable characters around, but they *are* the characters. There is, however, some reservation to claiming that a player *is* a character. Player identity and character identity cannot, of course, be precisely the same since, for instance, characters can have knowledge that the player does not and vice versa.

When players switch between frames they oscillate between different levels of meaning. Switching can happen rapidly, either by the player clearly stating the switch or by afterwards explaining the movement from one level to another. When playing pervasive games, players continually shift between different interactional frames in relation to the boundaries of the game. In this way, players also shift between taking part in and stepping out of the game, which involves shifting between being either immersed (in-game) or reflecting (off-game) on game experiences.

Narrating Game Experiences

In order to further understand how players create narratives based on their game experiences, we turn to Bruner's theory of the narrative construction of reality (Bruner, 1991). According to Bruner, constructing narratives about ourselves allow us to construct our identities. He defines a narrative as a connection of events and experiences that combine to tell a story. This theory of the narrative construction of reality is useful not only for understanding how players construct their real-world identities; it is also useful for understanding how players construct their character identities.

Bruner argues that knowledge can be constructed either through a narrative or a paradigmatic mode of thinking. In the *narrative mode* particular events are linked together, for instance when players encounter a series of ongoing game events. How players connect and assemble these events are represented in their player narratives. The *paradigmatic mode* of thinking refers to interactive systems that require logical reasoning. In relation to games, this type of thinking is dominant in game mechanics based on logical structures, for instance when players try to solve a puzzle. In general, games involve both modes of knowledge as a player's individual perception of reality is constructed and then reconstructed. As examples, changing the rules in a game of chess or adding a different background story to a *Dungeons and Dragons* session, would change the perception of the games. However, we will primarily focus on games as narrative modes of knowledge in this chapter as the paradigmatic aspect tends to be less prevalent in pervasive games, which are more reliant on the players' experience of crossing different frames.

In our analysis, we will use Bruner's theory of the narrative construction of reality to distinguish between three different types of narratives: 1) *game narrative*, which is the designed narrative of pervasive games, 2) *individual player narratives*, which are not necessarily externalised or clear to other players and 3) *collaborative or co-constructed player narratives*, which are created through negotiation between players.

Reflecting Game Experiences

Finally, we wish to argue that pervasive game activities also involve potential for providing valuable learning experiences through *reflection*. The open-endedness of pervasive games both allows and sometimes forces players to step in and out of the game frame as a part of the overall game experience. Because of this movement in and out of the game frame, pervasive games offer players a reflective mode for constructing and reconstructing their player narratives in relation to their game actions. This process can be understood using Dewey's (1933) theory of inquiry, which assumes that while as humans we experience unforeseen challenges through exploration of indeterminate situations, we may then turn our experiences of these challenges into ideas, hypotheses and strategies for creative problem-solving. A crucial aspect of the inquiry process is reflection, which is a meaning-making process that allows a learner to move from one experience into the next with a deeper understanding of relationships with and connections to other experiences and ideas (Rodgers, 2002). As we will show through our analytical examples, stepping in and out of a pervasive game tends to promote reflection among players on their game experiences. While being able to enter or leave a game by choice may promote reflection, not having the choice to enter or leave (perhaps because a player has been kicked out) can be quite a frustrating or challenging experience that is not in accordance with the players' immediate desires. Because of this contrast, it is relevant to examine how entering and leaving pervasive games may lead to reflective inquiry.

Analytical Examples

We will now present the reader with two analytical examples of how players construct narratives through framing, playing and reflecting on pervasive games. The first example concerns a group of players who attempted to play an unfinished game during a playtest session of an early prototype of the ARG *Hedeheksen*. The focus here is on how the players' own narratives differed from the intended game narratives and how the player's new line of narrative inquiry might inform a future design process. The second example looks closely at a game session of the educational pervasive game *Tough Road*, in which a specific student pushed the boundaries of the game system into an unforeseen and somewhat chaotic event that eventually caused her to be killed in the game. The focus here is on how the game facilitator managed to include the unforeseen game event in the overall game narrative and how the student turned her defeat into a reflective learning experience.

Example 1: Entering the Game

The following case demonstrates how four inexperienced players try to identify the frame and establish the narrative of an unfamiliar game, in this case a prototype of the ARG *Hedeheksen*, designed by one of the authors of this chapter. As our analysis shows, the players succeed in pursuing a game narrative but they are not able to establish a frame for the game. In spite of their difficulties with the not fully developed game, the players still engage in a collaborative effort by developing a common narrative through reflective inquiry.

The ARG *Hedeheksen* involves a non-player character (NPC) protagonist, Tommy, who in the beginning of the game engages in a conflict with three NPC witches. Tommy discovers an uncanny scene in the forest with the remnants from an occult ritual.

Tommy's encounter with the scene initiates the mystery of *Hedeheksen*: Who performed this ritual, and why are dark forces now harassing Tommy? Tommy then seeks help from players through articles in a local newspaper and on the newspaper's website to understand the mystery about why the witches are after him and how to solve it. As the players find, read and analyse the articles, the narrative unfolds for them as they engage with it.

Hedeheksen is constructed as a narrative that is pieced together through the discovery of multimodal information, clues and interactions. The physical and website articles in the newspaper Aalborg:Nu were the intended gateway (rabbit hole) for

FIGURE 10.1 The opening scene of the game *Hedeheksen*, where Tommy discovers an uncanny scene in the forest with the remnants from an occult ritual.

entering the ARG. These multimodal pieces were then collected on Tommy's blog, which acted as the hub of information. Players could interact with Tommy on the blog by posting comments or by interacting with some of the NPCs through email. Depending on how players interacted with the material, Tommy and the NPCs could influence how the narrative would be moulded to engage with the players' interactions. In the end, the players had the opportunity of keeping the conflict between Tommy and the antagonist witches from spiralling out of control.

The intention with the ARG was that players would feel intrigued and therefore be motivated to engage with the ARG when they first stumbled upon the articles and the initial clues. Once they had found the articles, the players would have enough information as to make contact with Tommy on his blog. Since the blog acted as a hub of information, the players were able to discover how far along the narrative had come.

In the playtest, four novice game players were provided three physical articles as a rabbit hole into the game. Without any introduction to the game, the genre or a clear goal, the players themselves had to figure out what the framing of the game and the game narrative was. In this process of iteratively framing and reframing their experience, both as individuals interacting with the game and as players understanding how the game worked, it was our hope that the players would be able to understand, engage with and enjoy the ARG.

However, the result was that the players, (Pete, Lea, Jamie and Rita, who were all students at Aalborg University), engaged with the game with a lot of confusion, frustration and difficulty. Despite this strained engagement, the players still worked in collaboration as they tested the game and explored it through reflective inquiry, coming up with ideas and hypotheses of what the narrative might be.

The players' very first challenge was to frame the experience as a game at all and thereby to establish the game narrative. Without this frame, the players would not be able to distinguish when they were in-game and when they were not. However, it became apparent when the players read the articles introducing them to the game that they were not able to establish such a framework.

These are quotes from a transcription of an audio recording made during the workshop with the players.

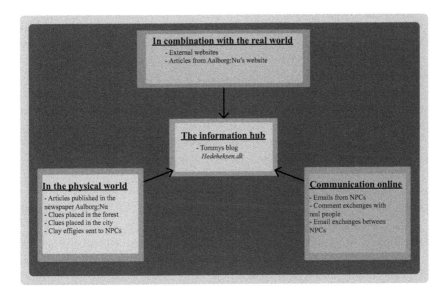

FIGURE 10.2 Map of different information sources used in the game *Hedeheksen*.

RITA: Okay, (pause) it [*the narrative*] is abstract.
PETE: You can say that.

JAMIE and Lea had a similar reaction when they, immediately after reading the articles, discussed their meaning.
JAMIE: I experienced among other things something supernatural uhm an unreal some kind of threatening. Something dangerous
LEA: Maybe even a little poetic because it is so abstract. It is incoherent.

Even though the players engaged with the game materials – articles, blog posts and websites – and thereby gradually engaged themselves with the game by reading, discussing, interpreting and analysing the game material, they were unable to understand the broader framing of it as a game. Because of this, it was not possible for them to understand the events through either the paradigmatic or the narrative mode. This was apparent in the interview conducted with them after the game test was finished.

LEA: So I really want to ask what is this thing [the game]?
JAMIE: Ha ha.
RITA: Yeah that is also what I am thinking (pause). Did we? Did we solve it?

As the example shows, the players were not able to frame their exploration of the game materials as something that could be part of a mystery game. They could not establish a particular connection between the events described in the material as a cohesive game narrative and thereby switch between frame levels. Instead of forfeiting, the players began to reconstruct the events and develop alternative narratives to those posed by the game materials. They started a collaborative process of reflective inquiry.

The game was designed to enable players to reveal a mystery about local myths and the Wiccan religion. But because the players struggled to frame the game as a game – thereby failing to access the intended narrative – their co-created narratives were only partially aligned with the intended narrative of the ARG. One of the reimagined narratives included the involvement of the Roman god Jupiter:

RITA: The King of the gods.
JAMIE: So it might be what do you say the gods. It might be light it could well be the moonlight.
LEA: Yeah it says something here about blah blah blah identified with the Greeks' Zeus and like him uhm. It is poorly formulated. Probably an Indo-European light thunder and weather god.
RITA: Light god.
JAMIE: Ahh uhm.
RITA: And weather god. (pause) Where? Where were we? How did we get to Jupiter?

While the involvement of Jupiter had a connection to the spiritual dimension of the Wicca narrative, it was not the designers' intended direction of the narrative. The game events did not include Roman religion directly, so Jupiter only appeared in the co-created player narrative because the players brought their own interests, knowledge and experience into their exploration of the open-ended game. Another unintended aspect to the narrative came about when Rita, a history student, applied her critical perspective competencies from her education to the game:

> Yes and there are probably some who have either died who may have been sacrificed. Back in the Viking Age or something like that. Perhaps someone is coming back from the dead or something weird like the thing he saw in his bedroom (pause). Maybe it's something quite concrete and we're just thinking too much about it. Maybe we are being too abstract?

In this next quote, Rita reflected on how the materials were connected. In elaborating on this, she applies information literacy acquired in her history study, and develop this interpretation of the story.

> Yes, we have begun to get some tasks in my study where you are handed fifteen sources and then you just have to figure out how it makes sense. It might be that the texts do not resemble each other and they might communicate completely different things. That was what I kept in the back of my mind when we analysed these texts (pause). Yeah, so it is a little reminiscent of that somehow.

As the players could not fully enter the game by establishing a framework for the game, they instead gradually engaged in co-creating narratives that could structure the events in the material they were engaging with in another way. As the examples show, the players used their own interests and knowledge – e.g. of the Roman god Jupiter – or competencies from their study programs to build these narratives. By co-creating these narratives through reflective inquiry, the players did not engage with the game as intended and their co-created narratives were not similar to the intended narrative of the game. By engaging with the game in this manner the players unintentionally broke down the game and started telling their own stories.

Example 2: Leaving the Game

Our next example focuses on how participation in an educational pervasive game may lead to unforeseen events that can turn into transformative player narratives. This example is based on earlier ethnographic field work conducted by one of the authors documenting a play session with the fully developed game *Tough Road*, which has been played several times at different Danish upper secondary schools (age 16–19) since its inception in 2010 (Ejsing-Duun, Hanghøj, & Karoff, 2013).

Tough Road is a pervasive game that mixes role-playing elements, storytelling and educational content. It is partially facilitated by a game master and partially by a digital game engine, which includes a computer simulation of financial markets, various functions for communication between players and the ability to keep track of the players' in-game transactions. *Tough Road* was developed by the small Danish organisation Coffee Road, which uses new media and communication strategies to engage people in the fight against global poverty. The educational aim of *Tough Road* is to provide players with a hands-on understanding of the complex dynamics of the global coffee trade.

The game is played as a whole day event at a school and involves between 75 and 200 players. At the start of the game, each player is provided with a character sheet that represents one of the following seven roles: farmer, trader, exporter, coffee brand company, café owner, banker or financial dealer. During game play, eight or more farmers from the same region are able to create cooperatives, which may offer them better prices when selling their coffee. The school is divided into different areas that correspond to the different roles – e.g. the farmers' villages, the banks or the financial market – and, based on their roles, the players can interact with one another in these different areas. In order to simulate the complexity of the global coffee trade, the game is supported by a digital game engine that keeps track of most of the transactions within the game. During the game, the game engine allows the game facilitators to trace the dynamic rise and fall of coffee prices, interest rates, company stocks and capital reserves. Due to the complexity of the game, it must be facilitated by several facilitators, which typically include a main game facilitator, a technical game facilitator and a handful of volunteers who have an interest in making students reflect on global trade. Prior to the game session the students' teachers at the participating schools are required to provide an introduction to global trade, as well as give a detailed introduction to the various game roles. The game unfolds over ten rounds and lasts a school day (6 or 7 hours). At the end of the game, the student who has made the relative largest increase (by percentage) in his or her assets is appointed the winner of the game.

FIGURE 10.3 Student making transactions in *Tough Road* that links the physical and virtual game economy.

Our focus here is on a particular game event from one of the game sessions that required the facilitators and players to negotiate the game frame itself and create a new player narrative that became known as "the failed cooperative". One of the main problems with this specific game session was a quite low student attendance of only 65 players. Consequently, there were insufficient farmers in the game to form cooperatives within each of the different global regions of the game scenario. As the game progressed, several farmers "died" from having insufficient money to pay their expenses – e.g. paying school fees for their children, buying condoms to prevent more children or acquiring new fields and harvesting crops. Moreover, it became clear to the farmers that their inability to form cooperatives due to the lack of players meant that they were cut off from getting the better prices for their coffee that they would have obtained by skipping the coffee traders in the game and trading directly with the exporters. One of the farmers, which we here will call Maria, was especially keen to form an international cooperative. She eventually persuaded the main game facilitator to form an unregistered international cooperative with 13 farmers across three different regions, which was not possible according to the game rules, while the game master tried to work out a solution with the "technical game facilitator", who was monitoring the game online.

The organisation of the interregional cooperative progressed for a couple of game rounds involving complicated workarounds for Maria, who creatively bypassed the game system by inventing new methods for analogue transactions between farmers and banks across different regions. During this process, several of the students playing bankers decided that the formation of the cooperative involved too much risk as it would lead to direct competition between the different banks as well as between their associated exporters and financial dealers. Eventually, Maria's affiliated bank decided her actions were foul play and terminated her account due to an insufficient balance, which then killed her character in the game. A few seconds later, Maria received a text message on her phone stating that her farmer character had died from AIDS as she was unable to pay for her medicine. Maria got quite frustrated at learning of her untimely death and asked the game facilitator to get her back into the game. In reply, the game facilitator insisted that since the cooperative had not been registered within the game system, it did not really exist and consequently had to be dissolved. Shortly after the incident, the game facilitator wrote and distributed a text message to all the players in the game that summed up and recategorised the event as a part of the overall game narrative and thus allowed players to associate the incident with the game and its learning goals:

> The cooperative that failed
> In spite of a foresighted farmer's vision for [creating] a cooperative, it proved impossible to create a cooperative across national borders. It is a blow against unions across the world. The farmer died in mysterious circumstances.

In spite of her initial frustration with her character being killed, Maria was able to reflect quite positively on her unexpected exit from the game, saying that "sometimes things simply must go wrong". She found it exciting to collaborate with other farmers in order to raise the coffee price, which helped those farmers that "were in a totally hopeless situation". Overall, she seemed to enjoy her attempt to create a global co-operative. After the game ended, the event was highlighted by the game facilitator, who prepared a speech that summed up the events by ironically telling a "nice story" about "all those things that went wrong today". In this way, the story of the "the failed cooperative" was recategorised as a key event in the facilitator's and the other players' collaborative narrative of this particular game session.

This example shows how pushing the boundaries of a pervasive game can create unforeseen game events that then feed back into the collaborative experience of the game. The facilitator first allowed Maria to explore and even transform the limits of the game; later, he reconceptualised the episode as a part of the game as it related to the learning goals of the game, that is, understanding how cooperatives work in a complex global economy.

The example of "the failed cooperative" shows how the facilitation of pervasive games in formal learning contexts can be bound up with dilemmas related to players' transgressions of flexible game rules. On the one hand, Maria's enthusiasm was clearly valuable to the game facilitator both because it let interesting narratives emerge from the game interaction and because it created awareness about how farmers may be empowered by forming cooperatives, which was one of the overall learning goals of the game. On the other hand, the game facilitator faced the technical constraints of the game engine, which prevented the formation of an international cooperative across different regions and banks. Moreover, his acceptance of Maria's international cooperative as an "illegal" solution within the game generated a cascade effect of new problems that emerged within the game system. The system did not embrace Maria's attempt to transform the rules of the conceptual space. This points to another learning goal of the game: teaching students that there are limitations to the influence of individual actors on the global coffee market chain.

The ambiguity surrounding the flexible rules illustrates an important premise about the facilitation of the *Tough Road* pervasive game. Namely, that no one – not even the game facilitator or the technical game facilitator – had a full overview of the unexpected events that can emerge from game sessions. One of the teachers, who acted as a co-facilitator, even described the game as a "monster" as no one had a clear idea of where the game would end. However, this teacher valued the chaotic and unpredictable aspects of the game as they forced students into unknown territory, which was difficult to achieve through more traditional forms of teaching.

Discussion

Our analysis of two pervasive games going wrong shows why the design and facilitation of pervasive games need to focus on players having agency and being independent as they interact with a game. The breakdown of pervasive games can develop into situations where players act upon their agency in such a way that it challenges the boundaries of the game. Such situations are present in our examples: in the first example when players did not understand the premise of the game they began scripting their own narrative; in the second example when there were not enough players for the game to work in the designed manner players challenged the boundaries of the game system itself. Though it is in the nature of pervasive games to challenge spatial, social and temporal dimensions of play, pervasive games still need boundaries such as rules to help players understand how the game works (Hinske, Lampe, Magerkurth, & Röcker, 2007). Understanding games as narratives and interpreting player narratives as valuable assets in the process of facilitating and designing games opens up the possibility for pervasive games to be transformative experiences as well as learning opportunities.

In the first case the players framed and reframed the game events by telling their own stories rather than following the designed game narrative. As the game framing broke down, they used their individual knowledge, experience and interests to fuel a process of reflective and collaborative inquiry through their own co-created player narratives. This process points to an important potential for game designers to adapt unfinished games to include player narratives. By adopting a process of co-created narratives with players, an ARG could be made easier to play for novice players with insufficient game literacy.

In the second case there was also a co-creative process between players, the game system and the game facilitator. As the game evolved into an enormous and complex monster, which no one was able fully to grasp, the boundaries of the game narrative were challenged as one of the players creatively tried to transform the game system to her own aims. One of facilitators tried to overcome this challenge by flexibly interpreting the player transgression not so much as a break or interruption in the game narrative, but rather as an opportunity to reframe the collaborative game experience in relation to specific learning goals. Reframing the game narrative in response to a transgressing player's narrative enabled a transformative experience to emerge.

Conclusion

In this chapter we have looked at two examples and have analysed how the design and use of pervasive games enables players to construct narratives through framing and reframing their game experiences. We have showed how players' meaning-making processes and reflections could both be important when players try to enter the mysterious world of a pervasive game, as in the first case, and when players are faced with overwhelming in-game challenges that force them to leave a pervasive game, as in the second case. In this way, we find that pervasive games may empower players through a strong sense of agency by giving them the ability to construct their own player narratives. In both examples these player narratives did not always resonate with the designed game narratives, and this conflict may have initially been problematic for the players, game designers and facilitators. However, by embracing player narratives that challenge the game narrative with either flexible facilitation or openness to a co-creative design process, pervasive games may allow players to acquire agency, transformative experiences and learning opportunities.

References

Ardito, C., Lanzilotti, R., Raptis, D., Sintoris, C., Yiannoutsou, N., Avouris, N., & Costabile, M. F. (2011). Designing pervasive games for learning. DUXU 2011. In *Lecture notes in computer science* (pp. 99–108). Berlin: Springer. https://doi.org/10.1007/978-3-642-21708-1_12

Bonsignore, E., Hansen, D., Kraus, K., Visconti, A., & Fraistat, A. (2016, October 15). *Roles People Play. Proceedings of the 2016 Annual Symposium on Computer-Human Interaction in Play. CHI PLAY '16: The annual symposium on Computer-Human Interaction in Play.* https://doi.org/10.1145/2967934.2968108

Bruner, J. (1991). The narrative construction of reality. *Critical Inquiry, 18*(1), 1–21. https://doi.org/10.1086/448619

Dewey, J. (1933). *How we think: A restatement of the relation of reflective thinking to the educative process.* Boston, MA: D.C. Heath & Co Publishers.

Ejsing-Duun, S., Hanghøj, T., & Karoff, H. S. (2013). *Cheating and creativity in pervasive games in learning contexts. Proceedings of The 7th European Conference on Games Based Learning*, pp. 149–156. Academic Conferences and Publishing International.

Evans, E., Flintham, M., & Martindale, S. (2014). The malthusian paradox: Performance in an alternate reality game. *Personal and Ubiquitous Computing, 18*(7), 1567–1582. https://doi.org/10.1007/s00779-014-0762-7

Fine, G. (1983). *Shared fantasy: Role playing as social worlds.* Chicago, IL: University of Chicago Press.

Goffman E. (1974). *Frame analysis: An essay on the organization of experience.* Cambridge, MA: Harvard University Press.

Gurzick, D., White, K. F., Lutters, W. G., Landry, B. M., Dombrowski, C., & Kim, J.Y. (2011). *Designing the future of collaborative workplace systems. Proceedings of the 2011 iConference on - iConference '11. the 2011 iConference.* https://doi.org/10.1145/1940761.1940785, 174–180

Hinske, S., Lampe, M., Magerkurth, C., & Röcker, C. (2007). Classifying pervasive games: On pervasive computing and mixed reality. Concepts and Technologies for Pervasive Games - A Reader for Pervasive Gaming Research, 1.

Jenkins, H. (2004). Game design as narrative architecture. In N. Wardrip-Fruin & P. Harrigan (Eds.), *First person: New media as story, performance, and game*. Cambridge, MA: MIT Press.

Kittl, C., & Petrovic, O. (2008). *Pervasive games for education. Proceedings of the 2008 Euro American Conference on Telematics and Information Systems - EATIS '08*. the 2008 Euro American Conference. https://doi.org/10.1145/1621087.1621093

Montola, M., Stenros, J., Wærn, A., & International Game Developers Association. (2009). *Pervasive games: Theory and design*. Burlington, MA: Morgan Kaufmann Publishers.

Muscat, M. (2013). *Blackgammon: A grounded participatory design of a preconception health promotion 'alternate reality game' for adolescent indigenous Australian women. CHI '13 Extended Abstracts on Human Factors in Computing Systems on - CHI EA '13*, 1949–1952. https://doi.org/10.1145/2468356.2468708

Rodgers, C. (2002). Defining Reflection: Another look at John Dewey and reflective thinking. *Teachers College Record*, *104*(4), 842–866. https://doi.org/10.1111/1467-9620.00181

Schmitz, B, Klemke, R., & Specht, M. (2012). Effects of mobile gaming patterns on learning outcomes: A literature review. *International Journal of Technology Enhanced Learning*, *4*(5/6), 345–358

Watson, J. (2012). *Reality ends here: Environmental game design and participatory spectacle*. University of Southern California Libraries. http://digitallibrary.usc.edu/cdm/ref/collection/p15799coll3/id/87218

11

VIRTUAL REALITY LEARNING EXPERIENCES ABOUT DEMENTIA

Anders Kalsgaard Møller and Markus Löchtefeld

Introduction

The increase in life expectancy and the demographic shift towards more senior citizens have resulted in a higher prevalence in age-related health issues. One such issue is the increasing number of people with dementia. Today approximately 50 million people are suffering from dementia and this number is expected to increase to over 130 million people in 2050 (Alzheimer's Diesease International, 2019). People with dementia have a brain disorder that affects their ability to remember things, think clearly, communicate with others and take care of themselves. In addition, the illness can change peoples' personality and behaviour (Alzheimer's Society, 2018).

It is often partners or children of the person with dementia who are taking up the role as the primary caregiver. As they most often don't have any formal education or experience in healthcare, they are usually referred to as informal caregivers. The swift change in the role from family to an informal caregiver can be both difficult and painful. They must cope with the potential changes in behaviour and personality of the person with dementia and at the same time, they must accommodate their own life to provide the necessary care for the person with dementia. This can be very frustrating and can eventually lead to mental illnesses such as stress and depression (Brodaty and Donkin, 2009). Providing the informal caregivers with more information and guidance about dementia at an early stage of the condition seems to help the informal caregiver to become less prone to physical, as well as psychological diseases (Cooper et al., 2007).

Tom Kitwood (1997) has developed a person-centred care approach, which differs from a strictly medical approach, by focusing on understanding the unique person, his or hers needs and challenges. Often the informal caregiver don't understand the sudden change in behaviour and the cognitive limitations as a consequence of the disease. This new situation can be both stressful and frustrating for the informal caregiver, something that might enhance negative emotions towards the person with dementia. Therefore, one way of improving the understanding and the empathy for the person with dementia, is by simulating those symptoms and feelings that the person with dementia experience.

In this chapter, we present and discuss different approaches to use Virtual Reality (VR) to inform informal caregivers about dementia, what it is and how it affects the person with the illness. We will also compare different approaches and derive a set of recommendations for using VR as part of the dementia care training.

Related Work

Both formal training, and internet courses that combine general information with specific caregiver strategies, have proven successful in helping people in their role as caregivers (Boots et al., 2014; Cooper et al., 2007). Simulating the cognitive and perceptual difficulties faced by people with dementia have proven to help caregivers to gain a better understanding of the challenges people with dementia face every day (Hayhurst, 2018) and helps with improving dementia-friendly characteristics (Julia et al., 2018).

There have been various attempts to show how people with dementia experience the world around them, e.g. by using low-tech solutions such as earphones playing white noise or glasses and gloves to simulate age-related impairments (Beville, 2002). This approach typically requires an equipment and an instructor visiting the caregiver or the caregiver visiting an instructor.

Lately, VR has proven to be a useful tool to support learning (Merchant et al., 2014) and applications such as VR, Augmented reality and 360° video has been used in various dementia applications to help people understand and experience dementia symptoms and the frustrations that follows the symptoms (Adefila et al., 2016; Alzheimer's Research UK, 2018; Hattink et al., 2015; Hayhurst, 2018; Wijma et al., 2018).

"Into D'mentia" (Hattink et al., 2015) is a transportable installation housed in a container. The installation uses augmented elements to give people an insight in the life of people living with dementia. After the experience the visitors have a debriefing session with an expert followed by a group session where the visitors can share their experience with others. One of the constrains of "Into D'mentia" is that the container has a limited capacity of 16 visitors per day making it a rather expensive solution (Hattink et al., 2015).

Utilising the idea of "Into D'mentia" Wijma et al. (2018) have developed a 360° interactive video named "Through the D'mentia Lens" that were combined with an e-course with the purpose of enhancing the understanding and empathy of caregivers. The evaluation showed an improvement in the participants' empathy and confidence in caring for the person with dementia. A walk through dementia is a similar application that combines information about dementia with 360° interactive stories that can be played from a smartphone (Alzheimer's Research UK, 2018).

Another VR experience is the "myShoes" (Adefila et al., 2016) where the participants enter a self-contained flat resembling a residential home. The participants are encouraged to carry out everyday tasks while simulating dementia- and age-related symptoms such as confusion and glaucoma. The evaluations showed an improvement in the participants' empathy towards the people with dementia.

The development of the latest VR applications has, at large, shown a potential to aid informal caregivers and other relatives to understand, and relate to, people with dementia. In this chapter we will explore this topic further, starting with two different virtual experiences and approaches developed at Aalborg University.

The Game Designs

To develop the two VR applications, we have worked closely with a former dementia nurse who now co-ordinates an organisation (Videnscenter for Demens) in the municipality. She gives guidance in questions related to dementia and teach courses for relatives as well as dementia advisors. We consider the person as an expert in dementia as well as to disseminate knowledge about the dementia.

The Grocery Shop Game

One of the scenarios of the smartphone application – a walk through dementia (Alzheimer's Research UK, 2018) – inspired the first game.[1] The target person is anyone who wants to know more about dementia. The scene plays out in

FIGURE 11.1   Overview of the grocery shop.

FIGURE 11.2 Images showing the symptoms. To the left the default layout, in the middle the double vision and to the right loss of colour contrast (colour saturation is decreased).

a grocery shop, and in the game the player takes up the role as a person with dementia from a first-person view. The objective of the game is to collect different groceries that appear on a shopping list.

In the game the player can move around by clicking on the spot they want to move to using the controllers. The groceries are placed on shelves in the shop indicated by blue cubes (see Figure 11.1). The next grocery on the list is indicated by a red cube.

As the player picks up the different groceries on the list, different symptoms associated with dementia gradually appear. These symptoms include the layout of the grocery store that is changing to show symptoms of memory loss and disorientation. During the game the player will gradually lose colour contrast and starts to see double making it extremely hard to read the items on the shopping list. Furthermore, the sounds in the store would gradually be distorted creating a blurred and stressful soundscape like what some people with dementia experience. Examples of how the symptoms appear is shown in Figure 11.2.

The game finishes after the players have found all the groceries and have found the exit to the grocery shop. This game was evaluated by 13 test subjects and the expert (the nurse mentioned above). In the evaluation the expert emphasised that the memory loss, double vision and loss of colour contrast all appeared to have the desired outcome, stressing and frustrating the user. By playing the game, people not living with dementia could gain an insight into what people with dementia experiences. These findings were supported by comments from the test subjects who expressed frustrations towards the symptoms while playing the game.

The House Game

While the first game could be played by anyone interested in knowing more about dementia, the second game[2] had the informal caregivers as the primary target group. In the game the player could move around by clicking on the spot they wanted to move to. Also in this game the player experiences dementia seen from a first-person perspective. The scene takes place in the house of a person with dementia, focusing on two different stories: the cup scenario and the distraction scenario.

The two stories involve a non-player character (NPC). The NPC represents a daughter to the person with dementia, who is also an informal caregiver. In the game the player starts in a hallway where he/she can enter the two scenarios by entering one of the two doors. The hallway is presented in Figure 11.3. In the

FIGURE 11.3 The hallway from which the player can enter the two scenarios. The posters on the wall contain information about dementia.

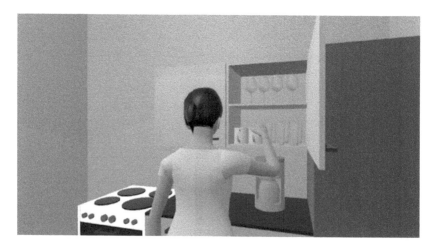

FIGURE 11.4 Images of the NPC retrieving the cup after the player failed to do so.

hallway the player could also go read the posters on the wall. The posters held information about dementia.

The Cup Scenario

In the beginning of the cup scenario the relative asks the player to bring her a cup. This cup scenario is used to show how difficult it can be for people with dementia to carry out everyday tasks such as locating objects cupboards or drawer and the frustrations that comes with it. The player's task is to locate the cup. However, due to the design of the game, the player will not be able to find it. In the end the NPC will find the cup by herself, being clearly frustrated about the players inability to locate the cup. An image from the cup scenario is presented in Figure 11.4.

Distraction Scenario

The distraction scenario starts with the NPC trying to have a conversation with the player. Meanwhile, the player gets disturbed by the increasing volume of the television and the light dimming. Consequently, the player is not able to concentrate on what the NPC is saying, followed by the NPC becoming very frustrated. The distraction scenario is used to show how people with dementia can have troubles with handling too many stimuli. Just like in the cup scenario it shows how the frustrations of the caregiver impact the person with dementia (see Figure 11.5).

After completing the two scenarios a new window appears with a debriefing session where the player's experiences in the previous scenarios are elaborated. In this case, 29 test subjects evaluated the application. The responses from evaluation

FIGURE 11.5 Image from the distraction scenario while the NPC talks increase the volume of the TV and the light dim to simulate how a person with dementia could experience to be distracted by different stimuli.

indicated that the game was an effective way to communicate the symptoms of dementia and the participants felt the game had increased their knowledge about dementia.

Comparison between the Two Game Designs

While having similar approaches, the two games differ in how they present different symptoms and frustrations. In the grocery shop game, the focus was on the player's experience of the symptoms of dementia, while the focus in the house game was on showing how difficult it is for a person with dementia to carry out everyday tasks – and how frustrating it might be when the caregiver gets upset about you. However, both approaches seem to be useful tools to evoke empathy towards the person with dementia, as well as helping the caregivers to better understand the person they care for.

According to the flow theory (Fullerton, 2008), a game can become too frustrating if the goal is too hard to achieve for the player. Therefore, game designer tries to balance the level between on the one hand being too boring and on the other hand being too frustrating. In the first case, we wanted the participants to feel frustrated with his/her inability to succeed, which also led to difficulties to complete the tasks.. In the house game, the tasks were deliberately designed in such a way that they could not be completed.

According to Kitwood (1997), it is important for the caregiver to be psychologically present without distractions from surroundings or disturbances from within, as giving "free attention". However, often enough people's own emotional baggage intervenes, and hinders, such a "free attention".

Another difference between the two games was that the grocery shop game included an in-game tutorial that helped the players to get started, while in the house game this was explained manually. The house game on the other hand included a debriefing session, which was done offline by a facilitator in the grocery shop game. The debriefing session was used to help the participants to make sense of what they had experienced. Other applications have also made use of a narrator for the same purpose (like Alzheimer's Research UK, 2018). Both approaches could thus minimise the risk of the caregiver feeling guilty about their relation to the person with dementia by building the tutorial and debriefing into the game. It would be possible for people to play the game on their own without the involvement of an instructor.

In terms of gameplay and graphical rendering it could be argued that the two games are rather simple, this does however not seem to affect the purpose of showing what a person with dementia experience. As explained by the dementia expert it is not about how accurately the symptoms are portrayed, rather the outcome showing how a person with dementia could get frustrated during daily activities. It is therefore possible with relatively simple means to create a useful scenario. The graphic rendering and gameplay may affect some people's inclination to use the application, something we could not go deeper into here.

VR and Learning Objectives

The learning objectives could be divided into three different categories: the first one concerns knowledge about dementia, i.e. what dementia is and how it affects a person, what kind of symptoms they experience and how it affects emotion and cognitive abilities; the second category involves strategies that help the informal caregivers with how to provide the right care and deal with specific situations; and the third category involves therapy sessions, which help the informal caregiver to handle their own emotional "baggage" (Kitwood, 1997).

Most of the available VR applications today, including the two presented in this chapter, mainly address the first objective that involves knowledge and symptoms of dementia (Adefila et al., 2016; Alzheimer's Research UK, 2018; Hattink et al., 2015; Wijma et al., 2018). Instead of just *explaining* the symptoms and frustrations related to dementia, the virtual games also *show* the symptoms and allows for *experiencing* both how the world appears for a person with dementia, and how the surrounding environment reacts to this.

While most of the applications today are concerned with the first objective we also see a potential for using VR scenarios with the purpose of showing how caregivers can apply certain strategies to deal with specific situations. The combination of VR applications with formal training and therapy sessions could lead to more knowledge and a better understanding of the person with dementia, increase the empathy and provide the necessary care strategies to improve the care. Doing so would improve the situation for both the person with dementia and the informal caregiver. And, probably, in a near future, we might also see telepresence consultancy addressing the third objective.

Conclusion and Prospects for the Future

In this chapter we have given examples of how VR experiences can be used to help relatives/informal caregivers to improve their understanding of a person with dementia. VR applications have proven useful as it allows us to show the symptoms of dementia, as well as how people in the surrounding environment may react to these disturbances, and thereby help the relatives to both understand and relate to people with dementia. VR games and applications may in the future be integrated into different courses and learning programs, targeting both informal caregivers and the general population. So far we have demonstrated some possible ways to use contemporary technology, which gives some insights for the future development of technology-enhanced learning.

Notes

1 The game is developed using the Unity game engine and uses the HTC Vive VR Head-mounted display system.
2 The second game was also developed using the Unity game engine and using the HTC Vive VR Head-mounted display. For the VR aspect of the game, Steam VR and ViR Toolkit were used and the 3D models were created using Autodesk Maya. The work related to the game and evaluation has previously been presented in (Jensen et al., 2018).

References

Adefila, A., Graham, S., Clouder, L., & Ball, B. P. (2016). MyShoes - the future of experiential dementia training? *The Journal of Mental Health Training, Education, and Practice Brighton. 11*(2), 91–101.

Alzheimer's Research UK (2018). *Virtual Reality app offers unique glimpse into life with dementia*. Retrieved from http://www.alzheimersresearchuk.org/a-walk-through-dementia-news/ accessed May 23, 2018.

Alzheimer's Society (2018). *What is dementia?* https://www.alzheimers.org.uk/info/20007/types_of_dementia/1/what_is_dementia, Accessed May 30, 2018.

Alzheimer's Diesease International (2019). *Dementia statistics*, https://www.alz.co.uk/ Accessed May 19, 2018.

Beville, P. K. (2002). Virtual dementia tour helps sensitize healthcare providers. *American Journal of Alzheimer's Disease and Other Dementias, 17*(3), 183–190.

Boots, L., de Vugt, M., van Knippenberg, R., Kempen, G., & Verhey, F. R. (2014). A systematic review of internet-based supportive interventions for caregivers of patients with dementia. *International Journal of Geriatric Psychiatry, 29*(4), 331–344

Brodaty, H., & Donkin, M. (2009). Family caregivers of people with dementia. *Dialogues in Clinical Neuroscience, 11*(2) 217.

Cooper, C., Balamurali, T., Selwood, A., & Livingston, G. (2007). A systematic review of intervention studies about anxiety in caregivers of people with dementia. *International Journal of Geriatric Psychiatry 22*(3), 181–188.

Fullerton, T. (2008). *Game design workshop: A playcentric approach to creating innovative games.* Hoboken, NJ: Taylor & Francis Group.

Hattink, B. J., Meiland, F. J., Campman, C. A., Rietsema, J., Sitskoorn, M., & Dröes, R. M. (2015). Experiencing dementia: Evaluation of Into D'mentia. *Tijdschrift voor Gerontologie en Geriatrie, 46*(5), 262–281.

Hayhurst, J. (2018). *How augmented reality and virtual reality is being used to support people living with dementia design challenges and future directions* (pp. 295–305). Cham: Springer International Publishing, https://doi.org/10.1007/978-3-319-64027-3

Jensen, J. M., Hageman, M., Lausen, P. B. L., Møller, A. K., & Löchtefeld, M. (2018). *Informing Informal Caregivers about Dementia through an experience-based Virtual Reality Game, 3rd International Conference on Smart Learning Ecosystem and Regional Development - The interplay of data, technology, place and people*, Aalborg.

Julia, F.-M., Gilmartin-Thomas, J. M., Powell, A., Malone, D. T., Larson, I. C., O'Reilly, C. L., Kirkpatrick, C. M., Kipen, E., Petrovich, T., Ryan-Atwood, T. E., & Bell, J. S. (2018). Qualitative evaluation of how a virtual dementia experience impacts medical and pharmacy students' self-reported knowledge and attitudes towards people with dementia. *Dementia (London), 19*, 205–220.

Kitwood, T. (1997). *Dementia reconsidered – The person comes first.* Buckingham & Philadelphia: Open University Press.

Merchant, Z., Goetz, E. T., Cifuentes, L., Keeney-Kennicutt, W., Davis, T. J. (2014). Effectiveness of virtual reality-based instruction on students' learning outcomes in k-12 and higher education: A meta-analysis. *Computers & Education, 70,* 29–40.

Wijma, E. M., Veerbeek, M. A., Prins, M., Pot, A. M., and Willemse, B. M. (2018) A virtual reality intervention to improve the understanding and empathy for people with dementia in informal caregivers: Results of a pilot study. *Aging & Mental Health, 22*(9), 1121–1129.

12

CHILDREN'S PROGRAMMING OF ROBOTS BY DESIGNING FAIRYTALES

Eva Brooks and Jeanette Sjöberg

What is fantastic about today is that there is no one or two ways to go. Now things are more interesting in that they are completely open, and people do not have to restrain their imagination. For how can you restrain imagination?.

Irvine Arditti – Violinist and founder of the Arditti Quartet

Introduction

Through the lens of Vygotsky's theory on imagination and creativity, this chapter investigates children's programming of robots framed by fairy-tale designs. By foregrounding imagination and creativity, children's interest in programming are promoted and thus is expected to increase their knowledge within this area. In order to gain an understanding of this, we carried out a cross-case study on robot-supported learning using different educational robots, including Ozobot, Bee Bot/Blue Bot, Dash and Dot and KUBO. The study included ten different workshops with, in total, 300 children between 6–9 years of age: two 1st grade classes (6–7 years of age), four 2nd grade classes (7–8 years of age) and four 3rd grade classes (8–9 years of age) participated. Each school class of children worked in groups of 4–5 children in each group, resulting in six groups within each school class. The study was carried out in November 2017 and March 2018. The workshops took place in a school context and the children were challenged to work with programming activities using creative material, including a fairy-tale theme. In the empirical examples outlined in coming sections of this chapter, the two groups of children have worked with Ozobot robots. An Ozobot is a versatile robot designed to enhance interest in programming and thus suitable for STEM education (Science, Technology, Engineering, Mathematics).

The general idea for the children was to, in their groups, interpret a fairy tale and use different creative material to conceptualize and reproduce the story, using programming. The fairy tales were selected by the researchers beforehand and consisted of classical fairy tales, such as H.C Andersen's "The Little Match Girl" and European folklore "Little Red Riding Hood". In this chapter, the empirical material focuses on two groups of 3rd graders (one group consisted of three girls and a boy, and the other group included two boys and a girl) addressing the classical fairy tale of *What the old man does is always right* by H. C. Andersen. In the examples presented here, the Ozobots have been part of the material that the children used in the making of fairy tales. The coding was carried out analogously with different coloured sharpies. Other props consisted of creative material such as foam clay, modelling clay, crayons, markers, LEGO, cardboard, paper, yarn, glue, tape, scissors and post-its (see Figure 12.1).

Even though robotics is gaining increased popularity in the educational fields, the focus when introduced in the classroom is narrow and traditionally task-based approaches rather than grand explorations into unknown territories, or "forbidden seas" as Melville (1851/2003) puts it. The longing for these forbidden seas are elements in epic tales and classics, and a way to enter these territories is by introducing storytelling, music or arts to create different modes of engagement and exploration of available materials (Rusk, Resnick, Berg, & Pezalla-Granlund, 2007). The combination of craft and mechanical materials "can inspire both girls and boys to think more creatively about what is possible and what they

FIGURE 12.1 Coding scheme and coding sharpies (bottom), foam clay and LEGO creations together with code lines (top).

want to create" (Rusk et al., 2007, p. 61). Children naturally explore the material world through hands-on activities, where physical properties of materials afford them to expand and intensify meanings of what they want to create.

A strong reason why interest in computer programming and coding in school has increased recently relates to research showing that students who have experience in programming and coding have superior problem-solving skills and higher order thinking (Blackley & Howell, 2019). These are qualities that are desirable in a school context, which is why the realisation of potentials lie in activities that favour such skills appear. In addition to programming and coding, robots are increasingly used in teaching and learning activities, often referred to as educational robots (Barreto & Benitti, 2012). There is, e.g. an expanding attention for the usage of educational robotics as support for science activities (Komis & Misirli, 2016). However, the introduction of robots in a traditional school context is not completely without friction, but rather a challenging task (Mondada et al., 2017). An aspect of this has to do with the fact that the majority of contemporary educational robotic activities do not entirely meet formal educational requirements, but rather solely exploit the technical innovation (ibid.). Thus, just adding robots to a teaching situation in order to show the technicalities without any higher pedagogical aim, makes it difficult to tie robot activities to general educational goals. Consequently, other approaches have been adopted for the introduction of robots in school settings, where, e.g., research points to the benefits of using children's creativity in these contexts (cf. Barreto & Benitti, 2012).

Hence, in this chapter, we discuss how children creatively express themselves through programming activities with robots. In doing so, we draw on Vygotsky's concepts of imagination and creativity to argue the case that programming embraces *imaginative* and *emotional* interactions, which children learn within creative activities. This is how we try not to restrain imagination as Arditti puts it in the initial quote of this chapter.

We start by discussing these terms, followed by examples from an empirical study of children's learning of programming through representation of fairy tales.

Creativity and Imagination in Programming

How is it that programming can find its way to children's imagination and emotions? To find out, we begin with examining what *imagination* and *creativity* can be. Vygotsky (1993/2004, pp. 9–10) suggests that:

> /.../ imagination, as the basis of all creative activity, is an important component of absolutely all aspects of cultural life, enabling artistic, scientific, and technical creation alike. In this sense, absolutely everything around us that was created by the hand of man, the entire world of human culture, as distinct from the world of nature, all this is the product of human imagination and of creation based on this imagination.

There are difficulties in discussing creativity. Some people come to the subject of creativity with a belief that it is a mysterious and subjective topic, which is not possible to capture with scientific methods. With this view, we cannot define the term creativity or coherently discuss or study creative acts. Other people come to the discussion of creativity with the belief that even if we can define and study creativity, there is no meaning in doing so, as creativity emerges from particular personal characteristics. In this view, the people that show or present creative productions are equipped with gifts that ordinary people do not have. Aligned, then, is the view that creativity and imagination primarily are based on mental processes rather than being part of a concrete world. However, Vygotsky (1930/2004) explained that creative activity is based on an ability of the brain to combine elements in the form of imaginative actions. Also, he underlines that creativity is not isolated from our daily experiences, but is part of all areas of life and involves our daily activities whenever a person imagines, combines and creates something new. As such, imagination is a complex process that depends on experiences, where previous experiences are expressed through a creative reworking of acquired impressions combined to construct a new reality. This combinational act, to combine the old in new ways, constitutes a basis of creativity as an essential part of a social life. In their book *Vygotsky and Creativity*, Connery, John-Steiner, and Marjanovic-Shane (2010) present contemporary studies on creativity by applying Vygotsky's conceptualisation of imagination and creativity. They describe his notion of creativity as a profoundly social and transformative activity, where emotion and meaning are synthesised. This is what lies at the heart of a sociocultural conceptualisation of imagination, namely an understanding that learning and development cannot be separated from its social context, and learning is mediated through interactions with cultural tools and symbol systems (Vygotsky, 1978).

This intertwined and complex relationship between reality and imagination is the cornerstone of Vygotsky's four laws of imagination (Vygotsky, 1930/2004). The first law proposed that creative outcomes of imagination always are based on elements taken from reality, from a child's life experiences. The richer the variety of the experiences, the richer becomes the imaginative material that we as individuals have access to. Accordingly, imagination, and the creative activity associated with it, emerges by using materials supplied by reality. When the children in the present case study listened to classical fairy tales like "What the old man does is always right" by Hans Christian Andersen or the Grimm's version of "Little Red Riding Hood", they were engaged and could refer to elements of the story in their interpretations. Features such as horse, cow, apples, wolf, woods and house all exist in reality and the children could follow the storyline based on such concrete interpretations. However, wolves cannot talk and the trades that the old man did would not likely happen in reality, which is what Vygotsky referred to, when stating that it is the combination of different components from previous experiences that can create something new. So, the children's experience of, e.g. walking in the woods or eating apples gives the know-how for them to associate with the wolf or the old man's doings: "Every act of imagination starts with this accumulation of experience" (Vygotsky, 1930/2004, p. 15). The implication of this for learning to programme is the essential of building a foundation for the child's creativity and to broaden the experiences that are provided to the child.

The second law proposed by Vygotsky involves a more complex association between the imagination and real phenomenon by suggesting that imagination can expand reality. In other words, this law states that experience is based on imagination. This means that imagination is a way for children to get to know the world. For example, through books, fairy tales and images, they can learn about events or places that they have not experienced. With this, Vygotsky's (1930/2004) point is that imagination allows for an expansion of experiences informed upon experiences of others. Relating this to our study means that the children did not need to have experienced how the old man rode off to the market in town to sell his horse and how he, along the way, met different people and exchanged his horse for a cow and the cow for a sheep, and so on, to make sense of how he ended up with a basket of rotten apples. Through listening to the research assistant's explanation of the fairy tale as well as discussing with her about how a marketplace functions and about what can be the foundation of the choices people make when bartering things, the children could draw upon these mediated experiences to imagine how the issue of selling the horse by the end was bartered to a basket of rotten apples (Figure 12.2). In programming activities it is not always possible to directly observe the concepts, e.g. a line of red, green and blue colour together make up a code for Ozobot. So, the children have to

FIGURE 12.2 Children reading and talking about the fairy tale.

imagine this concept, which implies that without imagination, it is difficult to think about programming concepts.

Vygotsky's third law involves an emotional association between imagination and reality. Here, imagination is linked to a world-related (real) emotional life. Emotions are part of reality and therefore can influence the imagination, meaning that every experience has an image corresponding to it. "Emotions thus possess a kind of capacity to select impressions, thoughts, and images that resonate with the mood that possesses us at a particular moment in time" (Vygotsky, 1930/2004, pp. 17–18). For example, when the children listened to Linda (the research assistant) reading the fairy tale about "What the old man does is always right", one of the boys was bodily engaged, crawling up on the table, smilingly mimicking and gesturing to the other children. In doing so, he engaged emotions when he listened to the fairy tale as this resonated with experiences he has had or, in terms of Vygotsky, as if it was a real-life happening. However, in his writings, Vygotsky (1930/2004) pointed to a specific feature of this law, namely the double and mutual dependence between imagination and emotional experiences. So, while, as the above-mentioned quote states, emotions influence imagination, thus, imagination can, in other cases, influence emotion. This means that constructs, let us say in the form of images, that are linked with an emotion are often combined together to create an emotive image. Hence, what a person can imagine can have a real effect on his or her emotions, that is when a person laughs, cries or becomes anxious. Even if this image does not in itself correspond to reality, the emotions it evokes are feelings the person truly experiences. For example, when Emily and Anna in the below-mentioned vignette (Vignette 1), pointed to the old man's pathway to the marketplace and pointed out that it needed some flowers and shrubs on the side to look more like in the countryside. The image of how it looks in the countryside was created by the girls' imagination. In terms of Vygotsky (1930/2004), the image the girls created was not real, but their experience of it was a true one. What does this mean for the matter of programming? The examples show, among other things, that an expansion and reconstruction of emotions can offer a foundation for learning.

The fourth and last type of association between imagination and reality states that imagination becomes reality, meaning that imagination enables constructions in the real world. So, when an imaginary image has been given a material form, it becomes real. Vygotsky (1930/2004, p. 21) explained this: "Finally, once they were given material form, they returned to reality, but returned as a new active force with the potential to alter that reality. This is the complete cycle followed by the creative operation of the imagination". In the programming activity, the children should, by the end of it, present for the other children and for their teachers, their coded retelling or, representation, of the fairy tale. It would be possible to say that this representation, or retelling, took an iterative pathway, where the ingredients of the fairy tale as well as of the coding of Ozobot underwent a complex reworking ending up in the form of a material product of the children's imagination. This suggests that a full circle completed by imagination includes both a cognitive and an emotional dimension, both equally necessary for learning and development.

While Bodrova and Leong (2006) described imagination as a generative mental activity that allows children to create new ways of thinking, we point to environmental considerations in which creative doings are encouraged. By this we mean that it is crucial to provide children with opportunities to explore and experience new things, to draw upon the experiences of others, and, importantly, to offer them opportunities to create with their hands to, in this way, embody their imaginative thoughts. Referring to Vygotsky (1930/2004, p. 88), this constitutes a foundation for becoming creative: "The development of a creative individual, one that strives for the future, is enabled by creative imagination embodied in the present". We draw on this to argue the case that learning programming by means of creativity is a highly imaginative and emotional activity. Next, we exemplify this through an empirical case study.

Case Study: Learning to Programme through Fairytales

In the workshops where the empirical data for this chapter is gathered, the two groups of children were encouraged to interpret and materialise the classical fairy tale of *What the old man does is always right* by H. C. Andersen, assigning Ozobots to represent characters in the fairy tale. In this fairy tale, the plot is set in motion when the farmer's (the old man) wife tells him to exchange their horse for something more useful. But which should they do, sell or trade? "You'll know what's best, Father," said the wife. "It's market day. Come on, ride off to town, and get money for the horse, or make a good bargain with it. Whatever you do is always right; so be off for the market"! Each time the farmer encounters someone on the road with a different animal, he stops and thinks how much better their animal is than his. After a series of trades, the farmer ends up with a bag of rotten apples. People make a bet that the farmer's wife will be angry when he comes home with the rotten fruit. But, despite this, he gets a kiss from his wife when he is back home again. The message of the fairy tale is that it is the thought that counts.

The size of an Ozobot is at par with a golf ball and it can be programmed both analogously and digitally; using colour codes on paper with sharpies, in apps on iPad or using block programming in web browsers on computer or iPad. The colour codes are intended to teach basic coding concepts like, for example cause/effect and critical thinking. The coding was carried out analogously with different coloured sharpies. The structure of the programming workshops started with the researchers and teachers telling each of the groups of children their specific fairy tale. There was one researcher or teacher designated to each of the six groups. To come to a joint understanding of the fairy tale, this was followed by retelling bits of the storyline and discussing the meaning of the story. After this, the children were introduced to Ozobot and how it should be used as well as an exemplification of how the robot and the available creative material could be part of the children's reproduction of the story. The latter was the final part of the workshop, where the children retold their fairy tale to each other, the researchers and teachers. They were free to choose how they would like to do this. Central to the shared and explorative situations that emerged from this were joint investigations where the groups of children iteratively tried out different coding strategies aligned with using creative material such as foam clay, LEGO and markers to develop the fairy-tale environment.

The data collection included video observation, casual conversations and observational notes and pictures. We could identify imagination and creativity through the children's concrete and often playful "design doings" with the material and technology at hand. We relate such design doings to Vygotsky's (1930/2004, p. 11) statement of play, where "a child's play is not simply a reproduction of what he has experienced, but a creative reworking of the impressions he has acquired". In referring to design doings as play, we, in line with Brooks in Chapter 1 of this book, emphasise dynamic processes where a child can establish an intense relationship between imagination and reality.

Verbal and written consent from teachers and parents to participating children have been applied: all teachers and parents were informed about the study in writing and the parents agreed to let their child participate by signing informed consent forms. In addition, the children were informed that they could withdraw from participation in the workshops at any time if they, e.g. felt uncomfortable in any way. In line with ethical guidelines, all names of the children as well as of the schools are anonymised and, thereby, no identifying information is provided. All pictures used from the study have been approved for scientific publications.

The workshops were designed in different sequences and lasted for 2.5 hours including breaks. During the workshops, video observations were carried out to capture the activities as well as participating observations. The recorded video observations included in total, 4590 minutes (76.5 hours) of recording, and selected samples for further analyses are the recordings that contain workshops with the two groups of 3rd grade children working with the Ozobots and with the fairy tale *What the old man does is always right* by H. C. Andersen. These samples were transcribed and used in the analytical process. The analysis is based on IA (Jordan and Henderson, 1995) including four analytical steps. First, the empirical video data was reviewed by both authors to select interaction excerpts (IA, step 1). Next, we transcribed the selected excerpts (IA, step 2). In the next step, we coded the chosen episodes to find patterns (IA, step 3), which initiated the authors' analyses of excerpts (IA, step 4). This process resulted in the identification of three patterns: (1) Shared exploration, storyline and coding processes; (2) Bodily actions and fiddling; and (3) Expression of intense engagement. These patterns are unfolded in the below text.

Shared Explorations, Storyline and Coding Processes

Central to the shared and explorative situations that emerged from the workshop activity were joint investigations where the groups of children iteratively tried out different coding strategies aligned with using foam clay and LEGO to capture the fairy-tale environment. Through discussing the story, they tried to identify themselves with the characters and their actions to come up with coding solutions that would fit the storyline. In the below vignette, the group of three girls are engaged in coding actions, which are tightly coupled to their understanding of the fairy tale (Figure 12.3).

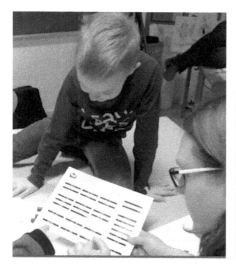

FIGURE 12.3 Ozobots in action together with foam clay and LEGO creations (left and mid image). To the right: coding scheme.

> **Vignette 1**
>
> Lisa, Anna, and Emily are busy coding with paper and sharpies to tell their Ozobot what to do. Their activity is framed by a classic fairytale, namely "What the old man does is always right" by H. C. Andersen. Together the children have coded the old man's (the farmer's) pathway from his home to the marketplace and back home again. They have colour coded on a piece of paper, so that Ozobot (who represents the farmer) shifts between moving fast to slowing down the speed between different people that he meets on his way to the marketplace. The girls used a big sheet of paper as a base to arrange the fairy-tale environment. They used foam clay to create some of the characters of the fairytale, i.e. the old man's wife and the house where they lived, as well as all the animals which the old man barted his horse to on his way to the marketplace (cow, sheep, goose, and hen) (Figure 12.4).

LISA: Ozobot can move quickly here [pointing to when Ozobot, i.e. the old man/farmer, has met the man with a cow and moves towards the man with a sheep], but must slow down when he [the old man] comes closer to here [pointing to the place on the paper where the old man meets a man with a sheep].

ANNA: Yeah, that works. Then, we can use both fast and slow code and we can let Ozobot move all the time [between the different tradings that the old man did] while we are telling the story. And he can get home to his wife in good time.

EMILY: But I don't think it looks like the old man is on his way to the marketplace. We need to make the area here [pointing to the area inside the coded pathway] more pretty, as in the countryside.

ANNA: Yeah, we have to make some flowers and shrubs. It's nice.

LISA: Hah, it is hard to believe that the old man actually received a kiss from his wife when he came home with almost nothing [laughing silently and smiling towards Anna and Emily].

Lisa's latter imaginary doubt was also reflected, with a sense of humour, by the other group (David, Eric and Marie) when they retold the story for the other groups:

MARIE: /.../ And they (the apples) were so heavy [her voice becomes playful and full of laugh].

DAVID: put the bag of rotten apples on top of the robot and put Ozobot into motion so that Ozobot, i.e. the farmer, arrives back home to his wife.

MARIE: Here you are, mother [with a pretend male voice].

David picks up the clay-apples from the bag of clay and puts them in front of the farmer's wife.

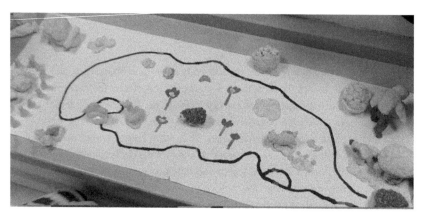

FIGURE 12.4 Ozobot representing the farmer on his way to the marketplace.

MARIE: Oh, help me, all apples are mashed [she laughs out loud].
RESEARCHER: What happened then?
MARIE: Strangely, she said that it does not matter, she thinks the farmer did the right thing.

Through the coding process, the girls identified themselves with the farmer when they intended to get him back home to his wife in good time. Here, they generated a coding narrative as part of the farmer's pathway to the marketplace. Also, while they were coding the farmer's pathway to the marketplace, they imagined that it should look like the countryside with flowers and shrubs. Here, the programming became a medium of communication opening up for imagination and creativity. The theme is summarised in Table 12.1

TABLE 12.1 Shared programming explorations.

Shared explorations, storyline and coding processes	
Expression of emotion in the fairy tale	*Expression of emotion in learning to programme*
The children identified themselves with the main characters of the story. Through this, they could share and reenact parts of the storyline alongside associated moral considerations and possibilities to reach a happy end of the story	Shared programming explorations: The children jointly developed knowledge of programming concepts, e.g. algorithmic thinking and debugging, and could express emotions when they shared explorations in groups to solve the problem at hand
The children sympathised with the fairy-tale character (the wife) and wanted to help another character (the farmer) to solve the problem of getting back home	In a learning to programme storyline, the children empathised with and wanted to help the characters to solve the shared programming problem

Bodily Actions and Fiddling

Particular bodily actions that emerged as important in the context of this case study are fiddling. This is typically small and repetitive body movements with and without objects in an ongoing task or situation (Witchel, Santos, Ackah, Westling, & Chockalingam, 2016). Examples of fiddling are tapping on the floor (or on a table) or playing with objects or handy tools (e.g. a pen). Although not purely hedonic, fiddling can be considered as play related (Treadaway & Kenning, 2015). Although bodily actions like fiddling can be associated with a decrease of attention, it can also be the opposite by, e.g. embody sustaining attention (Farley, Risko, & Kingstone, 2013). Bodily actions and fiddling are recognised to assist learning. For children, fiddling can, among others, help retrieve and articulate thoughts as well as engage in learning tasks. This is to say that fingers and hands are important means of, e.g. exploration, representing an access to children's life-world which perhaps could not have been established by other sensory modalities. This aligns with Vygotsky's description of how emotional expressions are part of children's imaginary processes. Examples of fiddling in the present theme are flipping Ozobot or passing it between the hands, tapping the paper with Ozobot coding guidelines, etc (Figure 12.5).

FIGURE 12.5 David fiddling (left and right).

Vignette 2

The group with two boys, David and Erik, and one girl, Marie, are sitting together with the researcher, Linda, around the table and Linda tells them the functionalities of Ozobot. She points to the coding guidelines and shows them how the robot can be coded to do different kinds of movement, such as fast, slow, zick-zack, etc. David taps with his finger several times at the coding scheme, points to one of the codes and asks Linda:

DAVID: Can I do like this with this code [at the same time spinning around with his finger]?

When Linda has confirmed David's question about making Ozobot spin, she shows how the robot can 'read' the codes. She points to the sensors under Ozobot and tells the children that these are cameras that can read different colours. David grabs Ozobot, investigates the sensors and passes it between his hands, turns it around, and again passes it between his hands. Linda informs them that they shall think about how they can code Ozobot to retell the story. She exemplifies by asking how Ozobot can move from the farmer's house to the marketplace and stop to exchange the horse for, for example, the cow.

DAVID: Can vi test it [energetically tapping on the spinning code]?

David is happy with his coding and is wiggling his upper body. Linda put forward a sheet of paper and said that they can try out different ways for Ozobot to get to the marketplace. She turns to Marie:

LINDA: Shall you try to code Ozobot to see how you can code the story?

Eric follows the coding attempts with concentration, he leans forward and his hands are moving back and forth on the table.

Below, Table 12.2 summarises the bodily action and fiddling theme.

Expression of intense engagement

The fairy tale embraced a wide range of anticipation aligned with the children's emerging emotional responses, e.g. of excitement. In identifying with the characters, not only the farmer, but also his wife, the children "lived" the emotions of the story through intense engagement. The below vignette (Vignette 3) shows

TABLE 12.2 Bodily action and fiddling.

Bodily action and fiddling	
Expression of emotion in the fairy tale	*Expression of emotion in learning to programme*
Through reflecting upon the fairy tale and how it can be reproduced, the children gain a sense of the farmer's movement in discussing with Linda. They clarify their own learning as they act out thoughts about how to reproduce the story. Through their embodied attention, the children could explore and articulate their thoughts connecting the fairy tale with the concrete world.	Through discussion and enacting of coding narratives and learning, the children could step-by-step anticipate their own actions, and along the way also the outcomes of the others' actions. This included verbal descriptions, but above all their bodily actions and fiddling, to pick up the programming solutions suggested by the researcher.

how the children became connected with the learning of programming as they took action to finding coding solutions. For Vygotsky (1978) the conceptualisation of imagination is a synthesis of emotion and meaning, which cannot be separated from its social context. The children could feel engagement and excitement of trying out different solutions and thoughts and, also, feeling the emotion

Vignette 3

The researcher (Linda) demonstrates how to code and exemplifies different possibilities of connecting the coding and the storyline. David is intensively engaged while following Linda's introduction to the activity. He is sitting on a chair, but gradually crawls up on the table and leaning towards Linda. Eric is concentrated and is laying with his upper body on the table, trying to come as close to Linda as possible. Linda explains the different coding that is possible to do with Ozobot. David slams his clasped hand lightly on the table, smiling and saying, 'yes, yes …' when Linda presents a code. Then, he lifts both his hands up in the air and down again towards the table smiling with his whole face. All three children intensively follow what Linda tells them. They cannot sit still, moving all the time and shouting 'yes'! to underline their excitement. David keeps laughing with excitement and clapping his hands when he can see that the code Linda is demonstrating actually works. David expresses. 'oh, this is great', Eric is half-laying on the table, and David is now sitting on the table while performing dancing movements with his upper body – just like Ozobot, which is spinning around. He looks at Linda saying, 'Now, can I try coding Ozobot?'

FIGURE 12.6 David intensively engaged.

of the characters, e.g. feeling joyful surprise when the wife actually was happy for a bag of rotten apples. This is also relevant to the issue of learning to programme as the children experienced an emotional response to this. The children became connected with the learning of programming as they anticipated that they could find a way to deal with it (Vignette 3).

Table 12.3 summarises the theme of expression of intense engagement.

TABLE 12.3 Expression of intense engagement.

Expression of intense engagement	
Expression of emotion in the fairy tale	*Expression of emotion in learning to programme*
While the children can be inside the storyline, "living" the story, here they are outside it acting as children eager to learn. They feel engaged and intensively happy when trying to find out how to coding the fairy tale.	The children are experiencing engaged happiness when following and wanting to explore a coding narrative. At the same time, they feel excited about learning new things and solving programming issues.

Conclusion

In concluding this chapter, we further elaborate on the relations between imagination, learning to programme and emotions by drawing on Vygotsky's four laws of imagination. Central to these laws are that these three concepts act as unified. This is to say that they cannot be separated. Often when programming or the 21st century skill of computational thinking are described in terms of teaching and learning, it is the learning side that is emphasised and embodied or emotional dimensions are more or less left out of the equation. In the present case study, we have identified how children emotionally relate to their social and material world while occupied with learning or problem-solving activities. So, conceptualising the matter of learning to programme as emotional and imaginary processes, means that we consider it as an indivisible unified experience of what the children brings to the activity, the environment and its situational character, and also how these events, for the children, are emotional as well conceptual learning processes. In relation to Vygotsky's theory on creativity and imagination, these processes unfolded as a unit of emotions, cognition and imagination as core dimensions of learning to programme. In the present study, the children developed various programming skills, such as algorithmic thinking, debugging and abstraction, as is shown in previous examples. Throughout the chapter, we have argued for not underestimating, but rather provide creativity and imagination as entry points into programming. Previous research has pointed to challenging issues when it comes to implementing educational robotics in a school context, e.g. that they primarily address technicalities without having any pedagogical strategies. Hence, our study claims that using classic fairy tales as a frame for learning to programme robots, stimulate creative expressions. This enabled the children to involve their emotions as well as their cognition and imagination, which triggered their interest and learning. By framing the programming activity with something that the children already knew about, such as classical fairy tales, contributed to the children's joint understanding which engaged them in intense collaboration and explorations. By introducing multiple pathways into programming, we argue that learning to programme becomes more likely to enhance the interest in STEM-related areas among children. Using classic fairy tales as a frame in schoolchildren's work with programming robots to enhance learning and to generate interest in programming as such, we seek to highlight the importance of allowing and including imagination and creativity in schoolchildren's work with programming.

References

Barreto, F., & Benitti, V. (2012). Exploring the educational potential of robotics in schools: A systematic review. *Computer & Education, 58*(3), 978–988.

Blackley, S., & Howell, J. (2019). The next chapter in the STEM education narrative: Using robotics to support programming and coding. *Australian Journal of Teacher Education, 44*(4), 51–64.

Bodrova, E., & Leong, D. (2006). *Tools of the mind: The Vygotskian approach to early childhood education* (2nd ed.). Englewood Cliffs, NJ: Prentice-Hall.

Connery, M. C., John-Steiner, V. P., & Marjanovic-Shane, A. (Eds.). (2010). *Vygotsky and creativity. A cultural-historical approach to play, meaning making and the arts* (pp. 3–15.) New York, NY: Peter Lang Publishing.

Farley, J., Risko, E., & Kingstone, A. (2013). Everyday attention and lecture retention: The effects of time, fidgeting, and mind wandering. *Frontiers in Psychology*, 4. https://doi.org/10.3389/fpsyg.2013.00619

Jordan, B., & Henderson, A. (1995). Interaction analysis: Foundations and practice. *Journal of the Learning Sciences*, 4(1), 39–103.

Komis, V. & Misirli, A. (2016). The environments of educational robotics in Early Childhood Education: towards a didactical analysis. *Educational Journal of the University of Patras UNESCO Chair*, 3(2), 238–246.

Melville, H. (1851/2003). *Moby-Dick or, the Whale*. Westminster, London: Penguin Classics.

Mondada, F., Bonani, M., Riedo, F., Briod, M., Pereyre, L., Retornaz, P., & Magnenat, S. (2017). Bringing robotics to formal education: The thymio open-source hardware robot. *IEEE Robotics & Automation Magazine*, 24(1), 77–85.

Rusk, N., Resnick, M., Berg, R., & Pezalla-Granlund, M. (2007). New pathways into robotics: Strategies for broadening participation. *Journal of Science Education and Technology*, 17, 59–69. doi:10.1007/s10956-007-9082-2

Treadaway, C., & Kenning, G. (2015). *Designing sensory e-Textiles for dementia*. In *Proceedings of the Third International Conference on Design Creativity (3rd ICDC)*. http://hdl.handle.net/10369/7470

Vygotsky, L. S. (1930/2004). Imagination and creativity in childhood. *Journal of Russian and East European Psychology*, 42(1), 7–97.

Vygotsky, L. S. (1978) *Mind in society: The development of higher psychological processes*. Cambridge, MA: Harvard University Press.

Witchel, H. J., Santos, C. P., Ackah, J. K., Westling, C. E. I., & Chockalingam, N. (2016). Non-Instrumental Movement Inhibition (NIMI) Differentially Suppresses Head and Thigh Movements during Screenic Engagement: Dependence on Interaction. *Frontiers in Psychology*, 7. https://doi.org/10.3389/fpsyg.2016.00157

13

THE TRANSFORMATIVE POTENTIAL OF SCHOOL-BASED MAKERSPACES

Novel Designs in Educational Practice

Kristiina Kumpulainen and Anu Kajamaa

Introduction

Lately, there has been an increased educational interest in "makerspaces" as potential sites for addressing the many demands surrounding learning and education in the knowledge society (Erstad et al., 2016). The Maker Movement and the broader "do-it-yourself" (DIY) culture celebrates hands-on innovation, creativity, personal fulfilment and community engagement across a wide array of genres, including crafts, robotics and computing (Peppler, Halverson, & Kafai, 2016). Makerspaces prescribe learner-centred pedagogies in which students can work on personally and/or collectively meaningful design projects, which supports interest-driven engagement and induces the emergence of student and teacher agency (Kumpulainen, Kajamaa, & Rajala, 2018, 2019). It is also considered that these technologically rich creative and participatory spaces offer a powerful context for students' agency, persistence, creative problem-solving and digital literacy in science, technology, engineering, arts and mathematics (STEAM) learning. Further, they provide arenas for utilising 21st century skills that are important for workforce development and overall functioning in the contemporary knowledge society (Peppler et al., 2016).

At the same time, emerging research suggests that makerspaces bring with them considerable tension when integrated into the educational practices of a school, creating both opportunities and obstacles for student-centred, participatory and creative learning (Kumpulainen et al., 2018, 2019). School-based makerspaces have also been criticised for their narrowly defined goals and culturally biased activities and, thus, for failing to attract and engage the broader population of young people (Peppler et al., 2016). In addition, researchers have warned about the wishful thinking that every child is a hacker and the erroneous dichotomisation of abstract thinking and play and further caution about a general ethos of more "doing" and less "thinking and reflection" in makerspaces (Blikstein & Worsley, 2016). How makerspaces contribute to new mindsets for innovative designs and educational practices is still an unexplored question.

In this chapter, we argue that in order to understand the opportunities and challenges of novel educational designs for learning and education, such as makerspaces, it is important to investigate how students and teachers participate and interact in makerspaces, as this information can shed light on the varied – and often contradictory – institutional and practice-related opportunities and constraints for implementing novel educational designs in practice. We address such issues in our chapter by drawing on a body of empirical research about longitudinal investigations into the interactional engagement of students (aged 9 to 12 years) and their teachers in a Finnish school that had recently introduced a novel design and making environment, the FUSE Studio, into its curriculum. The FUSE Studio comprises a choice-based digital infrastructure for students' creative activities, offering students opportunities to engage in STEAM design projects using a range of digital tools such as electronics, laser cutters and 3D printers (Stevens & Jona, 2017). In our chapter, we ask the following questions: How does the FUSE Studio, as a novel educational design, interact and come into tension with the more established educational practices of the school? What can we learn about the transformative potential of the FUSE Studio for student-centred, creative learning and educational change?

Conceptually, our work is grounded on sociocultural theorising (Hedegaard & Fleer, 2008; Vygotsky, 1987). From this perspective, we perceive the development and application of novel educational designs in education as culturally and institutionally situated and shaped. Further, we hold that students' and their teachers' participation in and experiences of institutional activities are shaped by their personal motive orientations and by the demands and history of the sociocultural setting. On this basis, we regard the students and their teachers as active participants who make sense of and influence the practices and learning opportunities in makerspaces while trying to accommodate their personal motives at the intersection of the novel makerspace and the more established institutional practices and demands of the school (Kumpulainen et al., 2019).

Our chapter offers insights into understanding how the innovative educational design of the FUSE Studio as one form of a makerspace interacts with and, at times, transforms existing school practices towards student-centred creative learning. Our chapter also provides useful information about implementing makerspaces in schools and discusses how teachers make sense of and adapt their work in relation to makerspaces. In addition, our work informs the future educational design of makerspaces for the advancement of students' 21st century skills and STEAM learning opportunities.

Study Overview

Our research stems from a Finnish city-run comprehensive primary school with 535 students and 28 teachers. Like any other school in Finland, this school follows the national core curriculum, which is defined locally. The local curriculum of the school strives for student-centredness and stresses design learning, which is targeted at enhancing students' creative problem-solving skills across the curriculum. As a response to the new curriculum requirements, the school introduced the FUSE Studio (www.fusestudio.net) as part of its elective courses in the autumn of 2016.

The education system in Finland has recently undergone a national curriculum reform with the introduction of new curriculum content, pedagogical approaches and learning environments. The new national core curriculum for the education of 7-to 16-year-olds emphasises the development of students' transversal competencies, including digital competencies, critical thinking skills and learning-to-learn, interaction and expression, multiliteracy, working life skills and entrepreneurship as well as social participation and influence. In addition, the national core curriculum recommends learning environments and pedagogies that are based on experiential, integrated and student-centred learning and that model real-life inquiries and problem-solving with relevant social and material resources (Finnish National Agency for Education, 2014).

The FUSE Studio

The FUSE Studio is a choice-based digital infrastructure for STEAM learning (see Stevens & Jona, 2017). The technological infrastructure of the FUSE Studio makerspace offers students different STEAM design challenges that "level up" difficulty like video games. Each design challenge has been developed in collaboration with a team of professionals in respective fields. The design challenges are accompanied by various tools, such as computers, 3D printers and other materials (e.g. foam rubber, a marble, tape and scissors), as well as instructions on how to process the challenges. The STEAM design challenges available to students include *Spaghetti Structures, Jewellery Designer, Robot Obstacle Course, Keychain Customiser, Electric Apparel, Coaster Boss* and *Solar Roller*. Figure 13.1 shows a student view of the FUSE challenges on a computer screen.

Each FUSE challenge is designed to engage students in different STEAM topics and skill sets. The design challenges have been carefully structured to introduce students to new ideas and to support them through more complex iterations of those ideas. Based on their own interests, students can choose which design challenges they want to work on, when and with whom. They can choose to work alone or with peers. There is no formal grading or assessment by teachers. Instead, using photos, videos or other digital artefacts, students can document their completion of a challenge, and the completion unlocks the next challenge in a sequence.

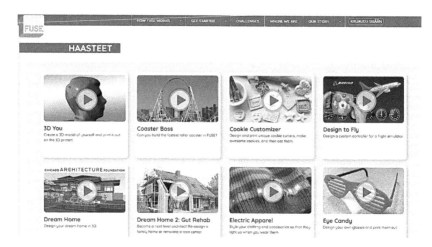

FIGURE 13.1   "My Challenges" student interface of the FUSE Studio

FIGURE 13.2   The students and their teachers working on the STEAM design challenges in the FUSE Studio

A combination of four elements in the FUSE Studio model makes it a distinctive makerspace: (1) an interest-driven approach in which students are free to select which design challenges to pursue and when to move on; (2) a levelling-up structure of challenges within sequences, following the basic logic of video game design principles; (3) a focus on STEM ideas and practices with a move towards STEAM, including artistic and design considerations in the criteria by which challenges are posed and judged; and (4) a core focus on cultivating interest in STEM ideas and practices among those who are not already affiliated with them, thereby aiming to broaden access to participation in STEM learning (Stevens & Jona, 2017). The FUSE Studio model differs from more open-ended makerspaces in which students are not typically offered choices of specific design challenges; rather, the work rests on the principles of design thinking, which dictate that the design is led by the identified needs of the context and/or community in question (Hughes, Morrison, Kajamaa, & Kumpulainen, 2019). Therefore, the results gained from our research need to be situated within the specific affordances and constraints of the FUSE Studio. Further research is necessary to address the integration of other types of makerspaces as novel educational designs in school contexts.

Next, we will discuss the core findings of a research project funded by the Academy of Finland and titled, "Learning by Making: The Educational Potential of School-Based Makerspaces for Young Learners' Digital Competencies" (iMake), in which we engaged in an ethnographic investigation of the adaptation of the FUSE Studio in a Finnish school. Specifically, we draw on a number of empirical studies to look into the teachers' agentic orientations for managing educational change in Finnish schools (Rajala & Kumpulainen, 2017); the agency-structure dynamics of the students' and teachers' participation in a novel school-based makerspace (Kumpulainen et al., 2018); the teachers' roles in a novel school-based makerspace (Kajamaa, Kumpulainen, & Olkinuora, 2019); and, finally, how a school-based makerspace mediates students' funds of knowledge and knowledge creation (Kajamaa, Kumpulainen, & Rajala, 2018).

The Transformative Potential of the FUSE Studio Makerspace for Student-centred Creative Practice

Our research findings provide evidence of student-driven creative STEAM practices in the FUSE Studio makerspace. Our studies show how the students creatively designed and utilised a constellation of materials and conceptual tools available in the FUSE Studio to pursue varied interests, build on each other's expertise and exercise creativity and agency (Kumpulainen et al., 2018, 2019). Many of the students and student groups creatively and agentively progressed with the FUSE Studio design challenges when interacting with various materials as well as with one another and their teachers. Many of the students found the design challenges intriguing and personally meaningful, and their engagement in design and making seemingly fulfilled their interests. In these cases, the makerspace environment successfully mediated the students' opportunities to draw on their personal "out-of-school" funds of knowledge to further their STEAM design and making activities and knowledge creation (Kajamaa et al., 2018).

Examples of student-driven creative resolutions included situations in which the students' work was first initiated by a FUSE design challenge; however, as their work progressed, they started to follow their own ideas and ways of working, which led to joint creative decision-making and products/end results. In these situations, it was important for the teachers to creatively and flexibly interpret the design challenges of the FUSE Studio not by focusing on the design of a specific, predefined object but rather concentrating on designs and processes that students found meaningful and engaging (Kajamaa et al., 2018; Kumpulainen et al., 2018, 2019).

When the FUSE design challenges resonated with students' interests, they worked on them enthusiastically and persistently, even when confronting challenges. In these cases, the students usually went beyond the instructions and demands of the FUSE Studio and of the teacher, generating new ideas and initiatives (Kumpulainen et al., 2018, 2019) and, at times, transforming the expected or customary practice. These situations represent "expansive learning experiences" for the students and resonate with the authentic making and design activities more typically found outside schools and in professional communities. For instance, when two students worked on a FUSE design challenge called *Spaghetti Structures*, they used several types of spaghetti and marshmallows to design and build large constructions. The students found the challenge of *Spaghetti Structures* so compelling that they simply forgot about the instructions and the time constraints of the school schedule and were instead driven by their collective motive to create something new (Kumpulainen et al., 2019).

One of our recent studies focused on the role of the teacher in the FUSE Studio makerspace. We were particularly interested in interactive situations in which the teacher(s) recognised the students' initiative and creative contributions and invited the students to reason out and explain them (Kajamaa et al., 2019). In these situations, the teachers also tried to balance and/or "glue together" the students' interests and ideas. This often helped the students to carry out their design work and overcome the difficulties associated with the instructions or lack of content knowledge that was required for pursuing a STEAM design challenge. The teachers also supported the students to find and/or use different materials and tools required for the design challenges (e.g. Tinkercad software, foam rubber, a marble, tape and scissors). Moreover, the teachers' interactive orchestration created opportunities for the students' relational engagement and expertise to develop (Kajamaa et al., 2019). In these situations, expertise became porous, flowing between the students and their teachers.

Further, we captured creative and agentive actions in teacher–student interactions (Kumpulainen et al., 2018, 2019). In these situations, the teachers typically attempted to support the students' creative design work based on the students' expertise and knowledge. In these interactive episodes, the teachers explored the students' existing knowledge and encouraged them to compare and test ideas as well as to identify conceptual or material resources for their design work and reasoning (Kajamaa et al., 2019). In some cases, the teachers and students jointly created an interactional space in which the students were able to deviate from the original rules and instructions of the FUSE Studio makerspace. This usually led to the creation of something new, such as a design that exceeded or expanded upon the original challenge criteria. For instance, instead of designing an earring as suggested by the FUSE Studio, the students designed a ring for a finger. In another situation, students used alternative software for their game design. Overall, these episodes were fairly rare in the data, but since such creative interactions are at the core of the makerspaces, we regard them as being important to document.

Tensions and Challenges of School-based Makerspaces

Even though makerspaces hold the potential to serve various students and their interests (Peppler et al., 2016), our research also makes visible how the students' participation in the FUSE Studio makerspace was not always straightforward and involved tensions and discontinuities. Moreover, there were students who did not find the design activities motivating, and these students demonstrated behaviour that required disciplinary actions (Kajamaa et al., 2019). Often in such cases, the more traditional teacher-centred practices superseded the novel student-driven creative practice (Kumpulainen et al., 2018, 2019). In fact, in our research dealing with the teachers' roles and intervention strategies in the FUSE Studio makerspace, the most common strategy applied by the teachers turned out to be authoritarian in nature (Kajamaa et al., 2018). In authoritative interactions, the teacher took charge of the cognitive work, typically dominating and/or controlling the students' learning activity. Often, this also meant that the teacher would not involve the students in problem-solving but rather would instruct them step-by-step towards a resolution. Sometimes the teacher even solved the FUSE design challenge on the students' behalf (Kajamaa et al., 2019).

The students themselves also frequently reinforced the traditional teacher-centred practice by turning to the teacher when they faced an obstacle or wanted to demonstrate their progress and/or outcomes (Kumpulainen et al., 2018, 2019). Our research shows that even though teachers took into account the students' initiatives and creative contributions, they also very often orchestrated the selection and provision of the materials for the students. This is a finding that contradicts the makerspace ideology, which underscores students' ownership over their learning activities by, for instance, being responsible for their materials and workspaces. These findings also suggest how, in an institution such as a school, it is typical that participants will draw on their customary ways of working in order to maintain stability, create coherence and address the complex realities of their everyday lives (Engeström, 2007).

Our research also suggests that the potential of the FUSE Studio to enhance student-centred creative learning is compromised if the teachers do not understand or appreciate the purpose and meaning of new designs for learning and education. Our interviews with the Finnish teachers in the school that introduced the FUSE Studio reveal that the teachers displayed different interpretations and orientations – namely, practical-evaluative, reproductive, critical-projective and creative-projective orientations – to manage and utilise the novel educational design in their practices (Rajala & Kumpulainen, 2017). The practical-evaluative orientation considered the practical realities of the teachers' strategies in relation to the new educational design and its use in practice. The reproductive orientation considered how the novel educational design of the makerspace could fit within the existing educational practices valued by the teacher. The critical-projective orientation displayed the teachers' future-orientated and transformative agency. In these orientations, the teachers identified the potential of the FUSE Studio makerspace for transforming their own educational practice and students' learning opportunities (Rajala & Kumpulainen, 2017).

Discussion

Our ongoing research makes visible how makerspaces – in our case, the FUSE Studio – can have the transformative power to develop existing educational practices in schools towards creative student-centred STEAM engagement and learning. Our work shows how makerspaces as novel educational designs challenge traditional educational practices, including teacher and student roles and positions. In this context, students and their teachers continuously encounter diverse motives and demands that they need to personally and collectively navigate and negotiate. Adding to the complexity, the learning process of students can never be fully preplanned in makerspaces; thus, both teachers and students need to be able to withstand uncertainty. Makerspaces ask both students and teachers to adopt novel mindsets to accommodate a variety of positions, skills and competencies intertwined into creative learning.

Furthermore, integrating makerspaces in schools requires rethinking how time is organised for students and teachers in these spaces. Attention also needs to be given to the nature of and overall pedagogy behind makerspaces. In particular, consideration needs to be given to considering whether a makerspace should be integrated into the school's core curriculum or offered as an elective or after-school activity independent of the core curriculum. The educational goals of makerspaces need consideration as well, and the nature of design challenges in makerspaces deserves further attention. Based on our research, it seems that students benefit the most if the design challenges exhibit variability, from specific to more open-ended activities. More structured design challenges may create an off-ramp to real making and support students as they learn to use advanced technologies for their design activities; however, it is important that maker challenges resonate with diverse students' interests and that these ultimately lead to their engaging in authentic design and making. Ideally, makerspaces would link students' personal interests to community-relevant problem-solving and active citizenship (Marsh, Arnseth, & Kumpulainen, 2018).

In order for teachers to develop and implement the new designs and learning opportunities advocated by makerspaces, they should increasingly exercise their professional agency and reflexive thinking to find a balance between old and new ways of working (Kumpulainen et al., 2018; Rajala & Kumpulainen, 2017). Moreover, such novel learning environments call for teachers to create flexible and more reciprocal ways of working with students and with one another. In sum, managing the opportunities and demands associated with makerspaces in schools requires constant efforts, from both the students and the teachers. Novel learning environments ask for institutional considerations about the timing and structure of schooling. We can conclude that the transformative potential of makerspaces requires a continuous process of collective creativity and learning at the level of teachers, students and institutions before such novel designs can make a sustained change to educational practice.

Acknowledgements

The research reported in this chapter was funded by the Academy of Finland Learning by Making: The educational potential of school-based makerspaces for young learners' digital competencies (iMake) project (no: 310790).

References

Blikstein, P., & Worsley, M. (2016). The maker movement: The last chance of progressive education? In K. Peppler, E. Halverson, & Y. Kafai, (Eds.), *Makeology: Makerspaces as learning environments* (Vol. 1, pp. 64–80). New York, NY: Routledge.

Engeström, Y. (2007). From stabilization knowledge to possibility knowledge in organizational learning. *Management Learning, 38*(3), 271–275.

Erstad, O., Kumpulainen, K., Mäkitalo, Å., Schrøder, K., Pruulmann-Vengerfeldt, P., & Jóhannsdóttir, T. (2016). Tracing learning experiences within and across contexts: A Nordic approach. In O. Erstad, K. Kumpulainen, Å. Mäkitalo, P. Pruulmann-Vengerfeldt, & T. Jóhannsdóttir (Eds.), *Learning across contexts in the knowledge society* (pp. 1–14). Amsterdam: Sense Publishers.

Finnish National Board of Education (2014). *Perusopetuksen opetussuunnitelman perusteet 2014* [National Core Curriculum for Basic Education 2014] Accessed from http://www.oph.fi/download/163777_perusopetuksen_opetussuunnitelman_perusteet_2014.pdf

Hedegaard, M., & Fleer, M. (2008). Studying children. *A cultural-historical approach*. London: Open University Press.

Hughes, J. M., Morrison, L. J., Kajamaa, A., & Kumpulainen, K. (2019). Makerspaces promoting students' design thinking and collective knowledge creation: Examples from Canada and Finland. In A. Brooks, E. Brooks & C. Sylla (Eds.), *Interactivity, game creation, design, learning, and innovation*. ArtsIT 2018, DLI 2018. Lecture Notes of the Institute for Computer Sciences, Social Informatics and Telecommunications Engineering (Vol. 265, pp. 343–352). Cham: Springer. https://doi.org/10.1007/978-3-030-06134-0_38

Kajamaa, A., Kumpulainen, K., & Olkinuora, H-R. (2019). Teacher interventions in students' collaborative work in a technology-rich educational makerspace. *British Journal of Educational Technology*. doi:10.1111/bjet.12837

Kajamaa, A., Kumpulainen, K., & Rajala, A. (2018). Digital learning environment mediating students' funds of knowledge and knowledge creation. *Studia Paedagogica*, *23*(4), 49–66.

Kumpulainen, K., Kajamaa, A., & Rajala, A. (2018). Understanding educational change: Agency-structure dynamics in a novel design and making environment. *Digital Education Review 33*, 26–38.

Kumpulainen, K., Kajamaa, A., & Rajala, A. (2019). Motive–demand dynamics creating a social context for students' learning experiences in a making and design environment. In A. Edwards, M. Fleer, & L. Bottcher, (Eds.), *Cultural-historical approaches to studying learning and development: societal, institutional and personal perspectives* (pp. 185–199). Amsterdam: SAGE Publications Ltd.

Marsh, J., Arnseth, C.-H., & Kumpulainen, K. (2018). Maker literacies and maker citizenship in the makey (makerspaces in the early years) project. *Multimodal Technologies and Interaction*. doi:10.3390/mti2030050

Peppler, K., Halverson, E., & Kafai, Y. (Eds.) (2016). *Makeology: Makerspaces as learning environments* (Volume 1 and 2). New York, NY: Routledge.

Rajala A., & Kumpulainen K. (2017). Researching teachers' agentic orientations to educational change in Finnish schools. In M. Coller & S. Paloniemi (Eds.), *Agency at work: An agentic perspective on professional learning and development* (pp. 311–329). Amsterdam: Springer.

Stevens, R., & Jona, K. (2017). Program design. *FUSE Studio -website*. Retrieved May 20, 2017 from https://www.fusestudio.net/program-design

Vygotsky, L. S. (1987). The collected works of LS Vygotsky. *Problems of general psychology*. Volume 1. New York: Plenum Press.

14

WHITEBOXING "BITS N BOTS"

How "Flawed" and Emerging Technologies can Facilitate Computational Play and Learning

Lykke Brogaard Bertel and Pauline Fredskilde

Introduction

Advanced and emerging technology such as social and educational robots, programmable electronic platforms (like Littebits), Virtual Reality and 3D printing are increasingly being introduced into the classroom with the aim of supporting collaboration, communication and creativity as well as critical and in particular, computational thinking (CT) (Wing, 2006). However, the current state-of-the-art in advanced and emerging technologies are by definition somewhat flawed and unfinished prototypes and beta versions, which in turn can lead to teachers and practitioners feeling insecure about introducing new technology into formal educational settings.

As the technology continues to advance and artificial intelligence becomes increasingly attainable, there is indeed a need to imagine future scenarios where robots and other emerging technologies are fully autonomous and intelligent and its operators potentially replaceable to explore potentials as well as ethical issues in such scenarios. However, in this chapter we argue, that the "in-between state" that researchers and practitioners may find themselves in, this "vacuum" between what emerging technology is able to do now and what we *want* it to do, is by no means a vacuum when it comes to *learning*. In fact, the emerging technologies' inherent immaturity and imperfection might indeed be the very thing that sparks children's curiosity and motivation to pursue careers in these fields. Thus, in this chapter we explore the possibilities and potentials in applying these emerging technologies "as is", that is, with their current limitations and 'flaws', and present different examples of how whiteboxing these "bits and bots" can facilitate playful inquiry, computational play and experiential learning.

Computational thinking – An essential life skill in the 21st century?

CT understood as the cognitive processes involved in the development of IT artefacts and programs is an important life skill for the future on par with language and mathematical skills (Dohn, 2021). This includes the development of not only algorithms and models, computer visualisations and programming, but also algorithmic thinking in contexts other than programming, e.g. in analogue algorithm construction and bodily anchored algorithmic interaction (Mikkonen, 2019).

When we discuss CT here, though, we do it in the context of many different understandings of the term. Gaining widespread attention since Wing (2006) described it as "*the thought processes involved in formulating a problem and expressing its solution(s) in such a way that a computer – human or machine – can effectively carry it out*", CT is quickly becoming a well-established concept and a desired competence generally accepted in modern education today. However, CT as an educational concept dates back as far as the 1980s and 1970s, and perhaps even 1940s (Denning & Tedre, 2019). In 1980, at a time when computers were mostly implemented in classrooms to "program children" through standardised testing, Seymour Papert (1980) developed the first educational robot to do the exact opposite; let children program the computer. Even further back, in 1970, Danish computer scientist Peter Nauer used the definition "datalogisk tænkning" (algorithmic thinking), which much like our understanding of CT today, included the importance of human aspects in computer science or "datalogi" (the subject experimentally taught in schools at the time) as well as its applicability in all subjects including language and art, not just Science, Technology, Engineering and Math (STEM) (Caeli & Yadav, 2020).

CT ≠ Programming!

CT is not programming. Dohn's (2021) definition of CT as "*the thought processes involved in the development of IT artifacts and programs to live in the world today*" involves the use of programs as much as the coding of such programs, and as such CT can be taught both analogically and digitally. CT is the thought process involved when solving problems using methods like decomposition, pattern recognition, abstraction and designing algorithms. These methods are fundamental to understand programming (Chongtay, 2018) but they are fundamental to other things, too; understanding algorithms and the way they affect our lives empower us to take part in shaping the future.

Thus, as an integral part of CT, Dohn places **computational participation** (Burke, O'Byrne, & Kafai, 2016) as a way to engage students in the field between using and coding programs, e.g. by remixing programs in Scratch or working with e-textiles (Kafai & Burke, 2013) with the purpose of facilitating **computational literacy**; a layered set of skills of which CT is considered the first and fundamental (Chongtay, 2018). This connects well with other more inclusive perspectives on the emerging field of CT such as **computational empowerment** (**CE**) (Iversen, Smith, & Dindler, 2018) which considers CE a merge between CT and the participatory design approach. Compared to the general understanding of CT, where children think and create digitally using CT skills solely to solve problems through coding, computational empowerment emphasises a focus on reflection and critical understanding of the role digital technology plays in society and, more importantly, in one's own life (Iversen et al., 2018). This is in line with the perspective that algorithmic processes should be understood as an integral part of the many social and emotional processes involved in living in the world (Dohn, 2021).

This is in line with the proposal in computational participation to go "*beyond the individual to integrate social networks and digital tools in a networked society*" (Burke et al., 2016; Bertel, Dau & Brooks, 2019), which redirects attention from specific code to creations and projects; from tools to communities: What do the children want to make and how can they get the help they need? Furthermore, computational participation promotes a move away from digital screens to the technological tangibles, with which de- and reconstruction leads to new understandings of not only emerging technologies, but the physical world in which they take part, thus becoming mediating artefacts and "objects to think with" (Resnick & Rosenbaum, 2013); tools among other tools, to create authentic formal and informal experiential learning opportunities.

Playful Learning and Objects-to-think-with

The outset of most learning activities involving emerging technologies is the experimentation with constructing or adapting "bits and bots" through coding. This method is also referred to as "tinkering", characterised by a "*playful, experimental, iterative style of engagement, in which makers are continually reassessing their goals, exploring new paths and imagining new possibilities*" (Resnick & Rosenbaum, 2013). Although tinkering can be hard work, it is aligned with play and a specific style of engaging with the world, in which boundaries and new possibilities are continuously tested through trial and error (Papert, 1980):

> (...)when you learn to program a computer you almost never get it right the first time. Learning to be a master programmer is learning to become highly skilled at isolating and correcting "bugs", the part that keeps the program from working.

Embedded within the tinkering concept, is the idea that the process of becoming "stuck and unstuck" facilitate a sense of authorship, purpose and deep understanding of the materials and phenomena it is exploring (Petrich, Wilkinson, & Bevan, 2013). However, much like with computational empowerment, the most tinkerable construction kit is only as successful as the context for tinker-ability, i.e. the activities, materials, facilitation, space and community supporting it (Petrich et al., 2013; Resnick & Rosenbaum, 2013; Caprani, 2016). We argue, that adopting a Playful learning (PL) approach to computational thinking is a way of doing just that; creating a context for tinkerability that facilitates imagina-tion, exploration and creativity while developing cognitive, social and emotional skills (Moyles, 1989).

PL as a concept is used very broadly in research with many different defini-tions. Historically, there has been a great interest in the relationship between play and learning (and objects); with examples such as Fröbel's playtools dat-ing back as far as 1837. We often associate PL with a constructivist approach to learning, where children's learning is directly connected to the people and things around them, which inspired Papert's focus on the construction of ana-logue and digital materials as objects-to-think-with and laid the groundwork for the way MIT Media Lab and many other "contexts for tinkerability" such as PlayLabs and makerspaces working with PL today. Here, **computational things** are understood as physical artefacts which interacts with their surroundings, typi-cally through sensors or actuators (Mikkonen & Fyhn, 2021) in particular, have been argued to offer new ways for play and learning with computers as tangible artefacts and tools to connect the physical and the digital and support children in expressing themselves creatively and collaboratively in playful, explorative ways (Johannesen, Brooks, & Borum, 2020) and to move from learning-by-doing to learning-through-making (Papert, 1980). These tangible, computational artefacts can include a variety of different types of technology, ranging from rebuilding the old and outdated and building new from spare parts and modular electron-ics in playful ways as is the case, e.g. with new concepts such as Hacker- and BreakerSpaces, or it can involve including new, emerging and often still proto-typical technologies and tools such as 3D printers and educational robots.

Bits, Bots and Breakables: Emerging Technologies in the Classroom

Advanced technology such as social and educational robots, electronic platforms (like Littebits), Virtual Reality and 3D printing are some of the computational tools we see increasingly introduced into the classroom, particularly in STEM teaching. Emerging technology as a concept covers what has been defined as "Eight Essential Technologies" (see Figure 14.1) which in addition to robotics and 3D printing includes artificial intelligence, Internet of Things, drones, block-chain and augmented/Virtual Reality (PWC, 2017).

In this chapter, we present examples of computational play using the 3D printer and different examples of educational robots. The 3D printer is probably one of the most common "computational things" to find its way into maker-spaces, schools and libraries. Still, it remains "emerging" in the sense that what these printers are able to do changes constantly. In contrast to educational robots and hands-on robotic kits, the 3D printer is not originally intended nor designed to be a pedagogical tool. Thus, schools buy them often in the hope that pedagogical practices might emerge with the access to them and that teachers will invest time in learning how to use them and how to engage children in learning with them.

Educational robots, on the other hand, are specifically designed with the purpose of teaching robotics-related courses in STEM and to translate abstract theoretical concepts through embodied interaction and experimentation (Alimisis, 2013) often through project-based learning (Resnick & Rosenbaum, 2013). Most often these are robotic kits or simple modular robots, but it can also include socially interactive and even humanoid robots. In previous research, a divide between robotic kits in STEM teaching and social robots in special needs education has been identified (Bertel & Rasmussen, 2013). However, as socially interactive robots become more increasingly affordable and adaptable and the value of hands-on programming equally discovering in special needs education, this seems to bring these two fields closer, e.g. with specific purposes in mind such as facilitating inclusion through robot-supported collaborative learning (Bertel, Dau & Brooks, 2020). There is, however, still the challenge that many of these robotic devices stem from an understanding of the user as a "consumer" rather than a "prosumer", meaning that these robots are subjected to blackboxing to a much higher degree than hands-on robotic construction kits in general (Bertel & Hannibal, 2015).

Blackboxing as a theoretical concept stems from Bruno Latour's (1999) more general definition of blackboxing in society, as something that occurs when scientific and technical work is made invisible by its own success:

> When a machine runs efficiently, when a matter of fact is settled, one need focus only on its inputs and outputs and not on its internal complexity. Thus, paradoxically, the more science and technology succeed, the more opaque and obscure they become.
>
> (Latour, 1999)

When blackboxing happens in educational robotics, it is often based on the misconception that construction and programming is by definition too demanding for children to take part in (Alimisis, 2013; Blikstein, 2013; Resnick et al., 2000). Whiteboxing, in contrast, is the activity through which the black box of technology, its wires and narratives, is unpacked and unconcealed; opened for examination, reconfiguration and transformation (Jabbar & Bjørn, 2019) which is supported by constructionist methodologies in education recommending a transition to the design of transparent (whitebox) technological systems where users can break-and-make, construct and deconstruct objects and/or imaginaries and we argue that this is particularly important when implementing emerging technologies that are by definition somewhat opaque and obscure.

Thus, we argue that just like in constructivist approaches to science and technology studies, much can be gained from "whiteboxing" emerging technologies, that is, "opening the black box" and attempt to describe and understand the internal workings of the system (computational thinking) and to be able to critically reflect, redesign and reconfigure these systems (computational participation) for the purpose of enjoyment and (computational) play.

Emerging (and Surprising) Practices of Computational Play

In the following, we will describe and discuss four different examples of computational play with different emerging technologies, including 3D printers and different educational robotic platforms. The purpose of these examples is not to cover the entire range and variations of types of computational play, but rather to provide examples that emphasise the inherent diversity in the initiation, purpose and nature of computational play in practice.

3D Jewellery: Playful Computational Making-and-Breaking

In a workshop for young girls (aged 7–13) titled "*From sketching to 3D printing: making jewelry with the 3D printer*" in collaboration with the NGO DigiPippi (DigiPippi, 2021), we took advantage of an informal setting and the limitations of technology and space (with only one printer and ten girls, prints had to be small). Thus, instead of focusing on the technical aspects of 3D design software (e.g. Tinkercad), printing or prototyping, as is often the case with 3D printing in educational settings, we decided to focus on creativity and enjoyment while engaging the girls in 3D printing.

Upon arrival, the 3D printer was already on and the girls were free to give it a look; some very interested, some less. The girls were then presented with the theme and preprinted examples of jewellery after which they were able to draw their own jewellery design by hand, then photograph and convert it into a readable file for the printer (see Figure 14.1).

The girls were part of the entire process from drawing their jewellery designs (varying in complexity and originality), initiating and monitoring the 3D printer, removing the prints and decorating them before turning them into actual jewellery using available accessories such as chains, earrings, paint, nail polish and glitter and were able to create several pieces of 3D printed jewellery later presented to their parents in an exposition.

The creative aspects of the workshops clearly engaged the girls, which was expected, however what was surprising to observe was the girls' curiosity and awareness of the printer itself. This particular printer is not just a "click and print" printer, it is self-assembled and needs ongoing calibration. Thus, our own limited experience with this particular printer created a cyber-physical space for collaboration, play and mutual exploration rather than just teaching-and-learning. The girls got to use the printer just like we did; they touched and turned the buttons,

FIGURE 14.1   Girls engaging with 3D printed material and 3D printer.

stared at the print for minutes at a time to make sure the filament would stick; tried again when it failed; scraped off the print once it was finished or ruined. Despite some initial disappointment when a print failed, analysing what went wrong and how to fix it quickly became one of the most enjoyable and engaging activities. In a joint effort, we found common "mistakes" (like when a star that would "float" over a nameprint and thus end up like a botched up squiggle, or when holes inside a letter would "fall out" (see Figure 14.2)).

Thus, even in a highly individualised workshop, a community of practice emerged where the girls participated (computationally and collaboratively) in debugging and iterating and in which the girls' contributions and suggestions were just as valid and helpful as ours.

Computational Storytelling in Kindergarten with Jack the Penguin

In an experiment with kindergarten children and the company Guldastronaut (Guldastronauts Coding Class, 2021), we explored children's ability to learn coding through engaging in computational play merging computational activities such as coding, game design, analogue/digital construction and robot interaction with storytelling and play activities.

Jack the Penguin (JTP) is a pixel figure penguin "Jack" and his best friend "Unni" a pixel figure alicorn. JTP was originally primarily a platform game

FIGURE 14.2 An example of a "failed" 3D print.

created in Unity to teach older children game design, but is now a larger universe for all age groups containing both digital and physical artefacts including centi-cubes, hama pearls and, in this case, LEGO Duplo to create physical pixel figures before drawing them into the computer game.

In this workshop, the children build elements from the game universe in LEGO Duplo using various building sheets (starting from very simple to more complicated) (see Figure 14.3). The computational aspects came into play when the children got to explore computational language like *sorting*, *decomposition* and *pattern recognition* outside the digital too, i.e. in a cyber-physical learning space and used the different building sheets while engaging in discussions about colour matching and building optimisation.

It was easy for the children to build from the building sheets which motivated them to go beyond (see Figure 14.4), e.g. one girl builds a rocket with less blocks than the sheet stated, allowing her to playfully challenge the instructions. Another

FIGURE 14.3 Building sheets and "physical" computational thinking in action.

FIGURE 14.4 Presenting a new version of a rocket and the building of "Jack the Penguin".

child build Jack the Penguin without a building sheet, so that he could fit into his own story.

The pixel figures were then uploaded on the computer through a software program and the children got to play with their figures in a computer game (see Figure 14.5).

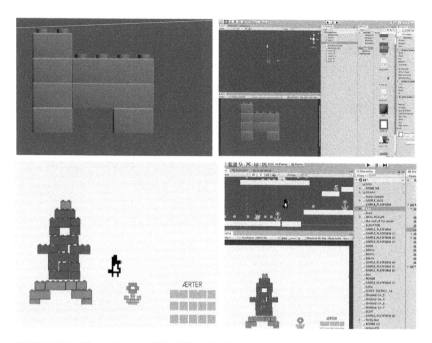

FIGURE 14.5 The rocket and "Jack" inside the computer game.

The children were excited to see and interact with their own figures on screen, immediately facilitating play. This example shows how computational play can transition the physical and digital and create a cyber-physical learning space inviting more co-creation and authorship (computational participation). Another interesting finding was that in similar workshops with older children, a much more visible distinction between the physical and digital space was observed. Whereas, the kindergarten children were engaged with and "inside" the JTP story (e.g. creating new characters) before watching it play out on the screen; older children tended to view the storytelling and building session as separate tasks from the game play.

Playful Linguistics: The Case of the "Dumb" Humanoid

The following example was an observation made during a study on the use of social robots as tools to facilitate dialogue among children about roboethics and technology in society. In this particular case, two different humanoid robots were used; an early generation NAO and the robot Keepon in a workshop with a 5th grade class at a local school.

After a preliminary introduction to the robot platforms, the children collaborated in a workshop in groups to construct robot "assistants" and applications by combining pictures of different social robots with varying attributes; "*roles*" (teacher, police officer, friend, etc.) and *actions* (read, listen, scold, etc.),

FIGURE 14.6 5th graders playing with NAO's text-to-speech function during the break.

which were then discussed in plenary, giving insights into the children's views of humanoid robots and their potential roles in society. However, it was actually in a break in between formal learning activities, that we observed interesting instances of computational play and learning.

In the break, the children were allowed to play with the robots with minimal interference from the teachers or researchers (see Figure 14.6) and particularly the text-to-speech system implemented in the NAO robot seemed to encourage the children to play with the formalised language, perception and concepts of cognition and artificial intelligence.

By programming sentences without syntax or with no semantic meaning such as "*Hej flødebolle træ*" – "*Hello cream puff tree*" and then observe the robot recite them with no apparent perception of the mistakes it just made, the children were playing and exploring while simultaneously assessing the robot's cognitive ability. This in turn made the children reflect and adjust their expectations towards the robot both in terms of technical maturity (e.g. whether the robot is artificially intelligent) as well as the severity of ethical issues that could arise from implementing this particular robotic system into their lives. For instance, upon realising that the robot is not (yet) able to perceive and analyse information intuitively, "trust" is not (yet) an issue. Telling the robot a secret, much like a pet dog, becomes harmless not because the robot leads the children to believe it is trust*worthy*, but because it is not (yet) technologically advanced or intelligent enough to pass on the information.

This is an example of how computational play can occur spontaneously and informally within a formal learning context and emphasises the need to assume the child's perspective on technology to identify the potential of emerging technology to facilitate reflection and learning, both in relation to the underlying logics of the system itself (computational thinking) as well as its effects on society as a whole (systems thinking and computational empowerment). In addition to highlighting the quality, and perhaps even *importance* of whiteboxing, of transparency in the flaws and failures of emerging technology such as social robots, these observations suggest that ethical issues often presented in relation to the introduction of social robots in education and society in general may lie less with the child's inclination to let herself be "deceived" by robots and more by designers (and researchers) tendency to want to compensate for the technology's current immaturity and inadequacies.

Confusing Coding: "Hacking" as Computational Play

This example was part of a case study on educational robots as tools to support inclusion in early childhood transitions. The small mobile robot KUBO used in this case is programmable through a tangible coding language; TagTiles with commands in the shape of puzzle pieces. The purpose of KUBO like most other educational robots for STEM teaching is to teach children the basics of coding (CT), however in addition to this, humanoid features such as eyes and a head as well as the assigned intention-driven coding tasks on the activity map invites social robotic narratives and frames KUBO within a social robotic context. This seemed to invite children with diverse needs and interests in PL scenarios, however the potential of these kinds of educational robots to support inclusion specifically, had yet to be explored in a systematic way.

In this specific case study, 16 2nd grade pupils (age 8–9) were teaching eight so-called "school ready" kindergarten kids (age 5–6) how to code using KUBO over the course of 3 weeks as part of an initiative to ensure more cross-disciplinary collaboration focusing on early childhood transitions. The older children spent two math classes preparing and working in pairs or groups of three to design programming tasks and exercises for the preschoolers to complete as well as accompany narratives involving the TagTiles and a designated activity map. However, it was actually in informal and rather unstructured instances of playful inquiry with the robot, that the most instances of computational thinking were observed. For instance, one child was testing the limitations of KUBO's perception by building code impossible to execute. When interviewed, the child explained trying to "confuse" or "hack" the robot. Similarly, the same child would then in the following week build a loop (without teacher's instructions) to "make the robot run forever" (see Figure 14.7).

FIGURE 14.7   Confusing coding with KUBO and the construction of a recursive function.

Towards a Conceptual Understanding of Computational Play: Positions and Perspectives

As shown in the above examples, great potential for computational play can be found in emerging technologies' inherently "unfinished" and flawed state, facilitating playful responses to interrelated processes of computational thinking, participation and empowerment. This approach to emerging technology in education is supported by constructionist approaches to learning recommending a transition towards transparent technologies as facilitators of computational thinking and creative mindsets, through curiosity and critical reflection, rather than ready-made (passive) and consumable technological products somewhat comparable to the traditional curriculum book. Thus, computational play cannot be easily orchestrated nor limited to specific (STEM) subjects or curricula but emerges spontaneously through playful exploration of both physical, digital and cyber-physical spaces and practices fueled by curiosity and creativity.

In this context we argue, that whiteboxing new and emerging technologies is essential to motivate such computational play, revealing not only the structures of the technology, its code and imaginaries and making it visible and available for scrutiny even for children at a young age; but also creating new spaces and communities; new emerging computational play practices, in the process. This is possible *because* of the technology's flaws and inconsistencies, not in spite of them;

through disconfirming events pushing for breakdown and inviting for transformation of the multiple digital and analogue artefacts and their narratives to provide an updated perspective that better reflect a current state worldview.

The interplay of these processes in computational play; when emerging technologies not only frustrate and disappoint us – but also puzzle, charm and fascinate us, carries the potential to challenge and change routines, encourage continuous experimentation, problem-solving and PL. Thus, the value of the unfinished and flawed lies in its potential to facilitate new ways of learning (playfully) and news ways of thinking (computationally). From this perspective, the current messy state-of-the-art of emerging technologies provides a unique perspective and opportunity of exploring a state in between what *was* and what (probably) will or *might* be.

As a final note, it is important to emphasise, that emerging technologies in this sense are considered accelerators rather than drivers of change in emerging practices, amplifying what we are already doing (Bundsgaard, Pettersson, & Puck, 2014). Thus, whereas an emerging technology might accelerate such a process by sparking curiosity and bringing forward the potential for computational play and learning, it is ultimately the practitioner, the one who introduces the technology and brings it into play with clear visions and goals; who is the true driver of change.

References

Alimisis, D. (2013). Educational robotics: Open questions and new challenges. *Themes in Science and Technology Education*, 6(1), 63–71. Retrieved October 4, 2020 from https://www.learntechlib.org/p/148617/.

Bertel, L., Dau, S., & Brooks, E. (2019). *Developing Robot-Supported Inclusive Education (ROSIE): A Play-Based Approach to STEM-teaching and Inclusion in Early Childhood Education.* In O. Levrini & G. Tasquier (Eds.), *Electronic Proceedings of the ESERA 2019 Conference.* The beauty and pleasure of understanding: engaging with contemporary challenges through science education, Part [part/strand number] (co-ed. [Editors of the strand chapter]), (pp. [page numbers]). Bologna: ALMA MATER STUDIORUM – University of Bologna.

Bertel, L. B., & Hannibal, G. (2015). Tema 2: The NAO robot as a Persuasive Educational and Entertainment Robot (PEER)–a case study on children's articulation, categorization and interaction with a social robot for learning. *Tidsskriftet Læring og Medier (LOM)*, 8(14). DOI:10.7146/lom.v8i14.22057

Bertel, L. B., & Rasmussen, D. M. (2013). On Being a Peer: What Persuasive Technology for Teaching Can Gain from Social Robotics in Education. *International Journal of Conceptual Structures and Smart Applications (IJCSSA)*, 1(2), 58–68. Publisher: IGI Global. doi:10.4018/ijcssa.2013070107

Blikstein, P. (2013). Digital Fabrication and 'Making' in Education: The Democratization of Invention. In J. Walter-Herrmann & C. Büching (Eds.), *FabLabs: Of Machines, Makers and Inventors.* Bielefeld: Transcript Publishers.

Bundsgaard, J., Pettersson, M., & Puck, M. R. (2014). *Digitale kompetencer: it i danske skoler i et internationalt perspektiv.* Aarhus: Aarhus Universitetsforlag. 220 s.

Burke, Q., O'Byrne, W. I., & Kafai, Y. B. (2016). Computational participation: Understanding coding as an extension of literacy instruction. *Journal of Adolescent & Adult Literacy*, *59*(4), 371–375. DOI:10.1002/jaal

Caeli, E.N., Yadav, A. (2020). Unplugged Approaches to Computational Thinking: a Historical Perspective. *TechTrends*, *64*, 29–36. DOI:10.1007/s11528-019-00410-5

Caprani, O. (2016). Tema 1: Mangfoldige læringsaktiviteter-ét robotbyggesæt. *Tidsskriftet Læring Og Medier (LOM)*, *8*(14). DOI:10.7146/lom.v8i14.22074

Chongtay, R. (2018). Computational literacy skill set: an incremental approach. In: *Designing for Learning in a Networked World* (pp. 158–174). Bonderup Dohn, N. (red.). London: Routledge.

Denning, P. J., & Tedre, M. (2019). *Computational thinking*. Cambridge, MA: MIT Press (Essential Knowledge Series).

DigiPippi (2021). *Bridging the Gap Between IT and the Next Generation of Women*. Retrieved March 8, 2021, from https://digipippi.dk/wp-content/uploads/2018/07/DigiPippi-Onepager-UK.pdf

Dohn, N. B. (2021). Computational thinking – indplacering i et landskab af it-begreber. In: Dohn, N.B., Mitchell, R. & Chongtay, R. (Eds.), *Computational thinking – teoretiske, empiriske og didaktiske perspektiver*. Frederiksberg: Samfundslitteratur. In press.

Guldastronauts Coding Class. (2021). Retrieved March 8, 2021 from www.guldastronaut.dk/codingclass

Iversen, O. S., Smith, R. C., & Dindler, C. (2018). *From Computational Thinking to Computational Empowerment: A 21st Century PD Agenda. In Proceedings of the Participatory Design Conference 2018*, Genk, Belgium [7] Association for Computing Machinery. DOI:10.1145/3210586.3210592

Jabbar, K., & Bjørn, P. (2019, May). Blockchain Assemblages: Whiteboxing Technology and Transforming Infrastructural Imaginaries. In *Proceedings of the 2019 CHI Conference on Human Factors in Computing Systems* (pp. 1–13). New York, NY: Association of Computing Machinery. doi:10.1145/3290605.330049

Johannesen, H., Brooks, E., & Borum, I. (2020). Perspektiver på børn, digitale medier og pædagogisk praksis. *Playful Learning - Digital Leg og Læring i Dagtilbud*. Aalborg: Aalborg Universitetsforlag. In press.

Kafai, Y., & Burke, Q.. (2013). *The social turn in K-12 programming: Moving from computational thinking to computational participation. SIGCSE 2013 - Proceedings of the 44th ACM Technical Symposium on Computer Science Education*. (p. 603–608). New York, NY: Association for Computing Machinery. doi:10.1145/2445196.2445373

Latour, B. (1999). *Pandora's Hope: Essays on the Reality of Science Studies*. Cambridge, MA: Harvard University Press.

Mikkonen, J. (2019). Bodygramming. Embodying the computational behaviour as a collective effort. *The Design Journal*, *22*(Suppl. 1), 1423–1437. doi:10.1080/14606925.2019.1594967

Mikkonen, J., & Fyhn, C. (2021). Læring af computational thinking ved udvikling af computational things gennem Storycoding. In: N. B. Dohn, & R. Mitchell & R. Chongtay (Eds.), *Computational thinking – teoretiske, empiriske og didaktiske perspektiver*. Frederiksberg: Samfundslitteratur. In press.

Moyles, J. (1989). *Just playing? The role and status of play in early childhood education*. Philadelphia, PA: Open University Press.

Papert, S. (1980). *Mindstorms: Children, Computers, and Powerful Ideas*. USA: Basic Books Inc.

Petrich, M., Wilkinson, K., & Bevan, B. (2013). It looks like fun, but are they learning?. In M. Honey @ D. E. Kanter (Eds.) *Design, Make, Play: Growing the Next Generation of STEM Innovators*. (pp. 55–70) New York, NY: Routledge.

PWC (2017). *The Essential Eight*. Retrieved March 8, 2021, from https://www.pwc.com/gx/en/issues/technology/essential-eight-technologies.html

Resnick, M., Berg, R., & Eisenberg, M. (2000). Beyond black boxes: Bringing transparency and aesthetics back to scientific investigation. *Journal of the Learning Sciences, 9*(1), 7–30. doi:10.1207/s15327809jls0901_3

Resnick, M., & Rosenbaum, E. (2013). Designing for tinkerability. *Design, Make, Play: Growing the next Generation of STEM Innovators*, 163–181. New York: Routledge. doi:10.4324/9780203108352

Waelbers, K. (2011). *Doing Good with Technologies: Taking Responsibility for the Social Role of Emerging Technologies* (Vol. 4). Springer Science & Business Media. DOI: 10.1007/978-94-007-1640-7

Wing, J. (2006). Computational thinking. *Communications of the ACM*, 49(3), 33–35. New York, NY: Association for Computing Machinery. doi:10.1145/1118178.1118215

15

DESIGNING VIRTUAL CASES FOR LEARNING AND ASSESSMENT

Uno Fors

Introduction

Virtual cases (VCs) is a phenomenon that has attracted a great deal of interest during the last 15 years from teachers and researchers in higher education and other areas. But what is really a VC, and what can the possibilities and challenges be for teachers, course directors, Universities and learners? And how to design VCs to allow as good learning outcomes as possible?

It all started about 50 years ago in medical education, when teachers and educational developers found a challenge of allowing students to practice with human cases in safe but still realistic educational environments. Healthcare education is usually based on a mix of theoretical lectures, skills training and practical rotations in hospitals. However, already in the 1970s were concerns raised regarding ethical issues, decreased access to "normal" cases suited for students at university hospitals, and the trend where patients started to become less willing to act as "guinea pigs" for students to train on. To this, additional challenges as increased restriction of time in curricula, economy and other issues further pushed for new educational interventions. There has also been an ever increasing wish to make access to good educational cases easier in many domains.

Therefore, educational researchers started during the 1970s to test if computer-based patient cases could be used as a part of the medical education (see e.g. Harless, Drennon, Marxer, Root, & Miller, 1971). The idea was to create a "bridge" between theory and practice but still allowing the students to meet challenging clinical situations and (patient) cases that were stimulating, engaging and motivating to learn from. The result became a new type of educational tool where students could freely interact with these VCsand automatically receive feedback from the system on actions they took. Thus, VCs were designed to mimic a real patient, where the learner could ask questions, perform physical exams and order lab tests as well as suggest diagnose before receiving feedback from the system.

In the 1970/80s, such systems were very difficult and expensive to develop, but still a number of pilot studies were performed, which gave encouraging results in terms of indications on increased motivation and engagement of the learners.

Thanks to the introduction of a new range of multimedia authoring tools in the 1990s and 2000s (see e.g. Bergin & Fors, 2003), the development process of VC systems became much easier and less expensive. Since about year 2005 and later, this technical development led to VCs becoming more and more common in healthcare education and were often referred to as "virtual patients" or simply VPs. Today, this type of VCs are rather common in many parts of the world and even made mandatory at many Universities.

During the recent years VCs have attracted interest from not only many other areas within higher education like healthcare education for nurses, physiotherapists and dentists but also from educators of law, social work, teacher education, special needs education, psychology and many more subject areas where learners need to prepare for encounters with humans where a professional need to discuss with a person, aggregate and interpret additional information, and to make more or less complex decisions.

A number of pilot tests in such areas have shown interesting and positive results, which has increased the urge to test VCs in even more areas, but even more to address questions regarding the design and development process of VCs.

What is a Virtual Case?

So, what is then a VC and which features do they commonly have? As mentioned above, the intention with all such learning systems is to visualise an interaction with a human being (patient, customer, client, etc.) where the user (learner) will encounter some type of problem (a sick patient, a client with a legal issue, a pupil with problems in school, a social welfare case or similar) and is supposed to interact with the virtual person to train to understand and solve this problem. In order to investigate the case and find out more about the problem, the learner can ask questions and receive answers, perform various "examinations" (like physical exam procedures in healthcare), order different tests (like lab tests or X-ray on a patient or order additional data in other domains). After investigating a case, the user is most often asked to suggest what the problem might be (e.g. the diagnosis in healthcare) and what to do to manage the situation (like treatment or medication in healthcare cases). Finally, most VC systems offer the learner to receive feedback on what he/she has done that was appropriate and what was less good. Thus, the general idea is that the learner by running a number of cases should be better prepared to meet other "cases" in the real world, meaning to develop better strategies to solve real-world problems or scenarios where human interaction is a central part.

A broadly accepted definition of VCs (or actually virtual patients) is "interactive computer simulations of real-life clinical scenarios for the purpose of medical training, education, or assessment" (Ellaway, Poulton, Fors, McGee, & Albright, 2008, p. 170). If we transfer this into something more general, a definition of what VCs are, could be: *Virtual cases are computer simulations of real-life scenarios featuring interactions with virtual humans for the purpose of training, education, or assessment.*

During the last 20 years, numerous (both commercial and academic) VC systems have been developed. Many of them are still in use while some others have been discontinued.

Features of a VC System

Of course, different developers have created many ideas of how VCs should look and feel, but if we take the example from healthcare education (where all started), a typical system might look like what is depicted in Figure 15.1. The learner can thus ask questions (or "interview") the virtual person and get answers in either text or as video clips. The questions can, depending on system, be entered as free text, chosen among preformed question options from menus, or something in between. The illustration in Figure 15.1A is from the rather unique system ISP where the user freely can type in questions in natural language via the keyboard and receive answers in video.

To gather more information, the user can also, e.g. perform physical exams (if healthcare cases), ask for lab tests (healthcare and other domains) or order additional written documents (legal cases, teacher education cases, etc.) as shown in Figures 15.1B and C. Finally, the users are almost always asked to formulate a decision on what the problem might be (a medical diagnosis, a legal decision, a school situation, etc.) and its basic reasons like in Figure 15.1D. In some systems, the user is also asked to justify the suggested problem description and/or suggest probable alternative solutions as well as to suggest what to do to solve the actual problem (medical treatment, legal advice, decision of social welfare or how to resolve a school conflict case, etc.).

The feedback to the learner can look and work very differently in different VC systems. Two examples are shown in Figure 15.2. To the left is a rather "typical" feedback given, where the learner gets feedback on which questions that were appropriate and which were missed, as well as similar feedback on appropriate further examination procedures performed (or not) and/or additional data ordered. The feedback section is the feature that works very differently between different VC systems and can even be focused on how the virtual person him/herself felt during the conversation and give hints to the user on, e.g. appropriate language used or not, trust, emotional reactions, ethical issues and similar. Such forms of feedback are often seen as important by many learners, see Figure 15.2B.

In terms of learning and training goals, it is important to realise that VCs mostly are intended for improving learners' critical thinking and reasoning (see

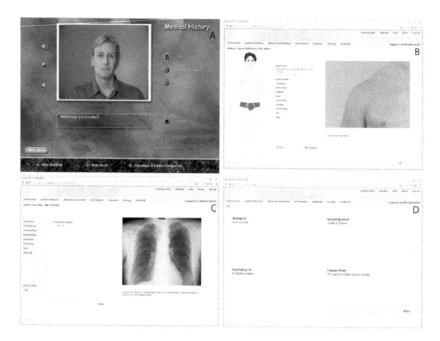

FIGURE 15.1 Examples on how virtual cases can look like. A: Dialogue; B: Physical examination; C: Lab/imaging tests; and D: Suggestion of problem description and justification.

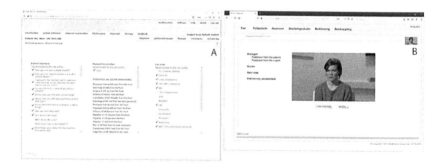

FIGURE 15.2 Examples on how feedback might be given. Left: Feedback on the user's actions; right: feedback given by the virtual person herself (translated from a Swedish system).

e.g. Zary, Johnson, & Fors, 2012), and are not good for practicing manual skills or for acquiring theoretical knowledge. Therefore most VC systems are implemented as one of many possible learning tools/methods in the curricula. It is uncommon that courses solely are based on VCs.

It is also important to understand, that most VC systems are focusing on user freedom, and practising an explorative approach, where the system seldom gives feedback until the user asks for it, making it possible to train alternative actions in a safe environment as well as allow the user to learn from mistakes. Therefore, VC systems are often used in problem-based curricula (PBL) or similar, where the teachers want the learners to be able to themselves discover issues that they need to improve or train. However, VC systems may also be used in most other educational settings, as long as the educator takes the features of the actual system under consideration.

VC Systems for Non-medical Domains

As have been demonstrated, VCs started in the healthcare domain and are still much more common there than in other areas. However, there are today many examples of VC projects that focus on totally different disciplines like teacher education, law, special needs education, social work, psychology, customer relations, insurance, police training, military training and interpreter education. Is all such domains, where there is a need to train and develop strategies on how to encounter other humans in a professional way and to train on how to make good decisions based on oral and written information, VCs might play an important role.

The only major difference between these domains and healthcare is that physical exams are unusual in other domains outside healthcare. However, such procedures can still be of interest, since it might be possible to find usage for this in, e.g. police cases, customs officer training or similar, where body examinations might be interesting to visualise and make decisions about.

At Stockholm University, we have for example worked with VC cases in teacher education, special needs education, social work as well as in law, where pilot studies indicate that such VCs have a good potential as both learning and assessment tools. For a number of examples, see e.g. Allodi, Linikko, and Fors (2012), Fors and Skoglund (2013) and Sunnqvist, Karlsson, Lindell, and Fors (2016). Please also refer to Figure 15.3 for additional examples.

FIGURE 15.3 Examples on two VC applications outside healthcare. A: VC case on refugee trauma and B: a school conflict case for teacher education.

Design and Implementation Possibilities

Regarding the art of designing and implementing VCs, there are two important design issues to focus on: 1. The curriculum design and case implementation; and 2. The design process of the VCs themselves. Both of these are crucial for a successful use of VCs for learning and assessment.

Curriculum Design and Case Implementation

Even if VCs started to be applied in PBL settings and similar, they are today used in many different educational set-ups. But still most of them are used in contexts where the learner is supposed to work independently from the teacher's direct supervision and to explore different possible actions (meaning not during traditional lectures). However, some teachers do use VCs during lectures or seminars, e.g. to illustrate special situations or scenarios that the teacher wants to demonstrate to the learners. This can be done to discuss matters during a lecture and can also be combined with "clickers" (student response systems) to activate the students who may "vote" about the next action to be taken.

More common, is that single students or groups of students are instructed to run a number of cases on their own and then come back to, e.g. a seminar where the groups of learners discuss their respective experience from the cases they have worked with, situations that they felt as challenging, alternative strategies to run the case as well as possible actions to take to solve the actual problem. To be able to discuss such matters during a seminar is usually seen as a positive learning activity by a majority of learners.

Since most VC systems today are web based, learners can run them from any place and at any time, and some teachers feel that VCs best are run individually, and others that they best are run by pairs or small groups of students. Here it is important to recognise that research studies often show that pairs or small groups of learners can be of advantage, since the discussion between the learners in front of the VC on what to do next, which new question to ask, how to interpret what has been revealed so far, etc. stimulate the learners to reflect on their knowledge and skills and help them to understand what they need to learn to become better prepared to handle such cases in real life. However, it is also important to realise that too large groups might be detrimental for the learning, since if you are more than four to five persons in a group, not all learners tend to become as active as others in front of the VC.

It is also important to realise that VCs will not work if the course director not plan and allocate both time for seminars like indicated above, as well as to make room in the curriculum so that the students really put both time and effort in using the VCs. A good example of this is the experience from the study by Edelbring et al. (2012), where four groups of students in the same course were asked to run a set of VCs, but where the instructions and time allocations were rather different: the group where the teacher [only] said that "it would be good if you as students use the VCs" put much less time and effort to run the cases as well as saw much less benefit from the VCs than a group that was instructed in detail on how to run the cases, which time to allocate and that they were supposed to discuss their experiences during a subsequent seminar. The students in the last group also were much more positive to VCs as a learning tool and also saw much higher benefit to their learning through the VCs.

Design and Creation of the Virtual Cases

A common question raised about VCs is how many cases are really needed in a course. In many pilot studies, only a limited number of cases (one to three) are developed. However, experience from studies and interviews with students and teachers indicate that a variety of cases are often desired. Rather often have teachers reported that students ask for more cases and also in other courses than where they met their first VCs. This is also good for avoiding creating too stereotype images of how a typical scenario in a certain domain might look like: if you have only met one case, it can easily be misunderstood that all other cases in real situations are to be solved in the same way.

Development of Cases as Learning Tasks

An interesting way to create VCs and at the same time create stimulating learning activities, is to ask students to create new cases on their own. This could not only be a good way to make the development process of new cases efficient, but also lead to good learning experiences. Since development of a case includes to decide on learning goals, to collect basic data, to draft the main features of the case, to define good and less good actions to take as well as formulate feedback texts on correct judgements and justifications, a learner need to master the subject domain rather good to be able to create a case. Therefore, many teachers have as a learning activity started to, as a part of the course curriculum, require students in small groups (or as individuals) draft one or more cases, including scripting the general case content, setting up learning goals, formulate feedback details, and collect data needed (images and other sorts of data) to develop the case(s). This type of VC usage is also most often seen as interesting and positive by learners, see for example the PhD theses by Botezatu (2010) or Forsberg (2014).

VCs for Assessment

A rather recent mode of use of VCs is the use for VCs as part of formative or summative assessment procedures. This idea is based on the fact that most VC systems have the possibility to follow the interaction by the user in detail, as well as a possibility to predefine which actions or decisions are important to perform, which that are improper and which are neither nor. This possibility to predefine actions and decisions that are good or bad is actually the base for making it possible to give the learners a personalised feedback after each session and is therefore available in most VC systems.

This functionality leads to a possibility to set up dedicated VCs for assessment. For example, the examiner can define that 15 questions are appropriate and needed to be asked, five are not appropriate and the rest are indifferent (the user can ask them or not), the assessment could, e.g. be based on that a user need to get at least 80% of the "important" questions correct and less than 10% of the improper questions asked to receive a "pass" grade. And together with similar settings for other actions like examinations, lab or other tests, a rather detailed assessment rubric can be developed. This potential assessment possibility is clearly different between different VC systems, some have no such possibility, some have a rudimentary assessment module and a few have a rather detailed and more full-fledged assessment module.

Figure 15.4 illustrates a VC system with a built-in assessment module (the Web-SP system). Here, the course director first assigns how many and which cases that should be available for the current exam (see Figure 15.4A), together with the actual grading and scoring rubric to use (here a 4-graded exam is chosen) as well as the percentage of correct actions to reach a certain grade. After the students have run the exam cases, the examiner enters the semi-automatic scoring and grading module (see Figure 15.4B), where he/she can see which scores the system is suggesting as well as changing the suggested scores and set the final grade. The examiner can correct the exam case-by-case or student-by-student, as he or she wants. The reason behind the semi-automatic scoring and grading of this system and not a fully automatic solution is both to ensure that no errors have been made by the system as well as to allow scoring and correcting the free text answers (here, diagnosis and treatment), which is difficult to automate.

This assessment possibility of some VC systems has led to that many Universities worldwide have started to use VCs also for assessment. Some Universities apply

FIGURE 15.4 Example of a VC system with a built-in assessment module. A: Here, the course director's view with the selected cases and the scoring rubric. B: Examiner's view with a case with system generated semi-automatic grading suggestions.

VCs as formative examination activities for students to practice and learn from by themselves (like self-evaluation), but some have since a number of years implemented high-stake summative exams based on VCs. The latter example then, of course, require that there is a stable infrastructure with backup systems so that no student runs into problems if, e.g. networks or computers breaks down during an exam. However, these are requirements that any kind of electronic summative exam system need to fulfil to be practically possible to implement. And – of course – students need to get the possibility to train before the real exam, so that they get used to the VC system that is going to be used during an exam.

The possibility to use VC-based exams is, as mentioned before, different from system to system, but is often well accepted by students as well as by teachers (see e.g. Botezatu et al., 2010a, Forsberg, Georg, Ziegert, & Fors, 2011). Students often tell that VC-based exams in a more appropriate way assess their abilities to solve real problems than ordinary written exams do. A possible challenge with VC-based exam cases is also that it often requires the exam cases to be new for each exam, so that students cannot tell each other what the correct actions are in a specific case. However, since the pure idea with VCs is that they are interactive and very detailed, it would probably be difficult to tell a fellow student exactly which actions that should be taken or not out of the often 1000 or more possibilities in a good virtual case. And if the course director uses a strategy to ask students to also create their own cases as a learning activity, the development of new cases would be facilitated. Additionally, it is rather easy to adapt an existing VC to a cloned case ("person") with another name, appearance, etc. without the need to develop everything from scratch. But there are also other strategies that can be used to create a multitude of cases, please refer to the last section on case creation of the future regarding new ideas.

Scientific Evaluations of VCs for Learning and Assessment

VCs have, as mentioned before, been developed and implemented at many Universities and other educational institutions since more than 30 years. However, since it all started in medical education and other healthcare areas, most studies are from such domains and there are still rather few studies from other areas, such as teacher education, law and social work. However, since the need of integrating VCs into curricula are similar regardless of discipline, most of the existing research and practical experience on the use of VCs in healthcare should be applicable more or less directly into other areas.

Learning Potential of VCs

First of all, do students learn from using VCs or do they just "play around"? As have been pointed out above, is this question dependent on how the VCs are implemented in a context and in the curriculum. If the course director plan ahead and make sure that there is both time and educational anchorage behind the use of VCs, most scientific studies have pointed out a great educational potential of VCs. For example, the study by Botezatu et al. (2010a) was among one of the first to really prove that students learn both better and faster using VCs as compared to traditional teaching.

Other studies like Botezatu et al. (2010b, c) and Forsberg, Ziegert, Hult, and Fors (2016) have shown that also learners and teachers most often are positive to the use of VCs for learning, since, e.g. engagement and motivation among students increase. As might be expected, there are also studies indicating that some students prefer traditional or other means of training than VCs, but that is the same as with any other mode of education – everything does not suit everyone (see also Cook & Triola, 2009).

Design of VCs and Realism

Another issue often brought up, is if a good VC system requires an aesthetic and realistic interface, with detailed interaction in free text (or even using spoken language) during the dialogue with the virtual person and answers with video clips featuring high-fidelity human appearance?

Initially, in the early years of VP system development (1990s and 2000s), the "authentic look and feel" of a VC system was an ultimate goal, as it was seen as a prerequisite of user acceptance and user engagement of VCs. However, the importance of this was unclear, and more and more VC systems started to focus on more low-key solutions with less use of video and less advanced dialogue features. This was both a reaction to the rather high costs for recording live actors for hundreds of possible answers as well as the tricky technology to interpret written or spoken questions to the virtual person. So, most developers turned to use only still images and text-based answers (like we did at Karolinska Institutet and Stockholm University when we during the early 2000s developed the Web-SP system after the experiences of the very advanced ISP-system). Surprisingly, very few users (teachers and students) told us that they lacked video-based answers or free text input of questions and indicated that the most important feature was the design and challenge of the individual VP case. The only exception to this, was if we showed that such possibilities were available before demonstrating a system where this was not possible; then many interviewees preferred the more advanced system with free formulation of open questions in natural language and video-based answers. However, when course directors were told that every case would take about ten times more in time (as compared to a system without this feature) to develop and about ten times as much money, almost all of them accepted the less advanced system with still images and preformulated question chosen via a menu (cf. Botezatu et al., 2010c). This was the case for both commercial and university-driven VC projects, and today rather few systems, if any, work with such advanced natural language processing solutions that the old

ISP system did. And as a matter of fact – almost all studies performed regarding user acceptance and engagement (cf. Botezatu et al., 2010c) are based on less advanced systems with no natural language processing or video-based answers (see also Cook & Triola, 2009).

Today, many systems still use video-based answers, since it often is easier to engage the user emotionally when the virtual person expresses also body language and an emotionally based dialogue/speech. However, research studies have indicated that the most important thing if a case should be engaging and motivating to be used by students, is the case story itself and also the mode of implementation into the curriculum. See for example Botezatu et al. (2010c) or Edelbring et al. (2012).

The Use of VC for Assessment

What about the use of VC for assessment then? Are not learners hesitant to this since it is so "technical"? On the contrary, most students seem rather positive to the use of VCs for assessment, as long as they have time and possibilities to prepare before the exam, see e.g. Gesundheit et al. (2009) or Forsberg et al. (2016).

However, as the use of VCs for assessment also involves scoring and grading issues, can different scoring rubrics influence how the results of an exam are interpreted, see e.g. Forsberg, Ziegert, Hult, & Fors, 2015). Other circumstances like the time allocation for the exams can also affect the results of VC-based exams, see Gunning and Fors (2012).

Using VCs for Special Applications

Up to now, much of the examples give have been focused on healthcare education, but as mentioned earlier, VCs have also been tested and implemented in a number of other domains and also for rather specific purposes.

VCs for Training Professional Language

One specific domain and purpose has been the use of VCs to train foreign professionals in, e.g. medicine or teacher education to work in a new country and/ or "professional culture". For example, a small-scale project was performed at Karolinska Institutet and Stockholm University targeting immigrating foreign healthcare practitioners and their interaction with patients in both a new language and a new professional paradigm. In that project, the starting point was that a healthcare professional need to use a different language than when you are talking to you neighbour or in a grocery shop; you need to use other terms, expressions and another "professional language" than in the everyday life. And the professional culture (meaning how you interact with a patient, a medical colleague or which procedures that are recommended) differs a lot between countries, cultures and regions. In that study, the implementation of VCs in Swedish, where foreign healthcare professionals freely could train encounters with Swedish (virtual) patients was seen as positive by most of the participants in the study. Almost all participants welcomed the use of VCs for training communication in healthcare Swedish and 73% of the users indicated that they considered that VPs should be mandatory to use in future courses (Fors & Courteille, 2015).

Transcultural VCs and Refugee Cases

Most professionals are good in encountering and managing cases from their own culture, meaning that, e.g. Swedish doctors are good in managing patients from Sweden. But what about the ability to understand cultural expressions, beliefs and other issues by persons from a totally different culture and history? An example of this is the challenging encounter between a Swedish physician and a patient with a very different background, which also could include severe mental and/ or physical trauma. This challenge is becoming more and more common in these days with numerous migrating refugees coming to Europe or USA. Other similar examples can be foreign teachers that need to encounter new school policies, national regulations and cultural expressions in a new country.

Experiences from pilot projects in both USA and Sweden have pointed out the possibility to use VCs for also such applications, meaning to prepare already practising professionals to encounter new challenges. See for example Pantziaras, Courteille, Mollica, Fors, and Ekblad (2012); Pantziaras, Fors, and Ekblad (2015) for more details.

The Future of VC Design and Development

So, since the early 1970s where the first VC systems were developed, until today, much seem to have happened. Or have it really? This is a tricky question to answer. Yes, the technology has changed and there have been numerous VC systems developed. However, the general idea of using VCs as a way to offer learners additional possibilities to "encounter" realistic and engaging cases to learn from is still the same (cf. Cook & Triola, 2009). Therefore, VC systems are still interesting to study and improve, and the demands of new applications for VCs are ever increasing.

However, there are a few challenges and also new possibilities to work with in the future. One such issue is the interesting question on how to make the case creation easier as well as the possibility to make the adaptation of existing cases into new curricula or courses more straightforward. Here, we can easily foresee the birth of new systems where teachers more easily can develop new cases as well as adapt to others without the need of programmers or technicians to develop the case for us teachers. A good start was (the now old) Web-SP system that was created in the early 2000s, where teachers after just 1 hour of training could create numerous cases themselves based on online templates and the adaptation of old cases. However, that system was designed for healthcare and thus not very usable for other domains, and new systems should be developed that makes the creation of cases for any domain as easy, or even easier.

Other issues that should be targeted are, e.g. translation and exchange of VCs between both Universities and systems (cf. Muntean, Calinici, Tigan, & Fors, 2013). Finally, possibilities with new technologies to apply animated but still very realistic characters should be explored (so that you do not have to record video clips of human actors) as well as new methods for natural language processing of questions.

Suggested Design and Implementation Principles

In this chapter, a number of possibilities and challenges regarding educational use of VCs have been discussed, as well as the need of a good curriculum integration to enhance the learning outcomes. A number of design possibilities and results from studies have also been put forward. But which design principles should then be followed if you want to implement, or even develop, a new VC system? The answer of that question is complex, and since the development and implementation possibilities of VCs vary a lot, there are few, if any, design principles that always must be followed. However the following list could be used as a guideline about things that should be considered when someone plans to implement (or develop a new) VC system:

- VC systems should preferably allow editing and creating cases by teachers themselves
- A good VC system should not require that programmers are needed to develop or edit cases
- Good VC systems should support dialogue using still images and text as well as video-based answers
- The dialogue function should support follow-up questions
- The feedback function should give feedback based on what the user actually have been doing, and even better, if different actions could be weighted different than other
- VC systems should support different languages
- It should be possible to use ready-made templates or old cases to develop new
- It should be possible to localise the cases, meaning that, e.g. terms and expressions should be possible to adapt to what the current institution prefers

Other features, although less common, that might give an advantage include:

- A possibility to follow a case over time
- VC systems that have built-in assessment functions
- A VC system that supports more than one specific domain (healthcare, law, teacher training, etc.) is often preferable

- A possibility to use various interaction methods, meaning to allow users to choose questions via a menu, free text inputs, multiple choice options or by other means
- The possibility to suggest the assessment (the decisions) of the case in different ways: in free text, from drop-down menus or via multiple choice items etc.

If you consider these recommendations above, the future of VCs is bright, for teachers and for VC system developers, as well as for educational researchers.

References

Allodi, M.W., Linikko, J., & Fors, U. (2012). *Simulation of establishing an individual education plan for a virtual pupil. EAPRIL conference*, Jyväskylä, Finland, November 2012

Bergin, R., & Fors, U. (2003). Interactive Simulation of Patients – an advanced tool for student-activated learning in medicine & healthcare. *Computers and Education, 40*(4), 361–376.

Botezatu, M. (2010). Virtual Patient Simulation: implementation and use in assessment. PhD Thesis. Karolinska Institutet, Stockholm, Sweden. ISBN: 978-91-7457-092-2

Botezatu, M., Hult, H., & Fors, U. G. (2010a). Virtual Patient Simulation: what do students make of it? A focus group study. *BMC Medical Education, 10*, 91

Botezatu, M., Hult, H., Kassaye Tessma, M., & Fors, U. (2010b). Virtual Patient Simulation for learning and assessment: superior results in comparison with regular course exams. *Medical Teacher, 32*(10), 845–850

Botezatu, M., Hult, H., Tessma, M., & Fors, U. (2010c). As time goes by: stakeholder opinions on the implementation of a virtual patient simulation system. *Medical Teacher, 32*(11), 509–516

Cook, D. A., & Triola, M. M. (2009). Virtual patients: A critical literature review and proposed next steps. *Medical Education;43*:303–311.

Edelbring, S., Broström, O., Henriksson, P., Vassiliou, D., Spaak, J., Dahlgren, L-O., Fors, U., & Zary, N. (2012). Course integration of virtual patients: follow-up seminars and perceived benefit. *Medical Education, 46*(4):417–425.

Ellaway, R., Poulton, T., Fors, U., McGee, J.B., & Albright, S. (2008). Building a virtual patient commons. *Medical Teacher 30*: 170–174.

Fors, U. G. H., & Courteille, O. (2015). Learner Acceptance of Using Virtual Patient Encounters to Train Foreign Healthcare Professionals in Swedish. *International Journal of Virtual and Personal Learning Environments, 5*(3), 18–32.

Fors, U., & Skoglund, Å. (2013). A pilot study of virtual cases in law education. *European Journal of Law and Technology, 4*(3).

Forsberg, E. (2014). Virtual Patients for Assessment of Clinical Reasoning. PhD Thesis. Karolinska Institutet, Stockholm, Sweden. ISBN: 978-91-7549-596-5

Forsberg, E., Georg, C., Ziegert, K., & Fors, U. (2011). Virtual patients for assessment of clinical reasoning in nursing – a pilot study. Nurse Education Today, *31*(8), 757–762

Forsberg, E., Ziegert, K., Hult, H., & Fors, U. (2015). Evaluation of a novel scoring and grading model for vp-based exams in postgraduate nurse education. *Nurse Education Today, 35*(12). DOI: http://dx.doi.org/10.1016/j.nedt.2015.04.005. Published Online: April 24, 2015

Forsberg, E., Ziegert, K., Hult, H., & Fors, U. (2016). Assessing progression of clinical reasoning through virtual patients: an exploratory study. *Nurse Education in Practice, 16*(1), 97–103. doi: 10.1016/j.nepr.2015.09.006

Gesundheit, N., Brutlag, P., Youngblood, P., Gunning. W. T., Zary, N., & Fors, U. (2009). The Use of Virtual Patients to Assess the Clinical Skills and Reasoning of Medical Students: Initial Insights on Student Acceptance. *Medical Teacher, 31*(8), 739–742.

Gunning, W.T., & Fors, U. G. H. (2012). Virtual Patients for Assessment of Medical Student Ability to Integrate Clinical and Laboratory Data to Develop Differential Diagnoses: Comparison of Results of Exams with/without Time Constraints. *Medical Teacher 2012; 34*(4), e222–e228.

Harless, W. G., Drennon, G. G., Marxer, J. J., Root, J. A., & Miller, G. E. (1971). CASE: A computer-aided simulation of the clinical encounter. *Journal of medical education, 46*(5), 443–448.

Muntean, V., Calinici, T., Tigan, S., & Fors, U. G. H. (2013). Language, culture and international exchange of virtual patients. *BMC Medical Education, 13*:21. http://www.biomedcentral.com/1472-6920/13/21

Pantziaras, I., Courteille, O., Mollica, R., Fors, U., & Ekblad, S .(2012). A pilot study of user acceptance and educational potentials of virtual patients in transcultural psychiatry. *International Journal of Medical Education, 3*:132–140.

Pantziaras, I., Fors, U., & Ekblad, S. (2015). Innovative Training with Virtual Patients in Transcultural Psychiatry: The Impact on Resident Psychiatrists' Confidence. *PLoS ONE, 10*(3): e0119754. doi: 10.1371/journal.pone.0119754

Sunnqvist, C., Karlsson, K., Lindell, L., & Fors, U. (2016). Virtual patient simulation in psychiatric care - A pilot study of digital support for collaborate learning. *Nurse Education in Practice, 17*, 30–35. doi:http://dx.doi.org/10.1016/j.nepr.2016.02.004

Zary, N., Johnson, G., & Fors, U. G. H. (2012). Impact of the virtual patient introduction on the clinical reasoning process in dental education. *Bio-Algorithms and Med-Systems, 8*(2), 173. ISSN (Online) 1896-530X, ISSN (Print) 1895–9091, DOI: 10.2478/bams-20r12–0011, January 2012

EPILOGUE

Lessons from Inclusive and Empowering Participation in Emerging Technologies

Eva Brooks, Susanne Dau and Staffan Selander

We started out by saying that we live in an era that can be characterised by its strongly expanding digital presence, which encompasses more or less everything that matters in our lives. Digitisation not only changes social and political control systems, but it also expands the conditions for creative development in different learning landscapes. The idea behind this boom was to discuss and give examples of this.

Throughout the different chapters in this book it becomes clear (at least we hope so) that inclusive and empowering participation in emerging technologies has an influence both on how we can organise collaborative cultures and digital learning, and how we can develop new metaphors, theories and methodologies to study these processes.

An inclusive design approach involves new forms of relationship and calls for new forms of collaboration between stakeholders. By way of inclusion, learning is based on heterogeneity in interests, capabilities and skills. Thus, learning not only allows for individual agency, but it also characterises transprofessional collaboration between researchers from different disciplines, as well as between researchers and professionals in different areas. And not the least, this approach entails implications on ethical issues, with respect to participants' voices and dignity.

However, participatory designs do not come out of nothing. In our view, this approach, which could be used in different educational and learning settings, must in itself be learnt – both theoretically and by way of open playful processes and systematically, but still flexible, design for participation in practice. In other words, we see a profound challenge to create new thinking and practices for future generations. We hope the book has unpacked some of these complexities that surround inclusive and empowering participation in emerging technologies, and we hope that the debates and research that can inform our understanding of these complexities can continue beyond the reading of this book.

INDEX

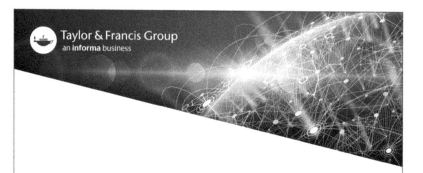

For Product Safety Concerns and Information please contact our EU
representative GPSR@taylorandfrancis.com
Taylor & Francis Verlag GmbH, Kaufingerstraße 24, 80331 München, Germany

www.ingramcontent.com/pod-product-compliance
Ingram Content Group UK Ltd.
Pitfield, Milton Keynes, MK11 3LW, UK
UKHW021449080625
459435UK00012B/422